Liv

BILL OF *Rights*

Also by Nat Hentoff

Nonfiction

The Jazz Life

Peace Agitator: The Story of A. J. Muste

The New Equality

Our Children Are Dying

A Doctor Among the Addicts

A Political Life: The Education of John V. Lindsay

State Secrets: Police Surveillance in America (with Paul Cowan
    and Nick Egleson)

Jazz Is

Listen to the Stories: Nat Hentoff on Jazz and Country Music

Does Anybody Give a Damn? Nat Hentoff on Education

The First Freedom: The Tumultuous History of Free Speech in America

John Cardinal O'Connor: At the Storm Center of a Changing Church

Free Speech for Me—But Not for Thee: How the American Left and Right
    Relentlessly Censor Each Other

Boston Boy

Speaking Freely

Fiction for Adults

Call the Keeper

Onwards!

Blues for Charlie Darwin

The Man from Internal Affairs

Fiction for Young Readers

Jazz Country

I'm Really Dragged but Nothing Gets Me Down

Journey into Jazz

In the Country of Ourselves

This School Is Driving Me Crazy

Does This School Have Capital Punishment?

The Day They Came to Arrest the Book

American Heroes: In and Out of School

Editor/Coeditor:

Hear Me Talkin' to Ya (with Nat Shapiro)

The Jazz Makers (with Nat Shapiro)

Jazz (with Albert McCarthy)

The Collected Essays of A. J. Muste

Living THE
BILL OF *Rights*

How to Be an
★ Authentic American ★

NAT HENTOFF

UNIVERSITY OF CALIFORNIA PRESS
Berkeley   Los Angeles   London

University of California Press
Berkeley and Los Angeles, California

University of California Press, Ltd.
London, England

Published by arrangement with HarperCollins publishers.
First California Paperback Printing, 1999

Designed by Nancy Singer Olaguera

Library of Congress Cataloging-in-Publication Data

Hentoff, Nat.
    Living the Bill of Rights : how to be an authentic American / Nat Hentoff.
        p.   cm.
    Originally published: New York : HarperCollins, c1998.
    Includes index.
    ISBN 0-520-21981-3 (pbk. : alk. paper)
    1. Civil rights—United States Popular works.   2. Constitutional
law—United States Popular works.   I. Title.
    IF4750.H46   1999
    342.73'085—dc21   99-13196
                                                                   CIP

Printed in the United States of America

08 07 06 05 04 03 02 01 00 99
10 9 8 7 6 5 4 3 2 1

The paper used in this publication is both acid-free and totally chlorine-free (TCF).
It meets the minimum requirements of ANSI/NISO Z39.48-1992 (R 1997)
(*Permanence of Paper*). ⊚

*To Anthony Griffin, for whom the Constitution is a
daily and demanding companion*

Why don't the schools teach why we are Americans? So few people know.

—Kathryn Sinclair, high school senior
in Murfreesboro, Tennessee, 1984

What constitutes the bulwark of our own liberty and independence? It is not our frowning battlements, our bristling sea coasts, our army and navy. These are not our reliance against tyranny. . . . Our reliance is the love of liberty. . . . Destroy this spirit and you have planted the seeds of despotism at your door.

—Abraham Lincoln, Edwardsville, Illinois, 1858

One day posterity will remember these strange times, when ordinary common honesty was called courage.

—Yevgeny Yevtushenko, Russian poet, 1969

We have in the U.S. produced several generations of cultural orphans who have little knowledge and even less appreciation of their heritage of freedom, or the struggles and sacrifices which produced it. . . . We have inadvertently engaged in a kind of unilateral intellectual disarmament which could well prove more devastating to the cause of liberty than would be the destruction of our defense arsenals.

—John A. Howard, *On Freedom*, 1984

★ CONTENTS ★

★ THE BILL OF RIGHTS ★

The First Ten Amendments to the Constitution of the United States of America

On September 25, 1789, Congress transmitted to the state legislatures twelve proposed amendments, two of which, having to do with congressional representation and congressional pay, were not adopted. The remaining ten amendments became the Bill of Rights and were ratified effective December 15, 1791.

AMENDMENT I.

Congress shall make no law respecting an establishment of religion, or prohibiting the free exercise thereof; or abridging the freedom of speech, or of the press, or the right of the people peaceably to assemble, and to petition the Government for a redress of grievances.

AMENDMENT II.

A well regulated Militia, being necessary to the security of a free State, the right of the people to keep and bear Arms, shall not be infringed.

AMENDMENT III.

No Soldier shall, in time of peace be quartered in any house, without the consent of the Owner, nor in time of war, but in a manner to be prescribed by law.

AMENDMENT IV.

The right of the people to be secure in their persons, houses, papers, and effects, against unreasonable searches and seizures, shall not be violated, and no Warrants shall issue, but upon probable cause, supported by Oath or affirmation, and particularly describing the place to be searched, and the persons or things to be seized.

AMENDMENT V.

No person shall be held to answer for a capital, or otherwise infamous crime, unless on a presentment or indictment of a Grand Jury, except in cases arising in the land or naval forces, or in the Militia, when in actual service in time of War or public danger; nor shall any person be subject for the same offence to be twice put in jeopardy of life or limb, nor shall be compelled in any criminal case to be a witness against himself, nor be deprived of life, liberty, or property, without due process of law; nor shall private property be taken for public use without just compensation.

AMENDMENT VI.

In all criminal prosecutions, the accused shall enjoy the right to a speedy and public trial, by an impartial jury of the State and district wherein the crime shall have been committed; which district shall have been previously ascertained by law, and to be informed of the nature and cause of the accusation; to be confronted with the witnesses against him; to have compulsory process for obtaining witnesses in his favor, and to have the assistance of counsel for his defence.

AMENDMENT VII.

In Suits at common law, where the value in controversy shall exceed twenty dollars, the right of trial by jury shall be preserved, and no fact tried by a jury shall be otherwise re-examined in any Court of the United States, than according to the rules of the common law.

Amendment VIII.

Excessive bail shall not be required, nor excessive fines imposed, nor cruel and unusual punishments inflicted.

Amendment IX.

The enumeration in the Constitution of certain rights shall not be construed to deny or disparage others retained by the people.

Amendment X.

The powers not delegated to the United States by the Constitution, nor prohibited by it to the States, are reserved to the States respectively, or to the people.

"Tell them stories about how our liberties were won and what keeps them alive."

One morning, while I spoke with Supreme Court Justice William Brennan in his chambers, his customary optimism about the resilience of the Constitution faded as we discussed the many Americans who were unaware of their liberties—and the liberties of others—under the Constitution.

"The Bill of Rights," he said, "never gets off the page and into the lives of most Americans."

I told him I was on my way to a series of schools in rural Pennsylvania to talk to the kids about the specific ways in which the Constitution affects their lives: their right to speak, their right to be protected from unreasonable searches by the police, their right to worship freely according to their faith, and their right to have no religion at all.

"But you've got to tell them stories," Justice Brennan said. "It's not enough to tell them what their rights and liberties are. They need to know—and this will get them interested—how these American liberties were won, and what it takes to keep them alive.

"And tell them," Brennan continued, "about the actual people out there now who are not afraid to fight to keep on being free Americans."

The idea for this book came from that conversation at the Supreme Court. And the reason for this book was underlined by a subsequent comment by Supreme Court Justice Anthony Kennedy in *The New Yorker:* "The Constitution needs allegiance and loyalty and renewal and understanding each generation, or else *it's not going to last.*"

The Americans whose stories are told in this book understand the Constitution and are renewing it, often against the will and power of other Americans who are either ignorant of the Constitution or disdain it.

Among the fighters keeping the legacy of the framers of the Constitution alive are a high school senior in Tennessee who is a born-against Christian; a black Texas lawyer fired by the state branch of the National Association for the Advancement of Colored People (NAACP) for representing a Klan member on constitutional grounds; Justice William Brennan himself; another Supreme Court justice, William O. Douglas, the preeminent supporter of the individual against the government; and a professional basketball star who, in conscience, would not be part of a display of mass loyalty to the American flag.

Also portrayed in this book are Dr. Kenneth Clark, a resolute black school integrationist at a time when more and more blacks are abandoning that goal; a Jewish teacher at a black university who spoke out compellingly against black anti-Semitism; a young white mother who refused to allow anyone to stereotype her or her children by their color; and a black high school student who did not rise to her feet for the Pledge of Allegiance because she believes there is not equal justice for *all* in this land. Also among these paladins of liberty is a southern lawyer with clients on death row whom he will not abandon.

The stories they tell make the Bill of Rights come off the page into the lives of actual Americans. And at the core of each story is this constitutional fact underlined by Justice William O. Douglas: "Restriction of free thought and free speech is the most dangerous of all subversions. It is the one un-American act that could most easily defeat us."

From freedom of speech and thought, all other liberties and rights flow. The people in these stories have learned that, and in the process, they exemplify Justice Louis Brandeis's description of the beginnings of our history:

"Those who won our independence by revolution were not cowards. . . . They did not exalt order at the cost of liberty."

Over time, getting to know the people portrayed in this book greatly energized my own sense of what it is to be an American, and I hope it will bring some of that life force to the reader's definition of *Americanism*.

The particular emphasis on the work of the late Justice William Brennan stems from his unique and extensive influence on the evolution of American liberties and rights. I have also given detailed attention to the life and works of Dr. Kenneth Clark; more than any other American, he has been devoted to integrating this nation's public schools, because he knows that if our children are not able to learn together, they will not be able to know each other.

SUPREME COURT JUSTICE
WILLIAM O. DOUGLAS

"Bill's life, like his law, was free."

*O*f all the Supreme Court Justices in our history, William O. Douglas was the most consistent and forthright defender of individual liberties against government's exercise of arbitrary power. His life, on and off the bench, exemplified constitutional Americanism as vividly defined by Alan Barth, a longtime illuminator of the Bill of Rights and the rest of the Constitution for the *Washington Post:* "Individual freedom is a means, an invaluable means, toward national security and survival. But it is an end as well—the supreme end which the government of the United States was instituted to secure."

Some constitutional scholars have faulted Douglas because he used few footnotes in his decisions, but Douglas did not write for scholars. He wrote clear, vigorous prose that anyone could understand because the Constitution was not made only for scholars.

Some of the scholars criticized him because, they said, he hadn't created, over the years, a coherent philosophy of constitutional law. But coursing through nearly everything he wrote was Douglas's unwavering conviction that the people of the United States are in charge of the government, not the other way around, and that each of us has the fundamental right to his or her own views, even if those views go against the moral or political conclusions of the majority. More of his philosophy of constitutional liberty is charted in chapter 2 in the story of a black Texas lawyer, Anthony Griffin, whose work exemplifies Douglas's insistence on protecting individuals against the government.

Douglas also continually warned of threats to our liberties from the government. In 1976, he wrote to the Young Lawyers Section of the Washington State Bar Association:

> The Constitution and the Bill of Rights were designed to get Government off the backs of the people—all the people. Those great documents . . . guarantee to us all the rights to personal and spiritual self-fulfillment. But that guarantee is not self-executing.
>
> As nightfall does not come all at once, neither does oppression. In both instances, there is a twilight when everything remains seemingly unchanged. And it is in such twilight that we all must be most aware of change in the air—however slight—lest we become unwitting victims of the darkness.

If enough of us are to remain aware of changes in the air, the words of the Constitution—especially of the Bill of Rights—must leap off the pages and into our lives. Yet to how many Americans is the Constitution *personal* and therefore worth protecting against its domestic enemies?

He looked liked his old friend Spencer Tracy and was amused when moviegoers, mistaking him for the actor, asked for an autograph. The thing about Tracy, William O. Douglas used to say, was that "he never talked bunk." Also, said the Supreme Court justice of the film star, "I never knew anyone more American than he."

Douglas could have been speaking about himself. Blunt, fearless, he scorned legalistic, euphemistic language. He was the same "Wild Bill," as his law clerks called him, on the bench as he was on the mountains he loved to climb: passionate, clear, and as rebelliously individualistic as the very framers of the Constitution. Indeed, the fiery main theme of the more than twelve hundred opinions he wrote during thirty-six years on the High Court—he served longer than any other justice in our history—was undiluted, revolutionary Americanism. And that is why he was the most crucially important member of the Court in our time.

But Bill Douglas's value to the nation was far more than as a jurist. In the brilliance and the sweep of his intellect, the boldness of his attacks on illegitimate authority—no matter how high or powerful—Douglas was in the direct line that included Thomas Jefferson, James Madison, Frederick Douglass, Eugene Debs, and Senator Bill Langer, the North Dakota maverick who supported Douglas when hardly anyone else would.

There is no voice now like that of Douglas, who in 1972 furiously asked this question: "Since when have we Americans been expected to bow submissively to authority and speak with awe and reverence to those who represent us? The constitutional theory is that we the people are the sovereigns—the state and federal officials only our agents. We who have the final word can speak softly or angrily. We can seek to challenge and annoy, as we need not stay docile and quiet."

This uncompromising Jeffersonian stance got Bill Douglas into a lot of trouble with those, in and out of government, who, if they had to vote on the Bill of Rights now, would condemn it for having gone too far (including the First Amendment, which guarantees freedom of speech, press, assembly, and religion, and the power of the people to confront government).

Three times there were moves in Congress to impeach the justice. One was in 1953, when he stayed the executions of Julius and Ethel Rosenberg. (His brethren immediately overruled him.) Acutely aware of the incendiary popular feeling against these convicted atomic-bomb spies, Douglas figured that his act might lead somebody to "take a shot at me," but he'd be damned if he'd be intimidated. Under the law, he said, the Rosenbergs couldn't be sentenced to death unless the jury had so recommended. And the jury had not. Therefore, Douglas declared with characteristic straightforwardness that "no man or woman should go to death under an unlawful sentence." The Rosenbergs were electrocuted anyway, but Douglas had no complicity in that judicial murder.

In 1966 another impeachment posse went after Douglas because the justice, then sixty-seven, had recently taken as his fourth wife twenty-three-year-old Cathleen Heffernan. It was always Douglas's unyielding view that he, like any other citizen, had the right to live his life anyway he chose so long as he didn't break the law. The Bill of Rights, as Douglas often said, was designed to keep the government off the backs of the people. And that meant Bill Douglas, too.

The final impeachment plot came in 1970, led by House Minority Leader Gerald Ford, serving as a ventriloquist's dummy for President Richard Nixon and Attorney General John Mitchell, who accurately considered this foremost paladin of the Bill of Rights their natural enemy. The charges included the scandalous fact that Justice Douglas had exercised his First Amendment rights by writing for such "pornographic" magazines as *Evergreen Review.* Another allegation had to do with a $12,000-a-year retainer Douglas was receiving for his work on a charitable foundation set up to promote international understanding by bringing foreign students to the United States to study the workings of American government. The businessman who had funded the project, it turned out, held a mortgage on a Las Vegas hotel and gambling casino. Therefore, Gerald Ford implied, Douglas had ties with the Mob. A House judiciary subcommittee entirely cleared Douglas.

Having had his high noon with Nixon, Mitchell, and Ford, Douglas kept on being his controversial self. And he continued to be a loner on the Court, for he never engaged in the customary bargaining there whereby a justice, to persuade enough of his brethren to make a majority, trades off bits and pieces of his own principles. Because Douglas would not dilute his opinions, he was wholly free to play to his greatest strength. As one of his former law clerks, Harvard Law School professor Vern Countryman, said of Douglas, "his capacity to get to the guts of the issue was his most distinguishing characteristic. He wouldn't get enmeshed in technicalities or doctrine. He would always see clearly what the issue was. And powering that extraordinary skill at penetrating to the heart of the matter was Bill Douglas's rage, until death itself, against injustice."

Justice Hugo Black, his longtime ally in many dissents that later become majority opinions, said that "Bill must have come into this world with a rush, and his first cry must have been a protest against something he saw at a glance was wrong or unjust."

For instance, three years after the Nixon team tried to have him thrown off the Court, Douglas became the first member of the High Court in history to order that American bombing of another nation be stopped. He didn't stop the bombing for long, because his appalled brethren reversed his decision, but the courage he showed—and the fundamental humanity of his opinion—particularly underscores what

Douglas meant to the nation. Although he was best known for his decisions giving full breathing room to the First Amendment, a body of work that will be a benchmark of liberty of speech and the press so long as this country exists, there was much more to Douglas, as the case of *Holtzman v. Schlesinger* reveals.

In 1973 Congresswoman Elizabeth Holtzman of New York and several air force officers serving in Asia sued to force the secretary of defense, James Schlesinger, to stop U.S. air operations over Cambodia. Why? Because Congress had not declared war on that hapless country. For years Nixon and Kissinger had secretly been destroying that land, and now it was being done openly. A lower court had agreed with Holtzman and the air force officers, but a court of appeals ruled that the bombing must go on until the case went all the way through the judicial system. The Supreme Court, however, was in summer recess, and so the lawyers for Holtzman and the other antibombers went to Douglas to get him to stop the killing. They found him in his beloved Goose Prairie, Washington (permanent population: eight), a place on the last natural frontier that he considered his permanent home.

Douglas examined all the arguments on both sides and said that, in essence, this was like all other capital cases. That is, when life is about to be lost and there is doubt whether due process has been followed in the imminent taking of that life, a stay of execution must be granted because "death is irrevocable."

Then Douglas spelled out his opinion in language so clear that all citizens could understand it:

> The classic capital case involves whether Mr. Lew, Mr. Low, or Mr. Lucas should die. The present case involves whether Mr. X [an unknown person or persons] should die. No one knows who they are. They may be Cambodian farmers whose only "sin" is a desire for socialized medicine to alleviate the suffering of their families and neighbors. Or Mr. X may be the American pilot or navigator who drops a ton of bombs on a Cambodian village. The upshot is that we know that someone is about to die.

Douglas granted a stay of the bombings. It wasn't up to him, he pointed out, to decide at this juncture whether the bombings were constitutional, but anyway, he let us know what he did think: "Even if the 'war' in Vietnam were assumed to be a constitutional one, the Cambodian bombing is quite a different affair. Certainly Congress did not . . . declare war against Cambodia and there is no one so reckless as to say that the Cambodian forces are an imminent and perilous threat to our shores."

The very next day the other members of the Supreme Court, polled by telephone, decided to let American bombers continue their killing in Cambodia. William Douglas, of course, was the only dissenter.

Douglas so often stood against the majority, in fact, that he filed more dissents—531—than did any other justice since the founding of the Court. And more of his dissents later became the law of the land than did those of any of the other Great Dissenters, including Louis Brandeis and Oliver Wendell Holmes.

Most often Douglas was alone or in alliance with Hugo Black in his total resistance to punishing people for their speech or writing, no matter how outrageous, offensive, or "subversive." Of all his dissents, he was proudest of what he said in *Dennis v. United States* (1951), when the High Court affirmed the conviction and jailing of eleven Communist Party leaders for "teaching" and "advocating" the overthrow of the government by force.

It was a time when much of the nation was transfixed by the fear of communism, and witch-hunts against domestic Reds, real and imaginary, were being conducted with at least as much fervor as in colonial Salem. Yet Douglas unequivocally declared that these Communist Party officials were fully protected by the First Amendment because all they had done was to discuss and teach certain books. They had only engaged in "speech, to which the Constitution has given a special sanction. . . . We have deemed it more costly to liberty to suppress a despised minority than to let them vent their spleen. We have above all else feared the political censor. We have wanted a land where our people can be exposed to all the diverse creeds and cultures of the world."

But these were *Communists!* That is precisely, said Douglas, why they, too, should be able to speak freely here. And he quoted, at the end of his dissent, from a 1938 book by the chief Soviet prosecutor

Andrei Vishinsky, *The Law of the Soviet State.* Vishinsky had warned the citizens of *his* country as follows: "In our state, naturally, there is and can be no place for freedom of speech, press, and so on for the foes of socialism."

"Our concern," Douglas emphasized, "should be that we accept no such standard for the United States." The quintessential difference between a free nation, as we profess to be, and a totalitarian state, is that here *everyone,* including a foe of democracy, has the right to speak his mind.

Douglas never got over the anti-Americanism of the majority of his brethren in that case. In 1973, speaking to students at Staten Island Community College in New York, the dauntless First Amendment warrior said of the convicted Communist leaders: "Those defendants were not plotting revolution, handing out grenades, making caches of rifles and ammunition and the like. They were teachers only—men teaching Marxism."

Not only was all political speech protected, said Douglas again and again, but *all* speech and writing was, as well. The First Amendment could not be more clear. There shall be no law "abridging the freedom of speech or of the press." Period. As Douglas thundered in the 1966 *Fanny Hill* case, "Publications and utterances were made immune from majoritarian control by the First Amendment, applicable to the states by the Fourteenth. *No exceptions* were made, not even for obscenity" (emphasis added).

Throughout his long term on the High Court, Douglas was appalled that his brethren took it upon themselves to police so-called obscenity. He himself never saw the movies or read the books that came up for decision, "because I have thought the First Amendment made it unconstitutional for me to act as a censor."

Back in 1957, when a majority of the Court first directly ruled that "obscenity" was not protected by the First Amendment, Douglas made his position utterly clear, and he never budged from it. Dissenting in *Roth v. United States,* the conservator of individual liberty proclaimed the following:

Any test that turns on what is offensive to the community's standards is too loose, too capricious, too destructive of freedom of expression to be squared with the First Amendment. Under that test juries can censor, suppress, and punish what they don't like, provided the matter relates to "sexual impurity" or has a tendency "to excite lustful thoughts." This is community censorship in one of its worst forms. If the First Amendment is to mean anything in this field, it must allow protests even against the moral code that the standard of the day sets for the community.

In obscenity cases and all other cases that came to him on the Court, Douglas was the strictest of constructionists, interpreting the Constitution as the guarantor of *individual* liberties it was fully intended to be. His decisions echoed the words of James Madison, the principal architect of the First Amendment, who kept emphasizing that the greatest danger to liberty in this free nation is to be found "in the body of the people, operating by the majority against the minority."

What particularly enrages the majority is any protest against its customs, values, and norms of proper behavior. As long as that protest was peaceful, however, Douglas not only supported but also encouraged it. For example, during the rise of the civil rights movement in the South, students were arrested in a small Florida town for assembling at a jail to protest the official segregation policies. In an opinion dissenting against the upholding of the protesters' convictions, Douglas delivered a classic endorsement of every American's right to take to the streets to exercise his freedom of speech:

> The right to petition for the redress of grievances is not limited to writing a letter or sending a telegram to a congressman; it is not confined to appearing before the local city council, or writing letters to the president or governor or mayor. Legislators may turn deaf ears; formal complaints may be routed endlessly through a bureaucratic maze; courts may let the wheels of justice grind very slowly.
>
> Those who cannot afford to advertise in newspapers or circulate elaborate pamphlets may have only a more limited type of access to public officials. Their methods should not be condemned as tactics of obstruction and harassment as long as the assembly and petition are peaceable, as these were.

This craggy six-footer from the West, who always looked directly at you with his gray-green eyes, continually insisted that the Constitution exists to nurture dissent and to protect the powerless. It was made to safeguard the heretic from the state and to give the poor at least a shot at justice. He was years ahead of his brethren, for instance, in urging that all criminal defendants be given free counsel if they couldn't afford a lawyer.

The intensity of Douglas's empathy with outsiders, even outcasts, did not come solely from an abstract reading of constitutional history. It came from his own life. As he once said, "I worked among the very, very poor, the migrant laborers, the Chicanos, and the members of the Industrial Workers of the World [IWW], whom I saw being shot at by the police. I saw cruelty and hardness, and my impulse was to be a force in other developments than cruelty and hardness in the law."

Douglas was born on October 16, 1898, in Maine, Minnesota. Soon after birth he was taken to California and then to a small town in Washington. His father, a circuit-riding frontier preacher, died there when the boy was six. Three years before, the child had contracted polio, and the doctors had gloomily assured his family that the stricken youngster would never walk again and would be lucky to live to the age of forty. Fatherless, growing up in poverty, Douglas spent much of his childhood forcing his limbs back into full use through hiking and mountain climbing. Along with instilling in him a lifelong tenacity of awesome proportions, this experience turned Douglas into an ardent admirer and protector of what was left of the wondrous wilderness.

An environmentalist before the term was known, Douglas was later, in dissent, to fight against any further exploitation of forests and streams, even claiming that all the forms of natural life should have a representative standing before the Supreme Court to defend their right to exist—"the pileated woodpecker as well as the coyote and bear, the lemmings as well as the trout in the streams."

Although the young Douglas felt at one with his surroundings out on the trail and on the ridges, he was acutely conscious of being "different" back in Yakima, Washington, where he grew up. The family was so poor, he recalled in his autobiography, *Go East, Young Man,* that he, his brother, and his sister were never invited to a single chil-

dren's party. "We grew up never seeing the inside of another home."
In retrospect, Douglas was glad that he had never become "united
with the elite of Yakima," because "to be accepted means living in the
right area, wearing the right hat, thinking the right way, saying the
right thing. What it means in the law is a Dean Acheson or John
Foster Dulles or a reactionary president of the Bar Association. They
cause all the beauty to disappear in pontifical emptiness."

Douglas never did become part of any elite. While he was on the
Court, his friends were mostly his old companions of the trail rather
than chieftains of the American Bar Association; and rather than din-
ing in expensive, exclusionary Washington clubs, Douglas used to
hang out at Jimmie's Cafe, an informal beer-and-sandwiches joint on
Pennsylvania Avenue near the Supreme Court. When not in his robes,
he looked like anything but an ultimate arbiter of constitutional law.
Once, at the end of a long hike down the Chesapeake and Ohio Canal
outside Washington, D.C., Douglas was refused service at an inn
because he was taken for a tramp. He never told those people he had a
job.

Another time, coming down from Mount Adams in the state of
Washington, the justice developed so painful a set of blisters that he
went into a doctor's office for relief. That worthy told the frontiers-
man, "We don't take care of the likes of you. There's a clinic down the
street that takes care of all the bums." When Douglas pulled out
twenty-five dollars, the doctor started calling him "sir."

"While he applied the bandages," Douglas recalled, "I told him
quietly how the law was way ahead of medicine, how, if he were dis-
barred for malpractice and was indigent, the highest court in the land
would take his case, would waive all filing fees and costs and name a
lawyer—'as good as Bethlehem Steel has'—to represent him."

"How do you know all that?" the doctor asked.

"Because, sir," Douglas answered, "I seem to spend a lot of time
there."

From boyhood on, Bill Douglas was most comfortable with those
who would never be part of the elite. As a teenager, during vacations
from school, he worked with harvest crews in the wheat fields of eastern Washington. And alongside him here, as well as on other laboring
jobs he had, were members of the IWW, also called Wobblies, who

believed in the abolition of capitalism and the establishment of a true socialism, under which hunger and want would also be abolished. To the good burghers of such towns as Douglas's Yakima, the Wobblies were dangerous, disreputable radicals, but Bill Douglas found them to be "warmhearted people" who had "higher ideals than some of the men who ran our banks and were the elders in the church."

Douglas also rode the rails with the Wobblies, picking up an acute distrust of the dedication of the police to justice that stayed with him all his years. "Most of the IWWs," he used to say, "had no criminal records and engaged in no lawless conduct. Yet, though few who rode the rods were criminals, we were all treated as outcasts or vagrants; we were even fired on by the police in railroad yards." (He was the only future justice of the Supreme Court to have had this experience.)

Douglas had to work to get through school. He graduated from Whitman College in Walla Walla, Washington, taught school in Yakima for two years, and then was accepted at Columbia Law School. He paid for half the journey to New York as a freight hand handling two thousand sheep. The rest of the way he traveled as a hobo, riding the rails. He arrived in New York City with six cents in his pocket.

Douglas worked his way through Columbia and graduated second in his class. Then came the most severe disappointment in his life to that point. He had fully expected to be chosen as a law clerk for Supreme Court Justice Harlan Fisk Stone, but the appointment didn't come through. There went his chance to see how the High Court actually worked. Looking for a job, Douglas applied to a number of prestigious and immensely powerful Wall Street law firms. At one of them he was interviewed by John Foster Dulles, later the most right-eous of the cold war secretaries of state.

"I decided against going with Dulles and his firm," said Douglas, "because he was so pontifical. He seemed to me like a high church-man out to exploit someone. In fact, I was so struck by Dulles's pomposity that when he helped me on with my coat, as I was leaving his office, I turned and gave him a quarter tip."

For a while Douglas did work for one of the elite Wall Street firms, but he hated it. "I looked around at the older men there, and I knew I didn't want to be like *any* of them. They couldn't climb a mountain, couldn't tie a dry fly; they knew nothing about the world that was closest to me—the real world, the natural world." Or, as his friend Yale Law School professor Fred Rodell was to say, "Bill's life, like his law, was free."

After a year practicing law back in Yakima and a brief teaching period at Columbia Law School, Douglas went off to a professorship at Yale Law School, where his swiftly rising reputation as an expert in financial matters led to his 1934 appointment to the Securities and Exchange Commission (SEC), of which he became chairman two years later. As the *Washington Post* summarized Douglas's tenure at the SEC, the mountaineer from the Far West "brought the giants of Wall Street to heel."

In 1939 Franklin Roosevelt, who had come to admire Douglas's keenness of intellect and natural egalitarianism displayed during many White House poker sessions as well as during his time on the SEC, appointed him to the Supreme Court. At forty Douglas was the youngest justice in more than a century. It was Louis Brandeis's seat he had taken, and the Great Dissenter had become a kind of mentor to the westerner during Douglas's Washington years. A Brandeis dissent that Douglas liked to quote had been written for the very first wiretap case, in 1928. Brandeis was unalterably convinced that wiretapping was an invasion of privacy, thereby violating the Fourth Amendment, and warned the following: "If the government becomes a lawbreaker, it breeds contempt for the law; it invites every man to become a law unto himself; it invites anarchy."

Douglas kept those words in mind as well as Brandeis's deep suspicion of the concentration of power, whether in government or in the private sector. "Brandeis said," Douglas pointed out in a 1972 CBS television interview, "if we continue in the way in which we're going, this nation will become a nation of clerks, submissive clerks, rather than independent, free men. And he was quite right."

So it was that nine years after he came onto the Court, Douglas himself sounded a warning in a characteristic dissent: "Power that controls the economy should be in the hands of elected representatives of the people, not in the hands of an industrial oligarchy. . . . It should be scattered into many hands so that the fortunes of the people will not be dependent on the whim or caprice of a few self-appointed men."

A single Supreme Court justice could not do much to fulfill this vision of economic democracy, but a president might. And in 1944 Douglas was almost placed in a position that could have made him president. Franklin Roosevelt told the Democratic Convention that either Douglas or Harry Truman would be acceptable to him as the vice presidential nominee. Douglas's name was first on FDR's list, but Robert Hannegan, chairman of the Democratic Party, reversed the names when he sent the list to the party leaders. If FDR died, Truman, who had come up through the party machinery, would be far more predictable and much less dangerous to the status quo than the wild card from the West would be.

Douglas used to claim that he never had any real interest in being president anyway, but when asked by lawyer-journalist Sidney Zion how his presidency would have differed from Truman's, he said this: "For openers, the atomic bomb wouldn't have been dropped on Hiroshima; there wouldn't have been a Cold War; there wouldn't have been the Korean War; there wouldn't have been loyalty oaths; there wouldn't have been the witch-hunts; there wouldn't have been a seizure of the steel mills; and we sure as hell would have recognized Red China."

In any event, Douglas, remaining on the Supreme Court, wielded the First Amendment like a giant broadsword against all who would try to tame the people of this nation. In 1949 he proclaimed the following: "A function of free speech under our system of government is to *invite dispute*. It may indeed best serve its high purposes when it induces a condition of unrest, creates dissatisfaction with conditions as they are, or even stirs people to anger. Speech is often provocative and challenging. It may strike at prejudices and preconceptions and have profound unsettling effects as it presses for acceptance of an idea" (emphasis added).

The work of the Court, however, hardly took up all of his time. When other justices, particularly Chief Justice Warren Burger, complained that the nine men were greatly overburdened, Douglas noted that it took him just four days a week to take care of his work there. But then, Douglas was a good deal smarter than his brethren. Abe Fortas, an old friend and a colleague on the Court, said, "His mind is a cutting instrument of fabulous sharpness. His intellect is a well-ordered, highly organized machine."

Accordingly, much to the annoyance of some of the other justices, Douglas, while hearing oral arguments along with his brethren, was able to write a good many of his books. Jotting away, seemingly oblivious of the jousting of the lawyers in front of the bench, Douglas would suddenly raise his head, ask the most penetratingly pertinent question of the morning, and soon go back to the next chapter of his work in progress.

With the time to roam, intellectually and geographically, Douglas wrote thirty books and traveled to every continent except Antarctica. A man who had conquered just about all fears, he still had one left when he was appointed to the Court: that he might become so enshrined there that he would not have enough *experience* to be a fully responsive justice. As Douglas once said to Eric Sevareid, a prominent CBS commentator, "The decisions we make on the Court are profoundly important to the people. And I think that the person who goes there and stays ten, twenty, thirty years, should be very active in life. Otherwise, he'll end up a dried husk, unrelated to anything that's going on in the world."

No other justice in American history was more active in life or had a wider range of knowledge than Bill Douglas. And because he refused to insulate himself within any one class or age group as he grew older, he never did lose his youthful curiosity and irreverence. Without being sentimental, moreover, Douglas tried to reach out to the young, writing in publications he figured they read. "People of my generation," he explained, "are bankrupt. Politically and philosophically bankrupt. Look at what they've produced: a system that makes war the alternative, a system that's highly stratified, that just pays off great sums of money. This is socialism for the rich. I'd like to reach the minds of the youngsters because this system doesn't have to be this way."

Once, in a recording distributed by Scholastic Magazines and Folkways, Douglas had a chance to speak directly to very young students. His advice essentially was to live as he had: "Learn to live boldly and adventurously, get rid of all the fears that slow people up and inhibit them. Come to the world with an open mind. Don't be afraid of it."

And in the epigraph to the first volume of his autobiography, Douglas, quoting a thirteenth-century Persian poet, added: "All your anxiety is because of your desire for harmony. Seek disharmony; then you will gain peace."

Bill Douglas actively and exultantly pursued disharmony for all his eighty-one years. The last six were extraordinarily frustrating, however, because a stroke he suffered on New Year's Eve, 1974, incapacitated him. With great reluctance, he resigned from the Court on November 12, 1975, after striving mightily, in intense pain, to continue his work there. And after he yielded that much to his infirmity, Douglas nonetheless tried to stay on as a "tenth justice." The Constitution, had no provision for such an arrangement, however, even for its most fervent protector, and Douglas was eventually persuaded to withdraw entirely.

His mind would not be confined, though, and Douglas continued writing, finishing the final volume of his autobiography. The book presents scathing profiles of certain justices, most notably the late Felix Frankfurter and then chief justice Warren Burger.

Until the end, Douglas kept up with his usual wide range of interests, which went far beyond the Court and the law. In May 1979, for instance, he commented trenchantly in a letter to the *Washington Post* on what had happened at the Three Mile Island nuclear disaster: "The message is clear. The benefits of nuclear power are far outweighed by the greater risks imposed upon an unsuspecting public. If we should treat the energy crisis as the 'moral equivalent of war,' then we should view the continued use of nuclear power plants as the 'moral equivalent of suicide.'"

On January 19, 1980, William Orville Douglas, after being hospitalized for a month with pneumonia as well as lung and kidney failure, died at Walter Reed Army Medical Center in Washington, D.C. He was eighty-one. His Court opinions fill 118 large volumes, a quarter of the entire production of the Supreme Court from its beginning. But Bill Douglas's opinions—and the thrusting spirit of liberty that powers them—are not just for study by constitutional scholars and historians. He reached, and will keep on reaching, Americans who continue to refuse, in Louis Brandeis's words, to become "submissive clerks" rather than remain contentiously independent citizens.

"The conscience of this nation," he used to say, "is the Constitution." Douglas was its keeper.

★ ★ ★

Characteristic of William O. Douglas was his view of affirmative action. He opposed affirmative action when it was based on race or gender, but he did not want to abolish the concept of giving particular support to people who had worked hard to overcome disadvantages. His view of affirmative action has not been widely adopted yet, but it keeps gaining adherents.

I learned of his concept of fair and constitutional affirmative action from the justice himself. We met, for the first and only time, in a dentist's office in New York in 1970. Both of us were patients.

It was before nine in the morning on a day that was dark with rain. Wearing a black raincoat that did not appear to have kept much of the rain off him, Justice Douglas strode into the office. With his craggy face and strong presence, he looked, as I've noted, very much like his friend Spencer Tracy looked in *Bad Day at Black Rock.*

Douglas was angry and obsessed that morning. The dentist introduced us and told Douglas that I wrote about constitutional law. I doubt that Douglas had ever heard of me, but he wanted to talk about what was on his mind; figuring I might understand something about what was troubling him, he spoke freely.

His brethren on the Supreme Court, Douglas told me, had put off a case concerning affirmative action, but he had wanted to deal with it right now. A white student, Marc DeFunis, had brought suit against the minority admissions program for entering classes at the University of Washington Law School in Washington State. An extra advantage was given to those who, filling out an optional question on their applications, stated that their "dominant" ethnic origin was black, Chicano, American Indian, or Filipino.

When DeFunis applied in 1971, he was rejected, although his scores (on the Law School Admission Test) along with his grades during his last two years of college were higher than those of thirty-six of the thirty-seven minority group students who were accepted.

DeFunis charged that the law school had violated the Fourteenth Amendment's guarantee that everyone is entitled to equal protection of the laws. Because a state court agreed with him, DeFunis was admitted. A higher state court reversed that decision, but because he had moved ahead in law school, he was allowed to stay.

By the time the case would have reached the United States Supreme Court for initial consideration, it was clear that DeFunis would already have graduated. Therefore a majority of the Supreme Court declared the case moot.

"This case is *not* moot," Douglas forcefully told me that morning in the dentist's office. "This is an issue that is inevitably going to come before us, and so we should address it *now.*"

When the Supreme Court had declared the case moot in 1974, Douglas wrote a dissent. His ideas in that opinion were ignored for a long time, but in the 1990s, as affirmative action based solely on race is increasingly being challenged in the courts and by many Americans, Douglas's reasoning in that dissent may well herald a new approach toward affirmative action across the board:

> The Equal Protection of the Laws clause in the Constitution commands the elimination of racial barriers—not their creation in order to satisfy our theory as to how society ought to be organized.
>
> A segregated admissions process creates suggestions of stigma and caste no less than a segregated classroom.
>
> One other assumption must be clearly disproved: that blacks or browns cannot make it on their individual merit. That is a stamp of inferiority that a state is not permitted to place on any lawyer.

Instead of a race-based admissions policy, Douglas strongly advocated "making decisions on the basis of individual attributes, rather than according to a preference solely on the basis of race:

> Such a policy would not be limited to blacks or Chicanos or Filipinos, or American Indians—although undoubtedly groups such as these may in practice be the principal beneficiaries of it.
>
> But a poor Appalachian white, or a second-generation Chinese in San Francisco or some other American whose lineage is so diverse as to defy ethnic labels, may demonstrate similar potential and thus be accorded favorable consideration by the [admissions] committee.

By "potential," Douglas meant the ability to overcome barriers of poverty or other handicaps. For instance, he noted, "A black applicant who pulled himself out of the ghetto into a junior college may thereby demonstrate a level of motivation, perseverance, and ability that shows an admission committee more promise for law study than the son of a rich alumnus who achieved better grades at Harvard."

William O. Douglas was passionate in detecting injustice, but he never fell into the trap of attempting to remedy injustice by creating another kind of unfairness.

2

ANTHONY GRIFFIN

"If you take the First Amendment from the Klan,
we, as black folks, will be the next to suffer."

The spirit of William O. Douglas can be found in certain teachers, editors of high school papers, union organizers, and lawyers. A particularly courageous defender of the legacy of the Bill of Rights is Anthony Griffin, a black lawyer in Texas. Like Douglas, Griffin believes that constitutional rights are the heritage of *everyone,* no matter how loathsome their ideas.

> *The Constitution protects expression and association without regard*
> *to the race, creed, or political or religious affiliation of the members*
> *of the group which invokes its shield.*
> —JUSTICE WILLIAM BRENNAN, *NAACP V. BUTTON,* 1963

> *It's very easy to give the First Amendment to groups we like and*
> *[that] make us feel good. It's very difficult to apply those principles*
> *to people who anger us, that we want to shut up. . . . But the First*
> *Amendment is not there to protect me from you—but us from the*
> *government. . . . If you start taking away First Amendment rights*
> *from the Klan, for instance, we as black folks will be the next to*
> *suffer. That law silencing them will come around to silence us.*
> —ATTORNEY ANTHONY GRIFFIN,
> GALVESTON, TEXAS, 1993

This is the story of Anthony Griffin, the rarest of all phenomena in American life these days: a person of unyielding integrity. Unlike Bill Clinton, and most everybody else, he does not bend his principles. As a result, the NAACP has fired him as its general counsel in Texas. On the other hand, the Thomas Jefferson Center for Freedom of Expression has given Anthony Griffin its first annual William J. Brennan Jr. Award, which "recognizes a person or group for extraordinary commitment to the cause of free speech in America."

Former University of Virginia president Robert O'Neill, director of the Jefferson Center, said recently that he first heard of Anthony Griffin from me, and I am glad of the result. An old friend of mine, high up in the NAACP, is not so glad because he knows that the NAACP undermined itself and its leadership by dismissing Griffin because he insisted on upholding a landmark Supreme Court decision, won by the NAACP in 1958, in Alabama.

This story begins with that decision. In the 1950s, the NAACP was regarded as subversive, at the very least, by the government of Alabama. The Alabama attorney general ordered the NAACP to turn over the lists of its members in the state. The NAACP refused, was judged to be in civil contempt, and was fined $100,000. This was no small sum for an organization that was rich in determination but not in money.

Delivering the Supreme Court's opinion in 1958, Justice John Harlan found for the NAACP. He pointed out that at stake in this case was freedom of speech and association. The NAACP, he wrote, "has made an uncontroverted showing that on past occasions, revelation of the identity of its rank-and-file members has exposed these members to economic reprisal, loss of employment, threat of physical coercion, and other manifestations of public hostility."

If the state can compel disclosure of the identities of the members of any controversial group, that group will lose members fast. Their First Amendment right to association will have been so chilled as to be meaningless.

NAACP v. Alabama was a mighty victory for all members of unpopular groups. Every once in a while, a state still tries to get away with subverting that Supreme Court decision. In the 1970s, the state of Texas tried to pry loose the NAACP's membership list there, but it was beaten off when confronted with *NAACP v. Alabama*.

Public officials eager to get hold of membership lists do not always have a malign purpose. In 1993, in Texas, the state's Commission on Human Rights went after the membership lists of another group, the Texas Knights of the Ku Klux Klan, for antidiscrimination purposes.

There was a federal court order to desegregate public housing in the town of Vidor, Texas, a place where many fierce racists live. Pressure by the bigots, including intimidation, caused the few blacks who moved in to leave. The Texas Commission on Human Rights wanted the Knights of the Ku Klux Klan's membership lists, mailing lists, and other information to find out if any Klan members were among those who were threatening blacks in Vidor.

Michael Lowe, grand dragon of the Texas Knights of the Ku Klux Klan, went to the American Civil Liberties Union (ACLU) affiliate in that state for help. He said he'd go to jail rather than give up the names of his members. ("These people could lose their jobs or businesses," the grand dragon pointed out.)

This was hardly the first time the Klan had asked the ACLU to protect it from government invasions of their rights under the Bill of Rights. This has happened in Mississippi and California, among other places, and it's a tribute to the ACLU that it defends the right to speak and associate of some of the vilest groups in the nation, because thereby it is defending the indivisible First Amendment. Jay Jacobson, executive director of the Texas ACLU—and one of the most impressive affiliate leaders in that organization—had no difficulty taking the Klan's case. He knew all about *NAACP v. Alabama,* and he knew that setting a precedent allowing a state to force a group to turn over its membership lists could eventually place the ACLU in that dragnet.

Jacobson then had to find a volunteer attorney to handle the case. He received a number of recommendations concerning Anthony Griffin. At that point, he did not know Griffin was black. Griffin had a powerful record of legal successes, as Thomas Korosec pointed out in the *Fort Worth Star-Telegram:*

> Since starting his general law practice in 1978, Griffin has pursued Voting Rights Act cases against the county, city, and school board to increase minority representation in Galveston, and hasn't lost one. . . .

His practice also includes civil and criminal work in Houston and Galveston and long-running civil rights or anti-discrimination lawsuits in courts from West Texas to Dallas to the Gulf Coast. . . . He has gone out of his way to take on cases involving AIDS, race, and sex-discrimination . . . (as well as fighting the practice of banks or businesses to avoid doing business in low-income neighborhoods).

He chose a career in law, he said, because it seemed a good way to make a difference in people's lives—black lives particularly.

When I spoke to Griffin about his record as a key civil rights lawyer in Texas, he reminded me of one of his victories that I'd written about some years ago, although I'd forgotten he was the lawyer. It was an unusual breakthrough in the area of the rights of citizens against their elected officials. A client of Griffin, a merchant, had people coming into his store complaining about the lack of rest rooms along the Galveston beachfront. The merchant printed up fliers listing the home phone numbers of city officials responsible for the paucity of these vital amenities. Soon the city officials were being called at all hours of the night by urgently complaining tourists. These officials tried to suppress the extremely annoying leaflets, but Anthony Griffin and the First Amendment prevailed. Public officials are public.

When he heard from Jay Jacobson of the Texas ACLU, Griffin immediately agreed to defend the grand dragon against the state's demand for the Klan's membership lists.

"The Klan," Griffin told the *New York Times,* "says some vile and vicious and nasty and ugly things. But the Klan has a right to say them. If you ask whether they have a right to organize, to assemble, to free speech, those people have such a right, and we just can't get around that. Because if you take away their rights, you take away my rights also."

The majority of the state board members of the Texas NAACP did not agree with Griffin, their general counsel. (He got no pay for the job, nor does he receive any fee as an ACLU volunteer attorney.)

Griffin told everyone who asked, "This case is not about race. It's not about whether I like Michael Lowe or he likes me. It's about the basic principle of his right to speak and organize."

In August, at a meeting of the state NAACP board in Galveston County, Raymond Scott, a Baptist minister and head of the Port Arthur NAACP, spoke for the angry majority: "You can't represent the NAACP and the Klan at the same time." There were other angry moments.

Griffin told the board that the issue was not debatable, all the more so because of the 1958 victory in *NAACP v. Alabama*. No, he would not apologize, nor would he resign. If he were forced to choose between his First Amendment principles and the NAACP, he would leave.

Supporting him, in the lonesome minority, was an editorial in the *Galveston County Observer News,* an African American monthly newsletter: "For those who do not want the Ku Klux Klan to have their rights protected, you should consider which of your rights you are willing to give up because the Klan has to give up theirs. It may be you giving up yours tomorrow."

The day before the state NAACP board met, there was a special event at the Black Heritage Festival in Galveston. There, Anthony Griffin was named Citizen of the Year. In his acceptance speech, he spoke of the possibility that he might have to stop being general counsel of the state NAACP. He said again that he would not back down and then he paused, looked up, looked down, swallowed, and wept.

The next day the state board, not having the courage to publicly abandon *NAACP v. Alabama* by firing Griffin, decided to let the national office make the decision. After a while, the national office, also without the courage to stand up for—or publicly deny—the principles of *NAACP v. Alabama,* shifted the buck back to the Texas NAACP.

The October 14, 1993, *Galveston Daily News* said this: "Galveston attorney Anthony Griffin has been relieved of his duties as the chief lawyer for the Texas NAACP because of his decision to represent the Ku Klux Klan in a civil liberties case."

"'Fired' is the wrong word," said Gary Bledsoe, president of the Texas NAACP. "We asked him to choose one or the other."

No one in the NAACP had the courage to tell Griffin to his face that he'd been removed. He was told by a reporter. Griffin then said he thought *fired* was indeed the right word.

I wondered what Thurgood Marshall, an unyielding champion of free association, would have thought of all this, particularly because the Texas NAACP actually filed a court brief supporting Texas's attempt to seize the Klan membership list.

In June of 1994, the Texas Supreme Court, citing *NAACP v. Alabama*, ruled that the Klan did not have to obey the subpoena. If the state of Texas appeals this decision, the U.S. Supreme Court is not likely to find a reason to overturn *NAACP v. Alabama*, a decision that protected the NAACP again in the 1970s when Texas commanded the NAACP to turn over its membership list.

I asked Anthony Griffin after the new decision came down whether his law practice had been affected by the controversy over his association with the grand dragon. "It was affected for about six months," he told me, "because I had to go on the road to defend my reputation and to attack the notion that the need to understand free speech does not apply to black people. So I didn't have much time to be a lawyer."

Griffin, by then a national figure, had been lauded by the ACLU and other national free-speech organizations, but, he says, "to the people on the streets, I was this crazy black lawyer in Galveston who had lost his mind. I had to respond to that. So I went on radio, and I talked to black groups and to students at colleges. I challenged the racism of those black folks who told me I should have let a white lawyer take that case. And I challenged the racism of Anglos who regarded me as some kind of oddity because I was a black man who had represented the Klan."

I asked Griffin if he felt he had gotten his reputation back.

"After six months of talking," he said, "I got it back. For instance, there was an NAACP meeting in Texas. As soon as I got in front of that audience, I knew how hostile it was—three hundred people who wouldn't even look at me. After ten minutes, some of them, now and then, looked sideways at me. After half an hour, some were laughing in agreement with what I was saying.

"Afterwards," Griffin noted, "two hundred people lined up to tell me, 'Now we understand, and we will tell others so that they will understand.'"

Of all the critical comments directed at Anthony Griffin during his defense of the First Amendment's guarantee of free association, the dumbest came from William Hale, executive director of the Texas Human Rights Commission, which was trying to force the Klan to give up its membership lists. Hale accused the Klan and Anthony Griffin of "hiding behind the Constitution." That's what Senator Joe McCarthy used to say when witnesses before his House Committee on Un-American Activities used the Bill of Rights to refuse to answer his witch-hunting questions.

3

SUPREME COURT JUSTICE WILLIAM BRENNAN, PART I

"The censorial power is in the people over the Government, and not in the Government over the people."

$\mathcal{I}$t was entirely fitting for Anthony Griffin to receive the first William J. Brennan Award. Justice Brennan was an extraordinarily influential member of the Supreme Court. He not only enlarged and secured the right to free speech but also strengthened much of the rest of the Constitution and expanded and deepened the meaning of constitutional rights and liberties.

It is not hyperbole to say that this would have been a different nation if William Brennan had not been on the High Court. Some of the changes he brought to the interpretation of the Constitution have been rolled back by later justices, but much of his work remains as further guarantees of individual liberty for all of us.

In 1984, the *National Review* paid gloomy tribute to Supreme Court Justice William Brennan. "No individual in this country, on or off the Court, has had a more profound and sustained impact upon public policy in the United States for the past 27 years," it said. From the perspective of the *National Review,* that influence, made all the stronger by what it described as "his engaging personality," was unfailingly pernicious:

A Catholic, he has played an instrumental role in the unfettered availability of abortion across the country; . . . appointed to the Court by a Republican because of his ostensibly conservative views and because of his experience as a state court judge, it is he who mandated the reapportionment of every state legislative system in the country; . . . the son of hard-working Irish immigrant parents, he nevertheless has made significant strides in elevating the welfare state to constitutional status.

This was hardly the first indictment of Justice Brennan as a powerful judicial activist. Years before, Brennan had even been disowned by the president who appointed him. Fred Friendly, the former head of CBS News, asked Dwight Eisenhower in 1961 if he had made any substantial mistakes during his presidency. "Yes, two," Eisenhower said. "And they are both sitting on the Supreme Court." The justices he had in mind were Earl Warren and William Brennan. Neither had turned out to be as restrained in his approach to the Constitution as Eisenhower had expected.

Brennan has not lacked celebrators. They agree with his critics that his influence on millions of Americans who know nothing about him has been wide ranging and profound. In a 1987 article in the *National Law Journal,* Norman Dorsen, the president of the American Civil Liberties Union, observed, "We would be living under a very different Constitution if Justice Brennan were not on the Supreme Court." Brennan's many landmark opinions, Dorsen wrote, have greatly strengthened freedom of expression and the rights of criminal defendants, and have expanded and deepened the principle of the Fourteenth Amendment's "equal protection of the laws," especially for racial minorities and for women. Brennan has often been on the dissenting side, increasingly so in the Rehnquist Court, but on certain fundamental questions of individual liberty he has so profoundly redefined the framework in which the issues are discussed that he may well be the most influential member of the Court in this century.

Brennan saw the fundamental purpose of the Constitution to be, as he told Bill Moyers in a 1987 interview for public television, "the protection of the dignity of the human being and the recognition that every individual has fundamental rights which government cannot deny him." It is because of this view of the Constitution that Brennan always entered a dissent against the imposition of the death penalty. He believed that it treats "members of the human race as non-humans," that "even the vilest criminal remains a human being possessed of common human dignity."

Brennan also believed in "the age-old dream," as he put it, that eventually no one anywhere will be denied his or her inherent dignity and rights. "The dream, though always old, is never old, like the Poor Old Woman in Yeats's play *Cathleen ni Houlihan*," Brennan told me in his chambers at the Court one afternoon. "'Did you see an old woman going down the path?' asks Bridget. 'I did not,' replies Patrick, who came into the house just after the old woman left it. 'But I saw a young girl and she had the walk of a queen.'" He smiled. "That passage has always meant a great deal to me. I've used it often over the last thirty years."

William Joseph Brennan Jr. was born in Newark, New Jersey, in 1906. His father, William Joseph Brennan, had come to New Jersey from County Roscommon, Ireland, in 1893. His mother, Agnes McDermott, was also an immigrant from Roscommon; she met her husband soon after moving, at age seventeen, to New Jersey to live with an aunt who ran a boardinghouse.

"My father settled in Trenton, where he stoked the boiler in a factory, but he later found work as a coal heaver in the Ballantine Brewery in Newark," Justice Brennan told me. "In those days, they had those monster furnaces that were served by hand and shovel.

"In short order, my father became quite dissatisfied with the way things were going at Ballantine's. But before he could do anything about it he had to find a place to live, and he came upon the boardinghouse where Agnes McDermott was staying. They met, and they married. Back at work, my father felt that Ballantine's was treating the coal heavers and the other employees unfairly. Remember, those were the days before we had the Wagner Act or the Taft-Hartley Act, or any of the other laws that protected workingmen in their efforts to organize. My father got into a great deal of trouble, but he went on to become quite prominent in what there was of a labor movement in Newark."

By 1916, the elder Brennan had become a member of the Essex

County Trades and Labor Council. "There was a transit workers' strike—trolley-car conductors and motormen," his son said. "They were up against a company owned by a family that you might say had a monopoly on the whole state. It was like a company state. One brother headed the biggest bank, another was in charge of the gas and electric companies, and the third had been attorney general.

"When the transit workers struck, the Newark police were on the side of the employers. My father came up with the idea. 'My God, it's the only way we're going to be able to take over the city government.' He sponsored a movement that resulted in the abolition of the mayor-and-aldermen form of city government and replaced it with five commissioners, each of whom was assigned to supervise a department. In the 1917 election, my father ran as a labor candidate, with the prospect that if he won he'd be named the director of public safety. That way, *he'd* have control of the police and fire departments, so there'd be no more strikebreaking." Justice Brennan was clearly savoring the story. He smiled and went on. "My father finished third out of eighty-six candidates, and was named director of public safety. He headed not only the police and fire departments but also the health and safety licensing department." The senior Brennan was reelected in 1921, 1925, and 1929. The last two times he ran, he finished first.

"There were eight of us," Brennan told me. "Four boys and four girls. One of the boys later became general counsel of Ballantine's. Raising a family that size on the kind of salary public officials got in those days was not easy. And my father was an honest man until the day he died. If there had ever been an honest official in the city of Newark, it was he. What got me interested in people's rights and liberties was the kind of family and the kind of neighborhood I was brought up in. I saw all kinds of suffering—people had to struggle. I saw the suffering of my mother, even though we were never without. We always had something to eat, we always had something to wear. But others in the neighborhood had a harder time."

Brennan went to parochial grammar school and to public high school. He was a good student and industrious outside school. Daniel Crystal, a New Jersey attorney and a chronicler of Brennan's life, says that the young Brennan made change for passengers waiting for trolley cars, delivered milk in a horse-drawn wagon, and worked in a filling station. After high school, Brennan attended the Wharton School of the University of Pennsylvania. He graduated cum laude in 1928 with a degree in economics, and that same year he married Marjorie Leonard, of East Orange.

He entered Harvard Law School in the fall. Since the newlyweds required an income, young Mrs. Brennan stayed in New Jersey, working as a proofreader and secretary on a newspaper. In 1930, Brennan's father died, leaving little money to his children. Brennan successfully applied for a scholarship in order to finish law school and waited on tables in a fraternity house. He received his LL.B. in 1931, graduating in the top 10 percent of his class. One of his professors at Harvard Law School was Felix Frankfurter, who frequently urged his students, "Think for yourself." Later, when both were serving on the Supreme Court, they often differed, and Brennan remembers, with a chuckle, that Frankfurter would sometimes say, "I always wanted my students to think for themselves, but Brennan goes too far."

While Brennan was at Harvard, he was at odds with his father over a court case, *Public Welfare Pictures v. Brennan*. The Brennan was William Brennan Sr., public safety director of Newark, and at issue was an educational film called *The Naked Truth*. "It was one of those films intended to teach children about sex, and a movie outfit called Public Welfare wanted to show it," Justice Brennan told me. "'No, sir,' my father said. 'Not that filthy thing!' He threatened to revoke the theater's license if the film was shown. Public Welfare went into the court of chancery and got an injunction against my father. He was compelled to let that film open. And that became a case that we studied in class."

On a visit home, young Brennan told his father that he believed that the court had ruled properly. "My father roared, 'WHAAAAAAAAT!'" Brennan told me, laughing. "I was never able to convince him that it was a good opinion. He was just as independent as a hog on ice. He had similar clashes with producers of plays and burlesque shows. He lost more of them than he won. He was an old-fashioned Irish Catholic who took a very dim view of the propriety of anything that touched on the sexual."

At Harvard, Brennan was president of the student legal-aid society, and his work there foreshadowed one of his chief concerns on the

Supreme Court: making due process of law attend every defendant, including those defendants with the fewest resources. But after graduating from law school, Brennan did not go into legal-aid work. Instead, he joined the large and distinguished Newark law firm of Pitney, Hardin & Skinner, sometimes known as "Pluck 'em, Hook 'em & Skin 'em," where he became an expert in labor law, that is, the management side of labor law.

One of his opponents in court was Morton Stavis, a labor lawyer and later a founder of the Center for Constitutional Rights. In the Passaic County Bar Association's journal, Stavis recalled two of his encounters with Brennan when he himself represented the employees' union of the Phelps Dodge Corporation of Elizabeth, New Jersey, and Brennan represented its management: "He was a vigorous, overwhelmingly able, and above all gracious opponent. I was inexperienced in litigation at the time and was guilty of a number of procedural oversights. Not only did he not take advantage of them, but he went out of his way to help me correct the record so that the cases would be fairly tried on the merits. Result: He won one case, I won the other."

In 1942, Brennan took a leave from Pitney, Hardin & Skinner to join the army, and he was given the rank of major in its ordnance department. He was borrowed by the Army Air Corps to settle some severe labor problems in the aircraft industry on the West Coast, and after a year of negotiating he brought peace to the dispute. He went on to become a manpower troubleshooter in other areas of conflict, and by the time he left the service, in 1945, he had been promoted to colonel and awarded the Legion of Merit. He had shown such proficiency at managing men and affairs that one of his wartime colleagues later said, "I would have expected that he would have become the president of one of our great corporations."

Instead, Brennan went back to his law firm and resumed his practice. The firm was renamed Pitney, Hardin, Ward & Brennan, but in 1949 Brennan resigned to accept an appointment from Governor Alfred Driscoll to the Superior Court of New Jersey. The appointment meant a considerable cut in income, and the reason Brennan decided to take it was that his large and growing law practice seemed to be affecting his health and didn't leave him enough time for his family.

While Brennan was on the New Jersey bench, he became known in legal circles for a particularly forceful dissent in *State of New Jersey v. John Henry Tune*. The defendant had been charged with murder, and the prosecution had a statement by him, made without a lawyer present, in which he confessed to the killing. Tune told his court-appointed lawyers that the statement had been exacted through force and through threats of violence to members of his family. His lawyers asked to see a copy of the confession before trial, but a majority of the New Jersey Supreme Court denied the request, on the ground that Tune might use the "opportunity to procure false testimony and commit perjury." Brennan's dissent emphasized the constitutional rights of defendants: "We must remember that society's interest is equally that the innocent shall not suffer, and not alone that the guilty shall not escape. . . . It shocks my sense of justice that . . . counsel for an accused facing a possible death sentence should be denied inspection of his confession which, were this a civil case, could not be denied."

Brennan might well have remained on the New Jersey Supreme Court for the rest of his career if Arthur Vanderbilt hadn't gotten sick shortly before he was to be keynote speaker at a conference in Washington, D. C., on the subject of court congestion. "It was in May 1956," Brennan recalled, "and the attorney general of the United States, Herbert Brownell, had convened a large assembly of judges, scholars, and others interested in improving the administration of justice through better court procedures everywhere in the country. For some years, the number one figure in that movement had been Arthur Vanderbilt. He became ill two days before the meeting, and I was pushed in to substitute for him. Having had so little time to prepare a speech, I spoke mostly off the cuff, for close to an hour."

Brownell was impressed by Brennan's performance, and four months later, when Supreme Court Justice Sherman Minton announced that he would retire in October, Brownell recommended Brennan as the successor, and President Eisenhower agreed. At the time, Brennan's qualifications were generally considered to include not only his ability but also the likelihood that in the forthcoming election the president might pick up some votes by nominating a Democrat who was also a Roman Catholic; furthermore, the bright, well-respected Catholic from New Jersey might take some of the play away from the rising senator John F. Kennedy.

When I asked Brennan about this, he laughed and said, "Well, I must say that didn't dawn on me. I read all about it days afterward. John Kennedy had almost taken the vice presidential nomination from Senator Kefauver. And Arthur Kock, of the *New York Times*—he was such a big wheel then—was conjecturing that even though the prospect of Adlai Stevenson's defeating the president was not that likely, Herbert Brownell, smart politician that he was, was not going to take any chances, and wanted to fend off Stevenson by putting a Northeast Irishman on the Court. Well, I did read a lot about it, but nobody ever said a word to me about it."

One of the opponents of Brennan's nomination was Senator Joseph McCarthy. "He knew about me," Brennan said, chuckling. "In 1954, when I was on the New Jersey Supreme Court, I was asked to address the Charitable Irish Society of Boston on St. Patrick's Day, and I spoke of certain things going on that were reminiscent of the Salem witch-hunts."

In 1955 Brennan spoke these words before the Monmouth Rotary Club in New Jersey on the subject of the Fifth Amendment:

> Frankness with ourselves must compel the acknowledgment that our resentment toward those who invoked its protection led us into a toleration of some of the very abuses which brought the privilege into being so many centuries ago. The abuses took on a modern dress, it is true—not the rack and the screw but the distorted version of the happenings at secret hearings released to the press, the shouted epithet at the hapless and helpless witness. . . . That path brings us perilously close to destroying liberty in liberty's name.

"Hell, when I made those speeches I had no idea I would ever to sit on the Supreme Court," Brennan told me. "And those weren't the only times I paid my respects to Senator McCarthy. I made speeches calling him all sorts of names before other groups around Monmouth County. So when Eisenhower announced he was going to appoint me, McCarthy issued a statement saying that I was supremely unfit for the Supreme Court. And, though he wasn't on the Judiciary Committee, he asked to sit with that committee so that he could interrogate me. I had a recess appointment, so they didn't get around to my hearings until I'd been on the Court for some four months.

"At first, there was resistance to McCarthy's sitting in on the committee. He was in decline. He had already been censured, and he died not long after my hearings. I thought that those who were against his sitting with the committee were wrong. There's absolutely nothing in the Constitution which limits the advise-and-consent function of the Senate. Nothing. And, because each senator has to cast his own vote on the matter, he should be able to interrogate the nominee if he wants to. And any senator, furthermore, is entitled to ask any damn question he wants—about ideology or whatever the hell it may be."

I asked Justice Brennan what kinds of questions Senator McCarthy had asked.

"Oh, just the craziest things." Brennan's voice took on McCarthy's heavy cadences, including the ominous pause: "'Do you mean to tell me you don't think the most *important* thing we can possibly do is rout out Communists, wherever they are?'"

During the hearings, McCarthy announced gravely to the committee that he had brought a document concerning the nominee. It turned out to be Brennan's St. Patrick's Day speech in Boston. "Do you approve of congressional investigations and exposures of communism?" the senator asked Brennan. "Show me one little word in any speech in which you ever approved of congressional investigations."

Brennan replied that he thought such investigations were a "vital function" of the Congress, but that since he was already on the Supreme Court his oath of office forbade him to make any comment on matters that might come before him. "I gather that those who heard the exchanges between us all that day did not think it was one of Senator McCarthy's finest hours," Brennan remarked to me.

Having been evaluated by the American Bar Association as "eminently qualified" at the time he was appointed to the Court, Brennan now received the approval of the Senate Judiciary Committee. On March 19, 1957, the United States Senate confirmed his nomination. The sole negative vote was cast by Joseph McCarthy. The new justice told one reporter that he considered himself "the mule entered in the

Kentucky Derby," and added, "I don't expect to distinguish myself, but I do expect to benefit from the association."

In a 1987 interview on National Public Radio, Brennan recalled his introduction to the other members of the Court this way: "Chief Justice Warren invited me to his chambers, and from there we went up to the third floor of the Supreme Court Building. In a small room, my seven new colleagues were sitting around a table having sandwiches. The room was dark, and he put on the light, and there they all were, watching the opening game of the 1956 World Series. I was introduced by the chief to each of them, and someone said, 'Put out the light.' They put out the light, and they went on watching the game."

In a 1986 article on Brennan in the *American Bar Association Journal*, Joel Gora, a professor at Brooklyn Law School, noted that in 1956, when Brennan came on the Court, it "had no clear direction or identity." He went on:

> The school desegregation decisions had not yet been imple-
> mented, and concepts like affirmative action had not even been
> articulated. First Amendment doctrine was mostly a function of
> ad hoc decision-making as the Court grappled with the issues
> posed by Communist Party advocacy and association. The rights
> of the accused, too, were determined by case-by-case adjudica-
> tion, and the major reforms that would protect defendants
> against the excesses of local law enforcement were years away.
>
> Notions of using the Constitution to protect private choice
> on intimate matters such as contraception, abortion and sexual
> privacy or preference would have seemed visionary. Problems
> raised by grossly malapportioned state legislatures were viewed as
> political questions not subject to constitutional measure. Indeed,
> constitutional restraints seemed largely irrelevant to the conduct
> of government at the state and local levels.

Through a blend of pragmatism and principle, with an ebullient, gregarious, and easy personal manner, Justice Brennan helped change all that. In the beginning, however, Brennan found it hard to feel comfortable on the Court. In a 1973 article in the *University of Chicago Law Review*, he wrote the following:

I expect that only a Justice of the Court can know how insepara-
bly intertwined are all the Court's functions, and how arduous
and long is the process of developing the sensitivity to constitutional adjudication that marks the role. One enters a new and
wholly unfamiliar world when he enters the Supreme Court of
the United States, and this is as true of a Justice who comes from
a federal court of appeals as it is of a Justice, like me, who came
from a state supreme court. I say categorically that no prior experience, including prior judicial experience, prepares one for the
work of the Supreme Court.

When I read that statement to Justice Brennan, he laughed. "Did
I say that? It's right, you know, every damn word of it. What I was
talking about reflects, I expect, more of my own background as a state
judge. Nonetheless, what I said is the sort of thing Felix Frankfurter
also used to say.

"For example, when I was on the Jersey courts, the judges, at
whatever level, had no occasion to keep abreast of the Supreme Court
in that dimension of criminal law that has to do with the Bill of
Rights. Those rights and liberties were not made applicable to the
states until I got here. For instance, the exclusionary rule—that ille-
gally obtained evidence cannot be used in a court, because it violates
the Fourth Amendment—was not extended to the states until 1961.

"But even today's state judges who come here have difficulty
adjusting to the Court at first. Take my colleague Justice O'Connor.
She was an Arizona state judge at the trial court and the intermediate
appellate court. Many of the cases she dealt with did have to turn on
the application of the Bill of Rights—as we had decided here—to
state law. But I know that even she will tell you that you simply don't
feel comfortable in this seat until you've been here for a while. One of
the reasons is that it's a pretty awesome feeling, believe me, to appreci-
ate that something you're doing, when it's decided, will have an enormous impact among two hundred-odd million people. And that feeling *never* leaves you. It just never leaves you." Brennan smiled. "It
takes a while before you can become even calm about approaching a
job like this. Which is not to say you do not make mistakes. In my
case, there has been the obscenity area."

He looked at the red-bound volumes of his opinions and said, "For sixteen years, it fell to me to write most of the obscenity opinions here. They were usually assigned to me. I won't say why, but they were."

"Why were they assigned to you?"

Brennan chuckled. "Because nobody else wanted to have anything to do with them."

Measuring obscenity against the First Amendment has been a challenge to Brennan since the days when he came home and argued with his father about censorship. Yet Brennan was not entirely at odds with his father: He believed that some forms of expression were indeed beyond the protection of the First Amendment. That notion became Supreme Court doctrine in *Roth v. United States*, for which Brennan wrote the majority opinion during his first year on the Court. A companion case, *Alberts v. California*, was decided the same day. Brennan's opinion, covering both cases, established him as the Court's spokesperson on a complex, emotional issue that was then, as it is now, intently followed by religious groups, civil libertarians, politicians, complaining constituents, book publishers, writers, and movie producers.

Samuel Roth had been convicted of mailing obscene advertisements and circulars as well as an obscene book. David Alberts had been convicted of "keeping for sale" obscene and indecent books and publishing an obscene advertisement for them. In his decision, Brennan emphasized that "sex and obscenity are not synonymous," and he tried to make as narrow as possible the area of speech that could be penalized. "The door barring federal and state intrusion into [freedoms of speech and the press] cannot be left ajar; it must be kept tightly closed and opened only the slightest crack necessary to prevent encroachment upon more important interests," he wrote. His solution was to adopt what struck him as a fair and reasonable test. Expression would not be protected under the First Amendment if "to the average person, applying contemporary community standards, the dominant theme of the material taken as a whole appeals to prurient interest."

Brennan believed he had set a reasonable course by which the Court could draw a line between obscenity and speech that the Constitution intended to be free, yet what Justice John Harlan later described as "the intractable obscenity problem" only got worse. Ten years after the *Roth* case, Harlan observed, "The subject of obscenity has produced a variety of views among the members of the Court unmatched in any other course of constitutional adjudication." By then, the Court had decided thirteen obscenity cases, and there had been fifty-five separate opinions.

In a 1966 case, *"Memoirs" v. Massachusetts*, Justices Brennan, Warren, and Fortas had used as a test of obscenity that the material in question be "utterly without redeeming social value." Justices Douglas, Black, and Stewart had concurred. In 1973, in *Miller v. California*, the Burger majority discarded the "utterly without redeeming social value" criterion and, in effect, largely removed the burden of proof from the prosecutor. It was up to the defense to convince a judge or a jury that the indicted material had "serious literary, artistic, political, or scientific value."

The *Miller* decision came down on the same day as the decision in *Paris Adult Theatre I v. Slaton*. In a long dissent in that case, Brennan took fundamental issue with the Burger majority, and in a rather rare confession by a Supreme Court Justice, admitted that his long effort to figure out the difference between protected speech and obscenity had been a failure:

> I am convinced that the approach initiated 16 years ago in *Roth v. United States* . . . and culminating in the Court's decision today, cannot bring stability to this area of the law without jeopardizing fundamental First Amendment values, and I have concluded that the time has come to make a significant departure from that approach. . . . The essence of our problem in the obscenity area is that we have been unable to provide "sensitive" tools to separate obscenity from other sexually oriented but constitutionally protected speech, so that efforts to suppress the former do not spill over into the suppression of the latter. . . . It comes as no surprise that judicial attempts to follow our lead conscientiously have often ended in hopeless confusion.

At that point, Brennan seemed to throw up his hands:

> I am reluctantly forced to the conclusion that none of the available formulas, including the one announced today, can reduce

the vagueness to a tolerable level while at the same time striking an acceptable balance between the protections of the First and Fourteenth Amendments, on the one hand, and on the other the asserted state interest in regulating the dissemination of certain sexually oriented materials.

Any effort to draw a constitutionally acceptable boundary on state power must resort to such indefinite concepts as "prurient interest," "patent offensiveness," "serious literary value," and the like. The meaning of these concepts necessarily varies with the experience, outlook, and even idiosyncrasies of the person defining them. . . . I would hold, therefore, that at least in the absence of distribution to juveniles or obtrusive exposure to unconsenting adults, the First and Fourteenth Amendments prohibit the State and Federal Governments from attempting wholly to suppress sexually oriented materials on the basis of their allegedly "obscene" contents.

"I put sixteen years into that damn obscenity thing," Justice Brennan told me early one morning in his chambers. "I tried and I tried, and I waffled back and forth, and I finally gave up. If you can't define it, you can't prosecute people for it. And that's why, in the *Paris Adult Theatre* decision, I finally abandoned the whole effort. I reached the conclusion that every criminal-obscenity statute—and most obscenity laws are criminal—was necessarily unconstitutional, because it was impossible, from the statute, to define obscenity. Accordingly, anybody charged with violating the statute would not have known that his conduct was a violation of the law. He wouldn't know whether the material was obscene until the court told him."

Brennan has had greater success in broadening the definition of the First Amendment. One of his landmark decisions in that area was *New York Times Co. v. Sullivan.* In 1960, L. B. Sullivan, the police commissioner of Montgomery, Alabama, had sued the *Times* for publishing an advertisement signed by writers, actors, labor leaders, and black Southern preachers. The text of the ad accused Southern authorities of conducting a "wave of terror" against black students demonstrating for their civil rights and charged the police with trying to intimidate Dr. Martin Luther King Jr. Although Commissioner

Sullivan's name was not mentioned in the ad, he claimed that he would be considered responsible for many of the actions listed there. A jury awarded him $500,000 in damages.

Until *New York Times Co. v. Sullivan,* libel was left to the common law of each state, on the ground that it was a private matter. Reversing the verdict, Justice Brennan established, for the first time in United States history, that "the constitutional protections for speech and press limit a state's power to award damages in a libel action brought by a public official against critics of his official conduct."

Brennan quoted the principal author of the First Amendment, James Madison: "The censorial power is in the people over the Government, and not in the Government over the people." And in a passage that is widely quoted, Brennan stated, "We consider this case against the background of a profound national commitment to the principle that debate on public issues should be uninhibited, robust, and wide-open, and that it may well include vehement, caustic, and sometimes unpleasantly sharp attacks on government and public officials."

Adding to the historic significance of the decision, Brennan addressed the Alien and Sedition Acts of 1798, which had criminally penalized speech defaming the government. In the 166 years since the passage of those statutes, the Supreme Court had not explicitly declared them unconstitutional. Brennan finally did.

New York Times Co. v. Sullivan did not foreclose all libel suits brought by public officials, but by insisting that such suits meet the "actual malice" test, the decision made them more difficult to win. Brennan wrote that a public official (and this was later broadened to include public figures in general) cannot recover "damages for a defamatory falsehood relating to his official conduct unless he proves that the statement was made with 'actual malice'—that is, with knowledge that it was false or with reckless disregard of whether it was false or not."

Another important First Amendment decision was Brennan's 1967 opinion on the right of New York State to impose loyalty tests on teachers in public schools, including public colleges and universities. The case, *Keyishian v. Board of Regents of New York,* involved a teacher named Harry Keyishian, an instructor in English at the State

University of New York at Buffalo, who had been threatened with the loss of his job and indeed was not rehired the following year when he refused to comply with various "loyalty" provisions enforced by the New York State Board of Regents.

Fifteen years before, the Supreme Court, by a six-to-three majority, had affirmed the constitutionality of the same set of loyalty tests in New York State. In his majority opinion, Justice Minton, Brennan's predecessor, saw nothing injurious to the First Amendment in a statute that said that no one could be employed in the public school system who spoke "any treasonable or seditious word or words."

There was also a law requiring the state's Board of Regents to compile a list of "subversive" organizations, membership in which would be "prima facie evidence of disqualification." The definition of *subversive* included the "advocacy" of the overthrow of government by violent or any other unlawful means as well as the utterance of seditious words.

In his opinion, Brennan wrote that the language in the anti-subversive statutes and regulations was unconstitutionally vague. Under the penal law involved, for instance, one commits a felony by "advocating, advising or teaching the doctrine that organized government should be overthrown by force, violence or any unlawful means." Brennan asked, "Does the teacher who carries a copy of the Communist Manifesto on a public street thereby advocate criminal anarchy?"

The civil service law also penalized the teaching of subversive doctrines. Brennan asked, "Does the teacher who informs his class about the precepts of Marxism or the Declaration of Independence violate this prohibition? . . . And does the prohibition of the distribution of matter 'containing' the doctrine [that government should be overthrown] bar histories of the evolution of Marxist doctrine or tracing the background of the French, American, or Russian Revolutions?"

With all the vagueness of the interlocking statutory and regulatory language, Brennan said, "it would be a bold teacher who would not stay as far as possible from utterances or acts which might jeopardize his living by enmeshing him in this intricate machinery."

Brennan went on to focus on the particular reason for safeguarding First Amendment freedoms in this case: "Our Nation is deeply committed to safeguarding academic freedom, which is of transcendent value to all of us and not merely to the teachers concerned. That freedom is therefore a special concern of the First Amendment, which does not tolerate laws that cast a pall of orthodoxy over the classroom."

Concerning the New York State law that membership in the Communist Party was prima facie evidence that a teacher was not qualified to remain in the educational system, Brennan emphasized that "mere knowing membership without a specific intent to further the unlawful aims of an organization is not a constitutionally adequate basis for exclusion from such positions as those held by appellants."

Twenty years later, Harry Keyishian was interviewed as part of the Bill Moyers series *In Search of the Constitution,* on public television. Keyishian told Moyers that as an undergraduate at Queens College in New York during the 1950s, he had seen a number of his professors fired for failing a loyalty test, and he said, "What struck me at the time, what I still carried as a kind of burden into the 1960s, was a sense of frustration and impotence, to watch these very decent, these intellectually talented and dedicated teachers vanishing from the system . . . and not being able to do anything about it."

The day the Supreme Court decision came down, Keyishian was awakened by a friend who worked at the *New York Times.* He told Keyishian the news. It was a five-to-four decision, however, and Keyishian told Moyers he had worried that the next time the issue came before the Court, the decision might not stand; after all, though the so-called McCarthy era had ended, the vote had been very close. As the years passed, and Brennan's opinion remained the law of the land, Keyishian realized that Brennan's "decisions have apparently been so well drawn and so well crafted that they've held up in very hostile environments in that Court, and I hope they'll continue to do so."

I saw Justice Brennan at the Supreme Court soon after he watched Harry Keyishian on the Moyers television program, and he was excited at having seen the actual person behind the name on the Court papers. "It was fascinating," he told me. "It was the first time I had seen him. Of course, it's rare that I ever see the people in the cases we deal with. The things he said on the program, the fight he and the other teachers put up—I had no idea how much they had to lose personally if the case had gone the other way. They would have lost everything they had ever done as teachers."

I asked Justice Brennan one afternoon whether the occasionally sharp exchanges in the published opinions of the Court were reflected in the justices' personal encounters in the Court's conference room, the chambers, and the corridors.

"It's hard to believe this, but none of that carries over, in the slightest, to our personal relationships," Brennan said. "It's remarkable, it really is, but it's absolutely essential in a small body of nine people who have to work as closely as we do, and out of sight of the public or the press or anyone else. You simply can't afford to let your convictions affect your personal relationships. I'm not saying it has *never* happened, but I can say this: I have sat now with about a fifth of all the Supreme Court justices there have been, and I have never had a cross word with one of them. Not with a single one of them.

"On the other hand, there's no question that Bill Douglas's relationship with Felix Frankfurter was very much affected by their conflicting views. They were more than distant." Justice Brennan smiled and added, "They were almost snarling at one another. You'll recall that when Felix came to the Court, everybody expected that he was going to be the great liberal champion. Of course, he turned out to be anything but. But Bill, who came on the Court just after Felix, started out as the great financial expert, the chairman of the Securities and Exchange Commission. His first work on the Court consisted of a number of really brilliant opinions in that field, and then he became a real champion—with Hugo Black—of the Bill of Rights.

"Felix regarded him as a turncoat. Consequently, their relations were very strained, to put it mildly. Before that, there was Justice McReynolds, who would not shake hands with Louis Brandeis or Benjamin Cardozo, because they were Jews. So there has been animosity between the justices in the past, but in my day, except for that between Felix and Bill, there has been none."

4

Supreme Court Justice William Brennan, Part II

"Schools cannot expect their students to learn the lessons of good citizenship when the school authorities themselves disregard the fundamental principles underpinning our constitutional freedoms."

*B*rennan almost never showed resentment at anything written or said about him, but he bristled when he was complimented for being the preeminent "politician" on the Court. "I am not a playmaker," he told me a number of times. "I don't go around cajoling and importuning my colleagues to go along with my point of view. When I have been able to draw a consensus, I have done it by the drafts I circulated among my colleagues. Rather than try to talk something out with another justice, I sit down and write concrete suggestions as to what I don't like about what he has done or what I do like about it. I suggest changes in their drafts, and other justices will suggest changes in what I've written. Every justice of this Court admits that holding on to a majority can be a very difficult thing, and what we all do is try to persuade each other by what we write to each other. From time to time, when I think I'm going to have a five-person majority, one of the four will write to me and say, 'I'll be happy to join with you if you delete this and this.' If you can, you do it. But there are times when I have to write back and say, 'I don't think I should, because then it wouldn't be what I wanted to say.' It's quite important to get these differences out by written exchanges."

Jeffrey Leeds, who clerked for Justice Brennan and is now an investment banker, says this about Brennan: "It's true that Justice Brennan didn't go around buttonholing the other justices, trying to persuade them to join one of his opinions. He doesn't have to do that. He gets *us* to do it; that is, he gets his clerks to talk to the other clerks and find out what their justices are thinking."

I told Brennan what his former clerk said, and he laughed loud and long. "Well, it's true," he said. "That's not the case with all my colleagues. Some of them hold tighter strings on their clerks' activities than I do. In my case, I'll take help wherever I can get it, and I think it's very helpful to have clerks exchange points of view with clerks in other chambers. It's helpful, when they know what I think about something, to attribute to me any view I may have. They're free to talk about anything we have here, about my position and their position and anything else. I've worked that way ever since I came here. It has always struck me as rather unfortunate that some justices will not let their clerks do that sort of thing. They will tell their clerks on given cases not to say anything about how the justice feels. I don't understand it. After all, we employ the clerks to help us. They are surrogates in a greater sense than is true of most associations."

A clerk beginning his tenure with Justice Brennan received a series of short orientation speeches from his employer. One had to do with the dress code of the Brennan chambers. "I walked into his chambers for the first time, and Justice Brennan said he was pleased to meet me," Leeds recalled. "Then he did this thing he does every year. He kind of grabs your necktie and says, 'Do you like wearing these things?' You say no. 'Then take it off,' he says. 'You'll spend plenty of time working hard in this building. You might as well be comfortable.'"

There was also the five-finger speech. It generally came when a new clerk asked, in dismay and outrage, how a majority of the Court arrived at a decision he or she felt was flagrantly unjust. Justice Brennan held up his hand, wriggled his five fingers, and said, "Five votes. Five votes can do anything around here."

All the more reason, before a final count in a case at hand, for his clerks to try to find out enough about the thinking going on in the other chambers. "While an opinion is being written in our chambers, we might talk to a clerk for a justice who we knew would be a tough fifth vote," Leeds explained. "And we would ask this clerk what was really bugging his guy about Brennan's draft. This information gathering can take place after oral argument in a case, when the justices hold their conference. That's where the preliminary votes are taken, before drafts of opinions are circulated. Or it can happen before a conference. We might find out, from his or her clerk, where a justice is leaning on a particular case. When we know what that justice is thinking, we keep that in mind when we write out two-page summaries of each case for Brennan to emphasize at the conference. The points he hits may be pitched entirely to that one justice."

Depending on the individual justices, clerks had varying input in the shaping of the written opinions. A first draft was almost invariably written by a clerk. One of them described the experience by saying, "You go back to your office, you take a deep breath, you stare at your computer screen, and you go, 'Holy shit, I'm going to write the law of the land.'" Brennan required that all his clerks—he had four—not only the author of the first draft, sign off on the analysis of the case before he saw it. That way, he got a range of viewpoints. After he read the draft, he told the clerk in private what he felt was lacking or just plain wrong. Brennan read every word in every change, and at times engaged in what one clerk called "dramatic rewriting."

His clerks, Brennan told me, never write the final draft. "But all of us need to make use of the contributions of the clerks," he said. "If we didn't have the benefit of their writing and research, we couldn't handle the workload here." For his first fourteen years on the Court, Brennan had only two clerks, and so did each of the other justices. The third clerk came in the 1970 term. "The reason is that John Harlan's eyes failed him, and his clerks had to read to him," Brennan explained. "We insisted that he had to have an additional clerk to help with the reading, and he was absolutely adamant that he would not take a third clerk unless the rest of us did.

"The reason we took the fourth clerk was Bill Douglas's stroke, in early 1975. He wasn't able to work, but he had already taken on new clerks, and we decided we didn't want those boys to lose out, so we just parceled them among us. It was done on a seniority basis, and I was one of three justices to get an extra clerk. Once some of us started with four, we said, 'Well, hell, everybody ought to have four.' A couple of us have cut down, but then we go back up again."

For his first dozen or so years on the Court, Brennan depended on Paul Freund, a professor at Harvard Law School, to send him the students he considered best qualified to be clerks. Brennan told me, "Then Paul came to me and said, 'Look, every law school in the country is madder than hell at you for taking law clerks only from Harvard. You ought to branch out.' So now I take them from everywhere. Hell, I've had them from night schools."

Brennan was proud of his alumni. He kept in touch with them, and they gathered for a reunion every three years, bringing their husbands and wives. Among Brennan's former clerks are federal circuit judges, a state supreme court judge, and law professors at Harvard, Yale, Columbia, New York University, and Boalt Hall, at the University of California at Berkeley. "Out of more than a hundred clerks, I've only had one lemon," he said. "Isn't that amazing? Only one who couldn't do the work. Every other one has measured up, and some of them brilliantly."

There was one exceptionally brilliant law student who, though he had been offered a clerkship by Brennan in 1966, was never able to serve, and some of the justice's warmest admirers consider what happened to the student an uncharacteristic surrender by Brennan to political pressures. Michael Tigar, now a law professor at the University of Texas and an active defense attorney, was a law student at Boalt Hall in California, where he had participated in a demonstration against the House Committee on Un-American Activities, and he had attended a youth festival in Helsinki, where some of the other participants were from the Soviet Union. Various right-wing individuals and organizations began to attack Tigar's appointment, and with talk of a congressional inquiry, Brennan withdrew the offer. Instead, Tiger went to work for the powerful Washington law firm headed by Edward Bennett Williams.

In the spring of 1988, when I asked Justice Brennan about Michael Tigar and the lost clerkship, he said, "That was a very sad occasion for both of us at the time. Mike and I have remained good friends. He's a great guy, a wonderful lawyer. What actually happened was a deluge. The right wing deliberately set up a program, a system of pressure, that involved Abe Fortas, who was on the Court then; J. Edgar Hoover; and, more particularly, Hoover's right-hand man, Clyde Tolson.

"They bombarded me with all kinds of letters, all having to do with Mike's participation in the Helsinki youth meeting. Probably, if I had just continued to face it down, the investigation would never have happened. But they had twenty-eight or more congressmen protesting Mike's appointment. Clyde Tolson came over to see Fortas, and Fortas came in to see me to tell me that if I went through with this there might well be an inquiry, which would be most embarrassing to Tigar and to me—and to the Court."

I said that I was surprised at Fortas's role, in view of his strong record in support of the First Amendment.

Brennan laughed. "He was very supportive of the First Amendment, but he was also very close to Lyndon Johnson, and also to J. Edgar Hoover," he said. "They used Fortas for a lot of things."

"At what point did you begin to seriously reconsider your appointment of Tigar?" I asked.

"When it got to the point where they were going to talk about a congressional inquiry," Brennan said. "Remember, a little before this happened, the Senate came very close to passing the Jenner bill, which would have stripped the Court of jurisdiction over cases involving the powers of congressional investigations, loyalty rules for teachers and federal employees, state antisubversion laws, and state regulations for admission to the bar."

I asked Brennan if Chief Justice Warren had been involved in deciding what to do about Tigar's clerkship.

"No. Aside from Fortas, the only one of my colleagues who said anything about it was Bill Douglas. He was furious. Oh, he was absolutely furious at me for capitulating. He said, 'You've got to stand up to those people.'"

I asked Justice Brennan if he'd had second or third thoughts about whether he should have taken Douglas's advice.

"I must say I've had a number of second thoughts," he said. "I suppose I should have treated it as something that would go away, but I didn't. I was very much concerned that, in the atmosphere of those days, if we got into this kind of thing it certainly would not have done the Court any good. That's what I said in the discussion I had with Mike at the time. A clerkship simply could not have that much significance—if it was going to hurt the institution."

"Did Tigar understand that?"

"Oh, Mike understood it perfectly." Brennan paused. "That's the only instance of anything like that I've had in all my years here."

All that Professor Tiger will say is, "I have enormous respect for Justice Brennan."

Brennan remained somewhat sensitive on the subject of his treatment of Tigar, but he kept on creating new ways of strengthening our liberties. In a 1977 *Harvard Law Review* article, Brennan wrote the following:

> It was in the years from 1962 to 1969 that the face of the law changed. Those years witnessed the extension to the states of nine of the specifics of the Bill of Rights; decisions which have had a profound impact on American life, requiring the deep involvement of state courts in the application of federal law. The eighth amendment's prohibition of cruel and unusual punishment was applied to state action in 1962. . . . The provision of the sixth amendment that in all prosecutions the accused shall have the assistance of counsel was applied in 1963, and in consequence, counsel must be provided in every courtroom of every state of this land to secure the rights of those accused of crime.
>
> In 1964, the fifth amendment privilege against compulsory self-incrimination was extended. And after decades of police coercion, by means ranging from torture to trickery, the privilege against self-incrimination became the basis of Miranda v. Arizona (1966), requiring police to give warnings to a suspect before custodial interrogation.
>
> The year 1965 saw the extension of the sixth amendment right of an accused to be confronted by the witnesses against him; in 1967 three more guarantees of the sixth amendment— the right to a speedy and public trial, the right to a trial by an

impartial jury, and the right to have compulsory process for obtaining witnesses—were extended.

In 1969 the double jeopardy clause of the fifth amendment was applied. Moreover, the decisions barring state-required prayers in public schools, limiting the availability of state libel laws to public officials and public figures, and confirming that a right of association is implicitly protected are significant restraints upon state action that resulted from the extension of the specifics of the first amendment.

One of Brennan's more difficult inner debates during this expansive change in the face of the law concerned the religion clauses of the First Amendment. The first clause prohibits "an establishment of religion." The second clause prevents the state from prohibiting the "free exercise" of religion.

In a 1968 *New York Times* interview, Brennan was asked by Jeffrey Leeds, his former clerk, to describe the hardest decision he had had to make as a justice. "The school-prayer cases," he said. "The 1963 *Schempp* opinion [a concurring opinion by Brennan] is some eighty pages long. The position I finally took took a long time to come around to. In the face of my whole lifelong experience as a Roman Catholic, to say that prayer was not an appropriate thing in public schools, that gave me quite a hard time. I struggled."

School District of Abington Township, Pennsylvania, v. Schempp addressed laws of the state of Pennsylvania requiring that "at least ten verses from the Holy Bible shall be read, without comment, at the opening of each public school on each school day" and providing that "any child shall be excused from such Bible reading, or attending such Bible reading, upon the written request of his parent or guardian."

The Supreme Court declared the laws unconstitutional, and Brennan ended his concurring opinion by going back to an 1856 speech on religious liberty by Jeremiah S. Black, a former chief justice of the Commonwealth of Pennsylvania. Brennan paid his respects to Justice Black's remarkably lucid analysis by quoting from it:

The manifest object of the men who framed the institutions of this country, was to have a *State without religion*, and a *Church without politics*—that is to say, they meant that one should never be used as an engine for any purpose of the other, and that no man's rights in one should be tested by his opinions about the other. As the Church takes no note of men's political differences, so the State looks with equal eye on all the modes of religious faith. . . . Our fathers seem to have been perfectly sincere in their belief that the members of the Church would be more patriotic, and the citizens of the State more religious, by keeping their respective functions entirely separate.

Since the 1963 decision, Brennan often emphasized in conversation that separation of church and state does not mean that the Constitution encourages hostility to religion. Nor, he points out, is he himself hostile to religion. Indeed, Brennan, a devout Catholic, still believed what he said in a speech he made before coming on the Court. "Whatever their religious belief, all Americans acknowledge with us the fitness in recognizing in important human affairs the superintending care and control of the great governor of the universe and of acknowledging with thanksgiving His boundless favors."

Brennan saw no contradiction between that belief and his votes against state-sponsored crèches and against permitting public school teachers, paid by federal funds, to go into parochial schools to provide remedial instruction. To Brennan, most of these cases have a bright line of First Amendment law running through them. Every American, he says, is guaranteed a free choice of his or her own religion or the choice not to believe at all. And the other religion clause in the First Amendment, the establishment clause, prohibits the government from, as Brennan puts it, "sticking its nose into how individuals should make that choice."

The extraordinary strengthening of the Bill of Rights, from the religion clauses to the rights of criminal defendants, during the Warren Court and to some extent thereafter grew out of the very belated acknowledgment by the Supreme Court that the Fourteenth Amendment meant what it said.

"The citizens of all our states," Brennan said, "are also and no less citizens of our United States." Accordingly, "this birthright guarantees our federal constitutional liberties against encroachment by government action at any level of our federal system, and . . . each of us is entitled to due process of law and the equal protection of the laws from our state governments no less than from our national one."

Brennan talks and writes about the Fourteenth Amendment with undimmed enthusiasm. In the 1987 interview with Bill Moyers, he said that because of the amendment there was "really a brand-new Constitution after the Civil War." But Brennan's celebration of the Fourteenth Amendment is tempered by apprehension that the Supreme Court will increasingly weaken that "egalitarian revolution."

Another concern of Brennan's was safeguarding the constitutional rights of young people. No other justice in the history of the Court has been more intensely involved in this area than Brennan. In one significant case in 1981, the Supreme Court denied a petition from a fifteen-year-old girl, for review of her case. Such refusals to review a decision by the lower courts are common, of course. Uncommon, however, was Justice Brennan's public rebuking of his colleagues in a printed dissent. It takes four members of the Court to grant certiorari, and Brennan could not understand why he was the only justice to feel strongly that the Constitution had been violated in this case. When cert is denied, the names of justices who wanted to review the case are often listed, but only rarely does one of them say why he or she voted for review. And even rarer are dissents as long as Brennan's in *Diane Doe v. Renfrow*. "I was really mad," Brennan told me recently.

In 1979, Diane Doe, age thirteen (her last name was not given, because she was a minor), was sitting in her classroom at Highland Junior High School, in Highland, Indiana. Next to that building was a senior high school.

Suddenly, all the classrooms in both schools were entered by school and police officials, along with police-trained German shepherds, who were undertaking a mass search for drugs and drug paraphernalia. No students in particular were under suspicion; all of them were under general suspicion. For two and a half hours, the students had to sit quietly with their hands on their desks and the contents of their desks in plain view. Reporters from newspapers and broadcast stations were present. Each student was inspected by a German shepherd. Justice Brennan wrote that when one of the dogs came to Diane, it "sniffed at her body, and repeatedly pushed its nose and muzzle into her legs." By its concentrated attention, the dog marked the girl as a person under suspicion. No drugs were found in her pockets, and she was taken to the nurse's office, where she was strip-searched. Again, no drugs were found. The German shepherd, it turned out, had smelled not marijuana but traces of a dog Diane had been playing with before she left for school.

Diane Doe sued several school district officials and the police chief, among others, claiming that her Fourth Amendment rights had been abused. No judge had issued a warrant for the dragnet operation, although the Fourth Amendment requires one for searches and seizures.

The Fourth Amendment also requires, Diane's lawyers argued, that the searchers have probable cause to believe that illegal behavior is taking place or has taken place on the premises and that the persons to be searched are involved in this activity. (Although the lesser standard of "reasonable suspicion" can be used in searches of students by school officials, once police are brought in, as in this case, the "probable cause" standard applies, Brennan said in his dissent, to public school students.) The Fourth Amendment also says that the place or the person to be searched must be "particularly"—that is, individually—described.

In their court papers Diane's lawyers wrote, "Being a teen-aged schoolgirl is neither a crime nor a cause for suspicion." The lawyers also charged that school officials, however well intentioned they may have been, had converted public schools "into police checkpoints."

A federal district judge threw out Diane Doe's case. The mass detention and inspection were constitutionally valid, he said, and although the search was so intrusive as to violate the Fourth Amendment, he refused to award damages against the school authorities, because they had been acting in good faith and trying to keep the school safe. As for the German shepherds, the judge ruled that being sniffed by a dog is not a search as defined by the Fourth Amendment. The dogs' only function had been to compensate for the inferior olfactory sense of the school officials and the police.

The judge thereby dismissed a point made by the student's lawyers: "If we are to understand the dogs' muzzles as mere extensions of the nostrils of the principal, then Highland's school administrators have been sticking their noses into some singular places. The dogs ran their noses along pupils' legs, between their shoes, and even into their crotches and buttocks, actually touching the bodies of the students. Surely it can be vouchsafed that no respectable school administrator would do the same."

Diane Doe appealed to the Seventh Circuit Court of Appeals, which agreed with the lower court except for denying immunity to the school officials connected with the strip search. She won damages for the strip search but did not win her constitutional case.

Justice Brennan approvingly quoted what the Seventh Circuit Court said about the strip search:

> It does not require a constitutional scholar to conclude that a nude search of a thirteen-year-old child is an invasion of consti-tutional rights of some magnitude. More than that: it is a viola-tion of any known principle of human decency. Apart from any constitutional readings and rulings, simple common sense would indicate that the conduct of the school officials in permitting such a nude search was not only unlawful but outrageous under "settled indisputable principles of law." ... We suggest as strongly as possible that the conduct herein described exceeded the "bounds of reason" by two and a half country miles.

In his dissent from the Supreme Court's denial of further review to the young woman, Brennan said that in his opinion the use of the dogs did indeed constitute a search. He recalled that Diane Doe had testified that "the experience of being sniffed and prodded by trained police dogs in the presence of the police and representatives of the press was degrading and embarrassing," and he wrote, "I am aston-ished that the court did not find that the school's use of the dogs con-stituted an invasion of the petitioner's reasonable expectation of pri-vacy."

Of the searches of all the students, Brennan said, "At the time of the raid, school authorities possessed no particularized information as to drugs or contraband, suppliers or users. Furthermore, they had made no effort to focus the search on particular individuals who might have been engaged in drug activity at school."

The last paragraph of Brennan's dissent was directed as much at his colleagues as at school authorities across the nation: "We do not know what class petitioner was attending when the police and dogs burst in, but the lesson the school authorities taught her that day will undoubtedly make a greater impression than the one her teacher had hoped to convey. . . . Schools cannot expect their students to learn the lessons of good citizenship when the school authorities themselves disregard the fundamental principles underpinning our constitutional freedoms."

For Brennan, as for one of his predecessors, Justice Louis Brandeis, the expectation of privacy is at the core of the Fourth Amendment. In conversation, Brennan sometimes recited the amendment, stressing each word: "The right of the people to be secure in their persons, houses, papers, and effects, against unreasonable searches and seizures, shall not be violated, and no Warrants shall issue, but upon probable cause, supported by Oath or affirmation, and particularly describing the place to be searched, and the persons or things to be seized." He repeated the words "probable cause," and said, "It's a high standard the framers wanted. And it means that no search may be conducted unless the official knows of facts and circumstances that warrant a prudent man to believe that an offense has been committed."

In Nina Totenberg's National Public Radio interview with Brennan in 1987, she played the devil's advocate, asking him, "Why do you let some of these creeps go? They do such bad things, and on some technicality you let them go."

"Honestly," Brennan said, raising his voice, "you in the media ought to be ashamed of yourselves to call the provisions and the guarantees of the Bill of Rights 'technicalities.' They're not. They're very basic to our very existence as the kind of society we are. We are what we are *because* we have those guarantees, and this Court exists to see that those guarantees are faithfully enforced. They are not technicalities! And no matter how awful may be the one who is the beneficiary time and time again, guarantees have to be sustained, even though the immediate result is to help out some very unpleasant person. They're there to protect all of us."

The essence of Brennan's fear that the Fourth Amendment is fading away can be found in a little-noted dissent to the Court's denial of review of a 1985 case, *McCommon v. Mississippi.*

Brennan began by stating that "this Court has long insisted that the determination whether probable cause exists to support a search warrant be made by a '*neutral* and *detached* magistrate.'" In *McCommon v. Mississippi,* he said, the judge who issued the search warrant "indisputably 'rubber stamped' the police request." The petitioner's car had been searched pursuant to a warrant, and a sizable quantity of marijuana had been found in the trunk.

Before trial, the owner of the car moved to have the evidence suppressed under the exclusionary rule, on the ground that there had not been probable cause for the issuance of the warrant. Brennan had carefully read the testimony from the pretrial hearing in Mississippi, and he quoted it in his dissent. The defense attorney asked the judge if he issued the warrant because officers of the law had asked for it rather than because of "any particular thing they told you."

"That's right," the judge said. "If Sheriff Jones walked in there and said, 'Judge, I need a search warrant to search John Doe for marijuana,' or drugs or whatever—liquor or whatever it might be—I'm going to go on his word, because he's—I take him to be an honest law-enforcement officer and he needs help to get in to search these places and it's my duty to help him fulfill that."

Brennan then reminded his colleagues of what he had said in his dissent in *United States v. Leon,* the year before, the majority having ruled that an officer's execution of a defective warrant does not violate the Fourth Amendment if the officer did not know that the warrant was defective; he said the following in his new dissent:

> I warned that creation of a good faith exception implicitly tells magistrates that they need not take much care in reviewing warrant applications, since their mistakes will have virtually no consequence. Today the Court tacitly informs magistrates that not only need they not worry about mistakes, they need no longer be neutral and detached in their reviews of supporting affidavits. The combined message of *Leon* and the Court's refusal to grant certiorari in this case is that the police may rely on the magistrates and the magistrates may rely on the police. On whom may the citizens rely to protect their Fourth Amendment rights?

In the years since, Brennan, in conversation, has continued to seem gloomy about the prospects of the exclusionary rule. Yet in January 1990, in a ruling so surprising that it made the front page of the *New York Times,* he succeeded in preventing a further restriction of the exclusionary rule, one that would have greatly weakened it.

In *James v. Illinois.* the defendant in a murder case had made incriminating statements to the police when he was arrested. But the arrest had been made without a warrant and without probable cause, and accordingly those statements were not at first admitted at the trial. However, a friend of the defendant gave testimony at the trial that was directly contrary to what the defendant had told the police. The prosecution moved, successfully, to have the defendant's original statement admitted in order to impeach the friend's testimony, and this exception to the exclusionary rule was upheld by the Illinois Supreme Court. In reversing the Illinois Supreme Court, the Brennan majority included Justice Byron White, who in the past had voted for a number of restrictions on the exclusionary rule and, indeed, was the author of the majority opinion in *United States v. Leon,* which had established the good-faith exception. I asked Brennan how he had persuaded White to join him, and he smiled. "It was hard," he said. "Very hard."

From the beginning of his time on the Court, Brennan was a persistent guardian of civil rights protections for blacks. What is surely the most dramatic opinion he drafted for the Court, *Cooper v. Aaron* (1958), was also signed by every other member of the Court: Earl Warren, Hugo Black, Felix Frankfurter, William O. Douglas, Harold Burton, Tom Clark, John Harlan, and Charles Whittaker.

Chief Justice Warren said later that he did not recall that ever happening before; usually, even when the Court is unanimous, the opinion is signed only by the other justices. But this time, Warren felt it important to get all the justices to sign because a governor was in contempt of the law and the Court, and it was vital for the Court to affirm powerfully the end of public school segregation.

The Court's unanimous 1954 decision in *Brown v. Board of Education*—ruling that segregated public schooling is inherently unequal—was being defied by Governor Orval Faubus of Arkansas and the Arkansas State Legislature. On September 2, 1957, Faubus had sent Arkansas National Guard units to block implementation of a plan by the Little Rock School Board to desegregate the public schools gradually, beginning with one high school.

For three weeks, the soldiers, standing shoulder to shoulder, forcibly prevented nine black students from entering Central High School. On September 25, the students finally got into the school, after federal troops were sent there by President Eisenhower.

The following February, the school board decided it would be safer, in view of undiminished white hostility, if the integration plan were delayed, and the federal district court agreed to have the plan postponed for thirty months. In *Super Chief,* a judicial biography of the Warren Court, Professor Bernard Schwartz of the New York University Law School described what happened next: "The Court of Appeals for the Eighth Circuit reversed [the district court], but stayed its order thirty days to permit the School Board [to appeal]. . . . The black students then filed a motion in the Supreme Court to stay the court of appeals postponement." With the school term due to begin in September and the Supreme Court's term due to start in October, the chief justice called a rare Special Term of the Court, which heard oral arguments in August and September.

The Court's subsequent opinion, as it was constructed by Brennan, was described by Schwartz as "one of the classic statements of the rule of law under the Constitution." It was read aloud at the Court by the chief justice on September 29, 1958:

> The controlling legal principles are plain. The command of the Fourteenth Amendment is that no "State" shall deny to any person within its jurisdiction the equal protection of the laws. . . . Article VI of the Constitution makes the Constitution the "Supreme Law of the Land."
>
> In 1803, Chief Justice Marshall, speaking for a unanimous Court . . . declared in the notable case of *Marbury v. Madison* . . . that "It is emphatically the province and duty of the judicial department to say what the law is." . . . That principle has ever since been respected by this Court and the country as a permanent and indispensable feature of our constitutional system. . . . No state legislator or executive or judicial officer can war against

the Constitution without violating his undertaking to support it. Chief Justice Marshall spoke for a unanimous Court in saying that: "If the legislatures of the several states may, at will, annul the judgments of the courts of the United States, and destroy the rights acquired under those judgments, the Constitution itself becomes a solemn mockery." A Governor who asserts a power to nullify a federal court order is similarly restrained.

As for the *Brown* decision itself, Brennan wrote:

State support of segregated schools through any arrangement . . . cannot be squared with the [Fourteenth] Amendment's command that no State shall deny to any person within its jurisdiction the equal protection of the laws. The right of a student not to be segregated on racial grounds . . . is indeed so fundamental and pervasive that it is embraced in the concept of due process of law. . . . The principles announced in [the *Brown*] decision and the obedience of the States to them, according to the command of the Constitution, are indispensable for the protection of the freedoms guaranteed by our fundamental charter for all of us. Our constitutional ideal of equal justice under law is thus made a living truth.

The *Times* noted that the Court's opinion in *Cooper v. Aaron* was written in "clear and simple language, understandable even to the most fanatic segregationist."

Justice Brennan also long regarded sex discrimination as violating the Fourteenth and Fifth Amendments, and he had been more insistent than any of his colleagues, until Ruth Bader Ginsburg became a justice, that such discrimination be given a high level of constitutional scrutiny. His reasons are vigorously expressed in a 1973 case, *Sharron and Joseph Frontiero v. Elliot Richardson, Secretary of Defense.*

Joseph Frontiero, attending college full time, was receiving benefits as a veteran of $205 a month. His wife, Sharron, was a lieutenant in the air force, and claiming her husband as a dependent, she applied for an increased housing allowance and for medical and dental benefits for her husband. Under federal law, male members of the uniformed services automatically received the increased housing allowance and the extra benefits for their wives, but a woman could qualify for the same extra housing and medical benefits only if she could prove that she was paying more than half her husband's living expenses. Sharron Frontiero was paying three-sevenths of her husband's living costs, and she was denied the extra benefits.

Brennan's opinion for the Court went further than some of his colleagues would have liked. The majority of the Court agreed that Sharron Frontiero had been subject to unconstitutional discrimination, but there was no majority for Brennan's view that discrimination by sex should be, like discrimination by race, examined by the Court with "strict judicial scrutiny." This is the highest standard in the Supreme Court classification of cases, and it places a heavy burden on the federal government or a state to justify unequal treatment.

In the Frontiero case, Brennan noted the following:

> There can be no doubt that our Nation has had a long and unfortunate history of sex discrimination. Traditionally, such discrimination was rationalized by an attitude of "romantic paternalism" which, in practical effect, put women, not on a pedestal, but in a cage. . . . Our statute books gradually became laden with gross, stereotyped distinctions between the sexes and, indeed, throughout much of the 19th century the position of women in our society was, in many respects, comparable to that of blacks under the pre–Civil War slave codes. . . .
>
> We can only conclude that classifications based upon sex, like classifications based upon race, alienage, or national origin, are inherently suspect, and must therefore be subjected to strict judicial scrutiny.

In his opinions, Justice Brennan often interchanged personal pronouns. That is, even in a case that concerned a male defendant or plaintiff, Brennan referred to the principal as "she" at times and "he" at others. "I do it purposely," he told me. "I've been doing it for two or three years. Why? Well, why should we males be the only illustrious participants in whatever events we've been talking about?"

Of all the developments in constitutional law since he started on the Court, Brennan regarded as among the most significant the grow-ing independence of the state courts.

Although a state cannot provide fewer protections of individual liber-ties than does the federal Constitution, any state can guarantee stronger protections for its citizens; in January 1987, for example, in an action warmly welcomed by Justice Brennan, Oregon's Supreme Court ruled that its state constitution mandates—the Supreme Court of the United States notwithstanding—that "obscene" material can no longer be pro-hibited or censored in the state. Oregon's Article I, Section 8, forbids the passage of any law restricting "the right to speak, write, or print freely on any subject whatever." The State Supreme Court said that "obscene speech, writing or equivalent forms of communication are 'speech.'"

I saw Brennan soon after that decision of the Oregon Supreme Court came down, and he started to reminisce about his role in the increasing independence of the state courts. He had been the primary force in getting more and more lawyers, legislators, and judges to think about the need for states to become aware of—and, if necessary, strengthen—their own constitutions.

"It all started around 1972," he said. "I initially suggested the idea in a speech very late at night to, I'm afraid, a quite inebriated meeting of the New Jersey State Bar Association. I was really concerned at the time about the way that things were going here at the Court, particu-larly in the area of the Fourth Amendment, but also in other areas of individual rights and liberties."

In 1977, Brennan wrote what proved to be a widely influential article, "State Constitutions and the Protection of Individual Rights," in the *Harvard Law Review.* "State courts cannot rest when they have afforded their citizens the full protections of the federal Constitution," he declared. "State constitutions, too, are a font of individual liberties, their protection often extending beyond those required by the Supreme Court's interpretation of federal law." Without "the indepen-dent protective force of state law," he said, "the full realization of our liberties cannot be guaranteed."

In 1986, addressing the American Bar Association's Section on Individual Rights and Responsibilities, in New York, Brennan was able to quote with satisfaction from a statement by Justice Hans Linde of the Oregon Supreme Court: "A lawyer today representing someone who claims some constitutional protection and who does not argue that the state constitution provides that protection is skating on the edge of malpractice."

Brennan, however, was far from entirely satisfied with the direction of constitutional law, both state and federal. In the same speech, he said something I have heard him say in his chambers and have read in many of his Court opinions, particularly in his dissents:

> We do not yet have justice, equal and practical, for the poor, for the members of minority groups, for the criminally accused, for the displaced persons of the technological revolution, for alienated youth, for the urban masses, for the unrepresented consumer—for all, in short, who do not partake of the abundance of American life. . . . The goal of universal equality, freedom and prosperity is far from won and . . . ugly inequities continue to mar the face of our nation. We are surely nearer the beginning than the end of the struggle.

Shortly before the 1988 presidential election, I reminded Justice Brennan that a number of liberals and libertarians had expressed concern for the future of the Court. If George Bush were elected, they pointed out, he might have several seats to fill, among them the seat of Justice William Brennan.

"Look," Brennan said. "This is an institution that has had its ups and downs for over two hundred years. By and large, it has done well, I think. There have been downturns from time to time. God help us, there was Chief Justice Taney and the *Dred Scott* decision.

"But we survived all that. So I don't see anything that serious, by way of changing jurisprudence, in contrast with what has happened in the past. And that's why I refuse to get sick about who might win. Anyway, whatever is to be, hell, we're a democracy. The only way the citizens can have their views felt nationally is through the Congress and the presidency. That's our system."

Also part of the system is access to justice, and of all the members of the Court in this century—and perhaps throughout its history—Brennan has been the most interested in making the courts accessible to as many people as possible.

"I have always felt that the courthouse door has been closed to too many people on the ground that they don't have sufficient reason for being heard," he told me. "Take the execution of Gary Gilmore, in Utah, in 1977. Gilmore insisted he wanted to die. He didn't want any more appeals. He had no patience for it. But his mother brought a case here trying to prevent the execution, and the Court refused to hear her on the ground that she had no standing to be heard. Good God, we can't refuse to discharge our responsibility to decide whether he should die or not. Anybody ought to have a right to be heard in a case like that. I've taken that position in many other kinds of cases, besides the death penalty."

Whenever I tried to engage Brennan in a broader discussion of his influence on the Court's direction over the years, he demurred. He discouraged such talk. Although he worked, as he must, case by case, he was keenly aware of the slightest nuance in the changing dynamics of the Court; however, it was not his habit to see himself as a marble figure in its halls. He regarded his job as one of trying to include as many people as possible within the protections of the Constitution and of determining how to get four other votes to agree with the opinions that could help do that.

Over the years, Justice Brennan made an invaluable collection of private Supreme Court history. Each term he, with the help of his clerks, documented the evolution of the justices' opinions in major cases. Included in his files are notes of what went on during conferences as well as draft opinions and memoranda circulated among the justices. Although historians urged Brennan to make these histories available eventually, he was not sure what he would do with them.

Just about every time I talked to Brennan, I asked him whether he had made up his mind about the fate of these histories. "It's a very troublesome question for me as to what the hell to do with them," he said. "I have a very clear memory of how angry Hugo Black and Bill Douglas were when Alpheus Mason used Chief Justice Harlan Fiske Stone's private notes in a biography about him.

"They were memoranda of cases, histories of cases—the voting, the reactions of the members of the Court, and so forth. Just like my own. Black and Douglas were furious. They insisted that Stone's histories were one-sided and didn't tell the whole story. They said it was all a goddamn lie.

"That's why Hugo Black insisted he was going to burn every damn paper of his. He said, 'I'm not going to have any colleague of mine in a position where he can say I've lied about what happened.' His instructions weren't carried out completely, but some of his papers *were* destroyed. What concerned Hugo Black bothers me, too.

"None of my colleagues have seen any of my memos. Nobody sees them except me. They cover the major cases from the time they're received at the Court. A lot of people want me to preserve them. For about ten years, I sat on the National Historical Publications Commission, and all my colleagues were very distinguished and well-known historians, and they were absolutely horrified at the thought that I might not preserve these histories."

"Me, too," I said.

"Well, there you are. One of these days, I'm going to have to make up my mind about what I'm going to do." He finally did. The notes are in the care of his son, William, and are not to be released until the deaths of all the justices with whom Brennan has served. But Brennan's son has, on occasion, allowed the notes of a particular case to be seen by a qualified writer on the Court.

I spoke to Brennan again at the end of the 1988–1989 Supreme Court term. There had been a series of civil rights decisions, all opposed by Brennan, that in the words of Barry Goldstein, the former director of the Washington office of the NAACP Legal Defense Fund, were "not just decisions limiting affirmative action but cases limiting the ability of women and men to prove discrimination, limiting the remedies once discrimination is proved, and limiting the opportunity to settle."

A majority of the Court had also ruled it constitutional to execute murderers who are mentally retarded and had decided that it is not "cruel and unusual punishment" under the Eighth Amendment to execute people who were sixteen or seventeen at the time they committed the crime. Moreover, the Court ruled that indigent prisoners on death row do not have a constitutional right to a lawyer to assist them in a second round of state-court appeals, even though such appeals often prove successful. I asked Brennan if he was still reasonably sanguine about the future of individual rights and liberties under the Court.

"Well, there is a pretty solid majority on the other side now, but it hasn't been an unbreakable coalition," he said. "I'm not discouraged to the point of giving up. I've selected my clerks for the next two years. I hope people don't overdo the suggestion that we're headed for perdition. This sort of thing has happened before, and the Court has finally righted itself." His voice brightened. "I agree the emphasis of the Court is not in my direction, but I'm not going to walk out and say the hell with it."

Next to the abortion decision—*Webster v. Reproductive Health Services,* which gave power to the states to broaden restrictions on abortions and in which Brennan dissented—the term's most controversial decision was concerning *Texas v. Johnson.* Brennan, writing the opinion for a five-to-four majority, ruled that the First Amendment protects burning the American flag as an act of political protest. He wrote, "If there is a bedrock principle underlying the First Amendment, it is that the Government may not prohibit the expression of an idea simply because society finds the idea itself offensive and disagreeable. . . . We decline, therefore, to create for the flag an exception to the joust of principles protected by the First Amendment."

It was characteristic of Brennan to use the word *joust.* He saw his life's work as a continual battle for five votes to help the words of the Constitution leap off the page, as he once put it, and into people's lives.

"Look, Pal," Justice Brennan told me at the end of our conversation. "We've always known—the framers knew—that liberty is a fragile thing." He smiled and went back to work.

5

SUPREME COURT JUSTICE WILLIAM BRENNAN, PART III

"The evolving standards of human decency will eventually lead to the abolition of the death penalty in this country."

$\mathcal{S}$itting across from Brennan in the chambers he still has at the Supreme Court, I find it difficult at first to realize that this short, decidedly informal man with so playful a wit ranks, according to Supreme Court historian Joshua Rosenkranz, with Justice Oliver Wendell Holmes and Chief Justice John Marshall in his impact on both the law and society.

William J. Brennan Jr. was entirely without pretentiousness. An ordinary member of a city council takes him- or herself more seriously than Brennan does. But the justice always took his job seriously. He described that job as requiring him to protect the dignity of each human being and to recognize that "every individual has fundamental rights that Government cannot deny him."

I have never known anyone who loved his work more. We were once walking out of the Supreme Court building, Brennan holding me by the elbow, and he looked around the marble hall and said, "It's just incredible being here—I mean the opportunity to be a participant in decisions that have such enormous impact on our society!"

When, in the summer of 1990, he suddenly retired because of the effects of a stroke, I wondered if he would ever recover—not from the stroke so much as from leaving the Court. "This is the saddest day of my life," he told a friend of mine.

When I talked with Brennan, it was clear that his was not going to be a passive retirement. His mind was still on the Court. In previous conversations, he had stressed his disappointment at the way the Court was covered by the press: at the inaccuracy of the reporting and the placing of decisions out of context. He had not changed his mind.

"I'm afraid," he said, "that most of your colleagues in the press simply don't do a good job." A key exception, he said, is Linda Greenhouse of the *New York Times:* "She's a whiz."

He kept returning to the failures of the press, because although the Court makes decisions affecting millions of Americans, many have only the dimmest notion of the content of those decisions and of how they were arrived at. And that, he thinks, is the fault of the press.

"What I would like to see," Brennan said, "is that [important cases] are covered from beginning to end, from before they get to the Court to the final result. But what you get in most papers are a few lines about whether there was a reversal or an affirmation of a lower-court decision."

I reminded Brennan that one way to enable more people to understand and become involved in the drama of the Court would be to have oral arguments before the justices seen on TV. The network C-SPAN has offered to carry all oral arguments in their entirety.

Brennan believes strongly that those arguments should be televised. Most of his colleagues, however, have refused to allow cameras in the courtroom. Since Brennan left, there has been no indication that the justices have changed their minds.

I asked Brennan about Sandra Day O'Connor—my sense was that she can be a good deal more impassioned than is indicated by her image as a cool, self-contained jurist.

"She can and does get quite passionate," Brennan said. And he mentioned *United States v. James B. Stanley,* which resulted in one of the most appalling decisions in recent Supreme Court history, although it received little press coverage. Brennan said that the case still deserves a great deal of attention. In 1958 James B. Stanley, a master sergeant in the army, had answered a call for volunteers who were to test the effectiveness of protective clothing and equipment against chemical warfare. He and the other volunteers were cruelly deceived. Secretly, the army doused them with LSD to find out how the drug worked on human subjects. In Stanley's case, the drug produced hallucinations, periodic loss of memory, and incoherence. Also, according to the Court record, Stanley would occasionally "awake from sleep at night and, without reason, violently beat his wife and children, later being unable to recall the entire incident." His marriage was destroyed.

Years later, when Stanley found out what had been done to him by the army, he sued for damages. Speaking for a majority of the Supreme Court, Antonin Scalia said Stanley had no redress, because military discipline and decision making could not be called into question without the entire military regime being disrupted.

O'Connor was furious in dissent, attacking the army's conduct as being "far beyond the bounds of human decency." The Constitution, she said sharply, guarantees even soldiers due process of law.

Brennan remembered his own dissent in *Stanley* very well. He emphasized that after the Nuremberg war-crimes trials, the United States Military Tribunal established the Nuremberg Code, which prohibits medical experimentation on unknowing human subjects. Yet the U.S. Supreme Court was putting its awesome constitutional imprimatur on similar experiments by its own armed forces.

So angry was Brennan that he ended his dissent these words: "Soldiers ought not be asked to defend a Constitution that, as interpreted by the Court, subverts their essential human dignity."

Reliving that case with me, Brennan said, "Wasn't that an outrageous case? It was incredible! Some of us were so shocked by it when it came down that we were fearful it had started a trend. But, thank God, it hasn't shown its head again—not yet, anyway."

Capital punishment, however, shows no sign of disappearing. In all of our conversations through the years, Brennan has predicted that "the evolving standards of human decency will finally lead to the abolition of the death penalty in this country." With more and more executions taking place, I asked him why he remained optimistic.

Brennan laughed. "Maybe because it's the way I want it to come out. I just have a feeling. Do you realize that we are the only Western country that has not abolished the death penalty? I can't believe that the leader of the free world is going to keep on executing people. I don't know when the change is going to come. I've never suggested it's going to be next week or five years from now. But I am absolutely convinced that it will happen. When I start doing some writing, I'm going to have quite a bit to say about capital punishment."

I told the justice that an Amnesty International report revealed that thirty-one prisoners in twelve states in this country were "under sentence of death for crimes committed before they reached their eighteenth birthday." And this nation is one of only four—including Bangladesh, Iran, and Iraq—that execute juvenile offenders.

"Isn't it horrible to be in that company?" Brennan said. "Good God!"

The Court also decided, I noted, that a retarded person can be executed.

"That's right," he said. "That's even worse. Well, I still believe that eventually we'll become more civilized. It would be horrible if we didn't. I wish there were more people arguing in the opposition."

Except for Thurgood Marshall, there are, with Brennan gone, no other absolute opponents of capital punishment on the Court. "Well," said Brennan, "people on the Court can evolve too. I give you the opinion for the Court by the chief justice in the *Hustler Magazine, Inc., v. Falwell* case."

Larry Flynt had a fake ad published in *Hustler* in which Reverend Jerry Falwell and his mother were depicted, with Falwell saying that his first sexual experience was with his mother in an outhouse. Both were drunk. The ad read: "I never *really* expected to make it with Mom, but then, after she showed all the other guys in town such a good time, I figured, 'What the hell.'"

A lower court awarded Falwell $200,000 for intentional infliction of emotional distress, but the Supreme Court unanimously reversed the decision, with William Rehnquist writing a passionate defense of free expression: "At the heart of the First Amendment is the recognition of the fundamental importance of the free flow of ideas and opinions on matters of public interest and concern." In the past, Rehnquist had not been one of the Court's notable defenders of free speech but in the *Falwell* case, he embraced Brennan concepts he had previously criticized.

In the 1989 flag-burning case *Texas v. Gregory Lee Johnson,* however, a year after *Hustler v. Falwell,* Rehnquist did a serious reverse with regard to the First Amendment. A parody of Falwell and his mother having sexual intercourse in an outhouse was one thing, wrote Rewnquest, but disrespect for the flag, the symbol of American freedom, must be punished.

I asked Brennan how much give-and-take there is at the conferences during which the justices tentatively decide how they will vote on a case they've just heard argued. Did he and Rehnquist, for instance, get into a substantive face-to-face discussion of the flag-burning case?

"No," said Brennan. "Contrary to belief, there's very little face-to-face debate. Our decisions are based on what we write, on the drafts we circulate to one another. What happens at the conferences is only a scratching of the surface. You really don't get into it until you have to write out your position, and then it changes back and forth as you read what the other justices have to say. Writing does a better job than if we were trying to decide a case just sitting around a table and arguing with one another. You're much more careful about what you're going to say if you write it down."

"You say the decisions are more careful," I said, "but it's still hard for me to understand how certain justices can *carefully* vote, for example, to execute the retarded or teenagers. Or permit [egregious] physical abuse of a child.

A particularly horrendous case, *Joshua DeShaney v. Winnebago County Department of Social Services,* one of the most poignant in the recent history of the Court, concerned a child, Joshua DeShaney, who had been beaten so often and so brutally by his father that he became permanently retarded and will need to be institutionalized for life. A county social worker who knew the boy was being abused took no action, so the county never took the child into custody.

Accordingly, a majority of the Court ruled that the child and his mother had no claim for damages because the *state* had not inflicted the violence on the child—the *father* had—and so it was not responsible. Although one of its agents had had continuing knowledge of what was going on, the state had not placed the child under its protection.

In his indignant dissent, Brennan said it was eerie that the county social worker had chronicled in detail what was happening to the child; indeed, when she heard about the last and most devastating beating, she said, "I just knew the phone would ring someday and Joshua would be dead."

Yet six members of the Court had failed to see, Brennan stressed in his dissent, "that inaction can be every bit as abusive of power as action. . . . I cannot agree that our Constitution is indifferent to such indifference."

Only Thurgood Marshall and Harry Blackmun were as appalled as Brennan at the majority view. In his dissent, Blackmun, in an anguished cry from the heart that is rare in the history of the Court's opinions, wrote, "Poor Joshua!"

Brennan's customary optimism and his conviction that the Court will one day fully live up to the Constitution did sometimes waver, for instance, when he was confronted by the coldness of some of his colleagues as in the case of *Joshua DeShaney*. But he kept bounding back. "You'd be amazed at the mail I've gotten since my retirement," he said. "Holy Moses! All these people agreeing with me about the way the Court and the country should be going. It's been an eye-opener for me."

Brennan saw much injustice in the land, but he always believed that the Constitution would be able to redress it when enough Americans understood the power and promise of that document.

"We can't give up," he told me. "We can't despair. We have to keep taking up the cudgels, and the first thing you know, by God, we'll abolish the death penalty and we'll make the Fourteenth Amendment come alive for everyone, so that there *will* be justice for all."

In this regard, Brennan vigorously advocated for years that law schools involve their students in clinics that deal with clients among the poor and those who are otherwise marginalized in this society. (The American Bar Association noted that 80 percent of Americans have no access to the legal help they need because they can't afford a lawyer.) However, Brennan began to see more and more law schools changing in ways he approved of. "The students are learning firsthand about how the law can actually affect people's lives," he said. "They learn not only from law books but from actual cases involving actual people. And that experience is going to lead to more improvement in the lives of many."

Eventually, perhaps, the words carved above the entrance of the Supreme Court—EQUAL JUSTICE UNDER LAW—may be more than rhetoric.

On the other hand, there are law students, I told Brennan, who out of decent motives—to combat racism and sexism, for example—have been working to establish speech codes on their campuses. The codes punish offensive speech and sometimes go so far as to lead to suspension or expulsion. Even some law school professors are supporting this kind of censorship.

I told him that at Stanford, student organizations advocate these codes, including the Asian Law Association, Black Law Students Association, Native American Law Students Association, Asian American Students Association, and Jewish Law Students Association.

Brennan shook his head. "I'll be damned," he said.

I asked him what he would do about these speech codes at colleges around the country.

"I can tell you what I think they ought to do," he said. "They ought to just abolish all of them."

Much of what Brennan has said will last, future justices will quote from some of the opinions of his that will shape the course of constitutional debate for as long as there is a Constitution. And the core of all William Brennan has said and done is his unyielding conviction that if freedom of expression is eroded, so, eventually, will be the rest of our liberties.

When I asked him if he had a favorite part of the Constitution, he replied, "The First Amendment, I expect. All other liberties and rights flow from the freedom to speak up. Its enforcement gives us this society. The other provisions of the Constitution merely embellish it."

On July 24, 1997, Justice William Brennan died. He was ninety-one. His casket was on display at the Supreme Court's Great Hall. One of the people in the viewing line, Jim Lyle, a law student from Columbus, Ohio, said that Brennan's work "affects you throughout your life, even though you don't realize it." One might add, even though most people did not recognize the scope and reach of what he did during all those years on the Court.

Indeed, most Americans didn't know his name, although his decisions reached into their lives. On a poll to find out how many people recognized the names of Supreme Court justices he had no more than 4 percent name recognition. This is not surprising because television covers the Supreme Court minimally, if at all, and most newspapers do not report on the Court in depth.

Nonetheless, Brennan did change the scope and depth of our Constitution. He called the Constitution "a sparkling vision of the supreme dignity and worth of every individual." And Justice Brennan strongly believed that the foundation of our democracy was a *living* Constitution. "Our task," he said, "is to interpret and apply the Constitution faithfully to the wisdom and understanding of the Founding Fathers. But often it is impossible to make a constitutional decision without basing certain findings on data drawn from the social sciences, from history, geography, economics and the like."

Adding emphasis, Brennan said, "The genius of the Constitution rests not in any static meaning it may have had in a world that is dead and gone, but in the adaptability of its great principles to cope with current problems and present needs."

One of those principles is the right to criticize government—the central meaning of the First Amendment." After all, the dignity and worth of each individual, a quality Brennan always found to be essential to the authentic American heritage, could not be fulfilled without the right of all Americans to criticize not only the government but also all other sources of authority—and nonauthority.

Justice Brennan was a consistent, indignant opponent of capital punishment: "Capital punishment treats members of the human race as nonhumans, as objects to be toyed with and discarded. It is thus inconsistent with the fundamental premise of the Constitution that even the most base criminal remains a human being possessed of some potential, at least, for human dignity. . . . On this issue, the death penalty, I hope to embody a community striving for human dignity for *all*, although it has perhaps not yet arrived."

Justice Ruth Bader Guinsburg said this of Brennan: "One of his major concerns was to take the preamble of the Constitution that says, 'We the people of the United States,' and make that 'we' an ever-larger group."

Justice David Souter, who took Brennan's seat on the Court when Brennan resigned, became a close friend of the older justice. At Brennan's funeral, Souter said:

"The life of the man is over. So is the liberal era when Justice Brennan's voice was the voice of the Supreme Court. But the law as he saw it will transcend his own time."

6

DR. KENNETH CLARK, PART I:
THE LAST OF THE INTEGRATIONISTS?

 $\mathcal{T}$ he oldest and deepest division in this nation is between blacks and whites. Although the Fourteenth Amendment to the Constitution (ratified in 1868) guaranteed—on paper—equal protection of the laws to all of us, as George Orwell might have put it, whites, by and large, remain more equal than blacks.

Dr. Kenneth Bancroft Clark has devoted his long life to bringing the Fourteenth Amendment into the lives of millions of black Americans. After what appeared to be a powerful triumph in the Supreme Court's decision in *Brown v. Board of Education* (1954), the rest of the journey so far has been deeply frustrating. If the years after *Brown* mark the end of Dr. Clark's hopes, then it is clear that the United States is a profoundly racist country—still.

On May 28, 1954, Dr. Kenneth Bancroft Clark, a thirty-nine-year-old associate professor of psychology at City College in New York, wrote out a brief statement for the press on the meaning of a unanimous Supreme Court decision, *Brown v. Board of Education of Topeka,* which had been handed down eleven days earlier.

Clark himself had been mentioned in the decision, in a footnote that cited him as one representative of "modern authority" supporting the Court's conclusion that segregation in the public schools generates in Negro children "a feeling of inferiority . . . that may affect their hearts and minds in a way unlikely ever to be undone."

Clark was somewhat disappointed that the Court, in citing his research, had ignored two other points he had made: that racism was as profoundly American as the Declaration of Independence and that school segregation twisted the personality development of white as well as Negro children.

Still, elated by the decision, he predicted in his statement that as a result of *Brown,* white youngsters could now look to a future "in which they will not have to spend so much valuable energy apologizing for injustices which they did not invent but for which they must share the responsibility." And young blacks, freed of the stigma of segregation, could now "be proud of the fact that they are Americans."

On a sunny morning in 1980, more than a quarter of a century later, Dr. Clark was on his way to a meeting of the Convocation for Competency, sponsored by the Public Education Association, at the Waldorf-Astoria Hotel in New York. In the years since *Brown,* he became the first black full professor at City College (he was now Distinguished Professor Emeritus of Psychology); served on the New York State Board of Regents; wrote a number of books—most notably, *Dark Ghetto*—that are widely used in colleges and universities; and received many professional honors. Also, although he keeps insisting that he has no constituency of his own, he became part of the inner councils of national black leadership.

For a long time, moreover, Clark had been serving another function—as a source of advice and revivification for younger black activists momentarily worn down. But there are times when Clark himself seems to be fighting a losing battle with gloom. On that morning at the Waldorf-Astoria, I was with Dr. Clark as he searched for the room in which he was to be a panelist—the topic was "Minimum Competency: A Community Strategy for Success-Based Schools"—and I thought he seemed gloomy.

"I swear, this is the last of these educational panels I'll ever be on," he said. "I've been to so many conferences, so many symposiums, so many seminars, and all they contribute is more alibis for why the schools aren't working and why society doesn't want to deal with this problem. I get so angry at being part of the damn charade, and then I get angry at myself for being so angry. All this talk all these years, and the percentage of black children going to segregated and inferior schools in the North is greater now than it was at the time of *Brown.* And the educational retardation gets worse and worse."

Then, as almost always happens when Dr. Clark is low in spirit, a further rush of anger lifted him out of his gloom into readiness for combat. "Damn it!" he said. "The school boards and public officials in the North are *much* more subtle and persistent in defending the racial status quo than those Southerners ever were. But the damage being done to the children is precisely the same as it was in the Southern segregated schools."

Clark entered a long, narrow room filled with educators and parents. When it was his turn to speak, he began, without notes, by recalling that he had first been elected to the New York State Board of Regents thirteen years earlier.

"I was told that I was the first black to be elected to that august body," he said, in a calm, rumbling voice. "I soon learned that we did more than preside over examinations. This was the body with the awesome power of responsibility for education at all levels, from prekindergarten to postgraduate. I decided to look particularly at the quality of elementary and secondary education in the state. And after two years I discovered that the State Education Department had been regularly giving examinations—Pupil Evaluation Program tests—in reading and mathematics at the third-, sixth-, and eighth-grade levels. But the scores were not publicized, because, the staff said, people wouldn't understand how to interpret the differences between schools. It took me two whole years to force the New York State Education Department to release those PEP scores, and when they did I found out why they had been so reluctant to do it.

"In the ghetto areas of New York City, from 80 to 85 percent of the children were not only below the norm but *significantly* below. I asked that those scores be made available to the legislators. At the time, Charles Rangel, now a congressman, was the assemblyman from a Harlem district. When he looked at the scores in the Harlem schools, he shouted, 'My God! My district is an educational disaster area.'"

Clark lit a cigarette, gazed at the audience, and went on. "One might think that once these scores had been presented to the regents and to the legislators there would have been an immediate demand for some kind of remedy to deal with so stark and flagrant a problem." He paused, then said, "Nothing was done. Some years later, the regents did begin to insist that certain standards of competency be demonstrated before a high school diploma is awarded, but that came about because of newspaper stories that *suburban* children were getting lower scores on the Scholastic Aptitude Tests for college. Apparently, this created greater concern in our democracy than the overwhelming evidence that many lower-class children were not even able to *take* the Scholastic Aptitude Tests, because their educational retardation was so profound.

"Not that I believe that competency tests given to the children are going to solve the educational genocide in our ghetto schools. We still have to deal with the competency of teachers and administrators. We have to make them accountable for what they do, and for what they fail to do. And that is not going to be easy, because it is a racist society that allows the public education system to produce hundreds of thousands of despairing, frustrated, functional illiterates each year."

A tall, lean, silver-haired man at the back of the room was shaking his head in disagreement or exasperation, or both. Dr. Clark looked at him and, without breaking the even flow of his speech, said, "The most frequent criticism I receive from colleagues is that I am not sufficiently balanced when I discuss what is happening in the schools. That I am too emotional. I am deeply disturbed, because I identify with the children who are being destroyed in those schools."

"But most middle-class educators are indeed balanced and cautious as they kept finding excuses for not educating these children. I have a hope that eventually our educational institutions will see as one of their responsibilities the training of human beings to be sensitive to what is done to human beings who are not like themselves. Until this happens, we will have one damn seminar like this after another, with no change in the status quo. I am sorry to have to say that it is really *not* a pleasure to be here."

The moderator of the panel asked for questions from the audience. The silver-haired man rose and identified himself as a retired principal of a New York City high school. Self-assured and angry, he declared himself deeply disturbed by what he called Clark's "emotional tone," and he denied that the school system had been indifferent to children in the ghettos. Pointing a long finger at Clark, he said, "To say that the schools are both incompetent *and* racist is a slander that destroys your credibility and alienates the support you might otherwise gain from the so-called middle class. Why, every effort has been made to deal with the problems of these children most sympathetically and effectively. There have been all kinds of programs."

The moderator asked Clark if he cared to make a response. With a slight, wintry smile, Clark said, "I first raised the question of the inferior quality of education in the schools of New York City in 1953. I had been doing research in Southern segregated schools for the NAACP in connection with a series of court cases that eventually led to the *Brown versus Board of Education* decision. I also testified in some of those cases, and on one such occasion a lawyer for the state of Virginia asked me during cross-examination, 'How dare you come and talk about the inferiority of our segregated schools here when you come from a city with segregated schools and you haven't done anything about them?'"

"I was really floored by the question. I told him, to begin with, that we did not have *legally* sanctioned segregation in the New York City public schools. And the second thing I said was, 'When I get back to New York, I'm going to find out whether the segregated schools in my city have the same negative educational and psychological consequences as the segregated schools in Virginia.' And that's what I did."

"Sure enough, the schools here had all the negative effects of the segregated schools of Virginia and the other Southern or border states. So I started trying to do something about it. I shall never forget one particular meeting at the New York City Board of Education headquarters, in Brooklyn. All the hierarchy was there, including a deputy superintendent who became very angry at me, getting so red in the face that I thought he was about to have an apoplectic fit. 'Dr. Clark,' he said, 'don't you understand that in this society we need to have hewers of wood and drawers of water, and that our schools have to be responsive to that reality?'"

"I was terribly embarrassed, and so were his colleagues. I got up to answer the deputy superintendent, but instead I left, and went back to the NAACP and the continuation of our struggle—a struggle I now know my grandchildren will have to continue after I am gone."

Dr. Clark looked directly at the man who had accused him of slandering the public school system. "Now, the gentleman back there said that the school system is providing these children with high-quality education. Therefore, their low academic achievement is a reflection of their inability to respond."

"I never said that." The silver-haired man was on his feet again. "Please do not misquote me."

"All right," Clark said, speaking very deliberately. "You said there have been all kinds of programs to achieve a very good school system. Yet this very good school system results in an intolerably high percentage of educational retardation among lower-status children. If they are *not* seen as inherently inferior, then their retardation indicates that the school system is not that good at all. It also demonstrates that these children are considered expendable, for why else would the failure of the *system* be allowed to continue year after year?"

There was no further comment from the silver-haired man.

A large middle-aged black woman rose. Gesturing toward the silver-haired man, she said in a strong, resonant voice, "Dr. Clark, the truth hurt that man over there. I am a voluntary teacher in an elementary school. And we have in there teachers who are not teachers. I say your competency tests should be given to the principals and right on down to the teachers. You would find that many teachers could not pass, because anybody who is teaching reading and writing and arithmetic—why, when a kid gets into the sixth grade he ought to be able to make a sentence and know a period from a semicolon and a comma. But the children do not know that. I resent a teacher miseducating a child, and I resent a teacher then saying there is something wrong with the *child*."

The woman continued, "They give us—the volunteers—children supposed to be going to a psychiatrist because those teachers can't teach them."

"The teacher will say to me, 'What are you doing with that child? She seems to be doing better since you have her.'"

"I say, 'Yes, she's a very intelligent child, so she's learning. I find her reading books all the day.'"

"The teacher will say, 'But you don't understand. We send her to a psychiatrist because she has a mental block and they are trying to find it.'"

"I say, 'When you find that block, what will you do with it?' I find that child a brilliant child—and she's not the only one. But those kids, our kids, they know when the teachers are not interested in them, and they respond accordingly."

Clark was nodding in agreement. The session ended soon afterward, and as Clark and I were making our way to the elevator he said, "What is this nation afraid of when it comes to really educating lower-status children? I don't know. I really don't know. In the entire society, this is the area most resistant to change. Of course, that woman was right about teachers, about how crucial they are. My God, they probably have the most important role in our society. I know, from my own life. Teachers certainly made a big difference in what happened to me."

Kenneth Clark went to elementary school and junior high school in Harlem. He was born, in 1914, in the Panama Canal Zone, and his mother, Miriam Clark, brought him and his sister, Beulah, to the United States when he was four and a half. Clark's father, Arthur Bancroft Clark, who was a general superintendent of cargo for the United Fruit Company, refused to go with his wife and children. A native of the West Indies, he had been told when he applied for a transfer that he could not be appointed to a job of equal status in America. "Learning that horrified my father," Clark recalled years later. "He couldn't understand why my mother would subject us to this kind of humiliation in a strange, racist country."

Miriam Clark, an indomitable woman originally from Kingston, Jamaica, was convinced that there would nonetheless be more and better opportunities for her children in the United States, especially in terms of education. She settled herself and the children in a small apartment in a Harlem tenement and found a job as a seamstress in a garment shop downtown, where she helped organize the workers and became one of the first black shop stewards for the International Ladies Garment Workers Union. At home, hearing his mother tell of the troubles and triumphs of her union activities, the boy caught what he later referred to as "the excitement of people doing things together to help themselves."

The classes in the Harlem schools were not yet all black. "We had plenty of Irish and Jewish kids," Clark recalled. "And the teachers were concerned with holding *all* of us to high standards, because they were convinced that *all* of us were educable.

"We had not yet come to that particular breakdown in the public education of minorities which is due less to flagrant racial bigotry than to the sloppy, sentimental good intentions of certain educators, who *reduce* learning standards for low-status youngsters, because they believe that these children's home conditions are such as to make it impossible for them to learn as much as suburban children. Thus, under the guise of compassion and understanding, these teachers reinforce educational disadvantage by treating the child as inherently inferior, as having real limitations of intelligence.

"And so each stereotyped child is denied his individuality and his potential; and the self-fulfilling prophecy of massive educational underachievement for these children is thereby perpetuated."

"But when I was going to public school we had teachers who did not consider themselves social workers, psychologists, and rationalizers of educational inequities. They were asked to teach reading, arithmetic, grammar, and they *did.* They understood that while there were individual differences in the children's ability to master academic subjects, these differences were not related to race or economic circumstances.

"I came from a broken home, but my teachers never asked me about that, or about what my mother did for a living. They were focusing on whether I was learning or not. For instance, when I went to the board in Mr. Ruprecht's algebra class, in junior high school, I had to do those equations, and if I wasn't able to do them he wanted to find out why. He didn't expect any less of me because I was black.

"There was an eighth-grade English teacher, Miss McGuire, who taught me to understand the beauty of an English sentence. And she didn't do it by worrying about my background. Also in the eighth grade, Mr. Mitchell, a blond, blue-eyed white Anglo-Saxon Protestant, taught us Shakespeare. Those plays came alive, right in the center of Harlem, as we took different parts. One day I was Macbeth, the next day I was Malcolm. It had nothing to do with color—the teacher's or ours. I do believe that it was because of my experiences with those teachers that I decided to become a teacher myself."

Not all of Clark's teachers were, as he put it, "fully developed human beings." By the time he was in the ninth grade, there were more black children in the classes, and the guidance counselor was advising them to go on to vocational school, where they could learn a trade. She wrote Clark's mother a note to that effect.

The next day, Miriam Clark did not go to work but instead showed up, with her fourteen-year-old son in tow, at the guidance counselor's office. "I was mortified, because I thought that my mother's coming into school like that would seal my doom," Dr. Clark told me. "On the other hand, I didn't want to go to any vocational school." He laughed. "I wasn't thinking about status—I just wasn't particularly adept at shop work. In any case, my mother marched in, refused to sit down, and stood there looming over the guidance counselor. Very slowly and very distinctly, my mother said, 'I don't give a damn where you send *your* son, but *mine* isn't going to any vocational school.' That was a turning point in my life. I went to Geroge Washington High School instead."

Dr. Clark continued, "At this point, I must tell you that I was by no means the brightest person in my classes in Harlem. I remember kids, particularly black kids—and not just in our fast class but in other classes and on the playground—who had minds like *that!*" He snapped his fingers. "And even though we did have some good teachers, there were others who shunted these black kids aside. The kids became bitter, because they were rejected. They didn't have anybody really fighting for them, you know. They didn't have a mother who was as daring as mine, a mother saying right out, 'Now, look, damn it! That's not going to happen to my son!'"

"When the child's mother does not or cannot fight for him, who can be the mother?" I asked.

He sighed. "All of us who are concerned with human beings must be the mothers, and must protect those who don't have anybody else to protect them. Does that sound corny? Well, that's what is on my mind when I go to board of regents meetings, when I write and talk about and work with schools. You see, the most horrible thing about Harlem—about all the ghettos—is the day-to-day destruction of human potential. In these concentration camps we build in our cities, the process of human destruction begins in the first and second grades. Back in the 1960s, I said in speeches and in papers that if there wasn't a dramatic improvement in the ghetto schools, all other civil rights gains would remain essentially empty promises. It did not require any particular brilliance to make that prediction."

Although Clark's own public school education was quite different from what has come to be the ghetto norm, he does remember one grievous setback, at George Washington High School. He is convinced that it occurred because of his color. Though it hardly destroyed him, it may have changed the direction of his career.

"In high school, I loved economics, and I read voraciously on the subject," Dr. Clark told me. "During my senior year, I was getting ninety-eights and ninety-nines on all the tests. The teacher always awarded an economics prize at the end of the year to the outstanding student, and everybody in the class was sure I was going to get that award. But when it came time for the announcement of the prize, someone else won. There was no question that I was entitled to it on the merits, but, as it turned out, the determining factor was color. A white student got it. I've never forgotten that teacher, because he was my first big disillusionment."

Clark did not question his teacher about why he had not been awarded the prize. "That sort of thing wasn't done then," he explained. "And, in any case, *I* certainly wouldn't have done it. I'll tell you what I did do, though. I never took another course in economics except for those courses that stressed the ability of human beings to refuse to be passive victims of so-called natural laws of economics. That fascinated me. Anything concerning human interaction with and *shaping* of the forces that affect our lives fascinated me."

In 1931 Kenneth Clark went on to Howard University, a black institution in Washington, D.C., where, in his junior year, he became the editor of the *Hilltop,* the campus newspaper, and organized a group of twenty Howard students to march on the Capitol—"to see if we could get them to treat us like loyal Americans. which we felt we were, by just giving us food in a public restaurant there." Food was denied, and the group was arrested.

Clark's most important experience at Howard, however, had to do with a professor of psychology. Clark had intended to go to medical school. "One day in my sophomore year," he recalled not long ago, "I was sitting, daydreaming, in Psychology I, looking out the window at two birds making love. When they flew away, I started listening to my professor, and I heard some very illuminating things about human behavior. From then on, I listened very hard to what he said, and I decided, 'To hell with medical school. This is the discipline for me.'

"What this professor, Francis Cecil Sumner, showed me was the promise of getting some systematic understanding of the complexities of human behavior and human interaction. In the physical sciences, understanding was achieving control—up to a certain point. And in the biological sciences, systematic understanding was providing the ability to manipulate the environment for the advantage of human beings. I saw no reason these kinds of possibilities should not extend to the social sciences. And although I do get depressed from time to time, I *still* believe that disciplined intelligence brought to bear on social problems can provide either the answers or the reasons we don't have the answers. The seemingly intractable nature of racism, for example, and its effects on children."

Clark continued. "Professor Sumner had *rigorous* standards for his students. And he didn't just teach psychology. He taught integrity. Once you had your facts, that was the basis on which you defended yourself. And although he led the way for other blacks in the study of psychology, Sumner would permit no nonsense about there being anything like 'black psychology'—any more than he would have allowed any nonsense about 'black astronomy.' In this and in many other ways, Sumner was a model for me. In fact, he has always been my standard when I evaluate myself."

Clark has said of Howard University, "It was the beneficiary of the idiocy of racism in American higher education. People like Sumner were not invited to teach at the University of Chicago or Harvard. They were black." Sumner had earned his doctorate at Clark University, under the preeminent psychologist of the time, G. Stanley Hall, who was the first president of the American Psychological Association and the leading national authority on educational standards.

Also on the faculty of Howard during Clark's years there were Ralph Bunche and the philosopher and cultural historian Alain Locke—"two more who were not invited to teach at white universities," Clark said. "Bunche, who had recently obtained his Ph.D. from Harvard, was chairman of the political science department. He became a great influence on me: his courage, his clarity, the standards he set for himself—and for his students. We became friends and saw each other often through the years after Howard. I especially remember one thing he said, about a year before he died: 'Kenneth, our leaders will never be taken seriously, and we will not be respected, and make any really fundamental move toward equality and dignity as a people, until we learn not to settle for crumbs.'"

Clark came under another lifelong influence while he was at Howard—that of Mamie Phipps, the daughter of a successful physician in Hot Springs, Arkansas. She arrived on campus as a freshman when he was a senior. "I knew right away I was going to marry her," Dr. Clark says. "It was her self-assurance. Her quiet self-assurance. Mamie had come to Howard to major in mathematics, and she was very good in the subject, but eventually I persuaded her to change to psychology. I wanted her in an area in which *I* felt more self-assured."

Mamie Phipps Clark, a slender woman of cool dignity, remembers that her initial impression of Kenneth Clark was that "he was very, very serious." She goes on to say, "And that was not characteristic of most of the male students on campus. I thought they were wasting their parents' money. But Kenneth seemed to be going someplace, and I admired that—all the more because I had rarely seen that kind of determination. Yes, he persuaded me to change my major. I got a C once, rather than the grade I had expected, and he told me that the teacher was prejudiced against women and that since the mathematics department was small, I would be stuck with that teacher unless I switched. Then he said, 'What are you interested in?'

"'Children.'

"'What are you going to do with mathematics and children?'

"'Teach it to them.'

"'If you want to work with children, you'll be able to do a lot more for them if you know psychology.'

"So I changed, married him when I was a senior, and later we became the first two black Ph.D.s in the history of the psychology department of Columbia University."

In 1936 Clark obtained an M.S. at Howard, and he taught psychology there for a year while Mamie finished her undergraduate work. Then, Clark said, it was time to move on. "Dr. Sumner, Alain Locke, and Mordecai Johnson, who was then president of Howard, all said to me, 'Kenneth, go get your doctorate and break the pattern. Teach at a nonsegregated school.' I was part of the next generation of black academics, and I was not to come back to Howard."

As the first black Ph.D. candidate in psychology at Columbia, Clark puzzled some members of the faculty by ranking first in the matriculation examination. "They had thought I would need some form of compensatory enrichment, or something of the sort, and couldn't figure out how I had done so well," he says. "Then they wanted to know about Francis Cecil Summer. Must be a pretty good teacher. All this puzzlement on their part fascinated me.

"Well, I went on to meet all the requirements and get a doctorate in experimental psychology. By then—1940—some of the professors who had been perplexed at my superiority to the other students were advising me to go back and share my knowledge with my people: I was to have a fine career in black colleges."

The new Ph.D. politely rejected this counsel. "I really want to teach where other Columbia Ph.D.s teach," he told his professors. Gardner Murphy, a Columbia faculty member with whom Clark had worked closely, was about to become chairman of the psychology department of City College, and Clark said he would like to join him there. At that time, there was no black on the regular faculty of any New York City municipal college. Clark was given a temporary appointment, for the summer and the following academic year.

"I taught there that summer, but then did something stupid," Dr. Clark recalls. "Instead of staying on in the fall, I accepted an invitation to build a department of psychology at Hampton Institute, a black college in Virginia. I was young and couldn't resist the chance to start something of my own." He stayed only six months at Hampton Institute. "A while after I came, the president told me he didn't want me disturbing and frustrating the students. I was to present my psychology courses in a way that would make these young black people adjust to and accept their status in the society. The president added that if I understood what he was saying, and acted accordingly, he would make me one of the best-known Negro psychologists in the nation. I told him I certainly did understand what he was saying, but no thanks, and I left."

Ralph Bunche meanwhile had moved to the Office of Strategic Services, and he arranged for Clark to get a job with the Office of War Information, as an assistant social-science analyst on its research staff. For about a year and a half, Clark traveled the country assessing the morale of the black citizenry in time of war. In 1942 he returned to the psychology department of City College. He became an assistant professor in 1949 and a full professor in 1960—the first black in New York City's history to receive a permanent appointment to a city college. In 1970, he was named Distinguished University Professor.

Throughout his teaching career, Clark has engaged in the kind of research that was encouraged by his professors at Howard—what he calls "the use of disciplined intelligence in achieving social justice." He served on Gunnar Myrdal's staff, for example, during the preparation of *An American Dilemma*, Myrdal's study of racism in the United States, which was sponsored by the Carnegie Corporation and was published in 1944.

In 1946 Clark and his wife set up a nonprofit organization in Harlem called the Northside Testing and Consultation Center. (It later became the Northside Center for Child Development.) Mamie Clark was the executive director, and Clark was in charge of research. At first, Clark told me, the Northside staff, which was made up of psychiatrists, psychologists, and social workers, tried to help emotionally disturbed children through the traditional one-to-one therapist-patient relationship.

"Over the years, however, it became clear to us that, given the realities of the ghetto, we could not believe we were really helping if we ignored those realities," he said. "If, for example, we tried to get individual parents and their children to *adjust* to schools so criminally inferior that they were dehumanizing. Or if we tried to get them to *adjust* to the kind of housing to which they had been sentenced by a society that had the economic but not the moral resources to do something about that housing."

"The families we were working with were not going to respond to umpteen years of lying on a couch and talking about ego and id," Mamie Clark told me. "They needed help with housing, welfare, health, money, and all those things."

Accordingly, the emphasis at Northside shifted, Dr. Clark explained. Individual therapy continued, but "within the walls of the clinic we also had to try to develop in the parents and the children the strength to attempt to change the social pathology around them—to work at problems of injustice and inequity," he said. "We felt that this was the only way in which they could really resolve the negative self-image that a racially cruel society had imposed on them and their children."

"One of the first social issues we got involved in at Northside had to do with an educational injustice," Mamie Clark recalled. "In the public schools, a great many children had been put in classes for the intellectually retarded. We tested them at Northside and determined that most of them were not retarded. So the families protested, we protested, and the children who should not have been in those classes were taken out."

During Northside's early years, Clark became increasingly active, elsewhere in the country, as a researcher and a witness in a series of court cases aimed at what he considered the most damaging of all educational injustices—legally segregated public schools.

When Mamie Clark was working toward her master's degree, she did her fieldwork among schoolchildren in Washington, D.C. She was studying the effects of race on the way the children felt about themselves. Kenneth Clark also became absorbed in the work, and together they broadened the field of research and began publishing pioneering studies in various social-science journals on how segregation affected preschool black children's sense of self-esteem. Today, when the results of such studies are taken for granted, it's hard to imagine a time when there was a need for such studies. In one series of tests, administered to children between the ages of three and seven in, among other places, Philadelphia, Boston, Worcester, and several cities in Arkansas, the children were asked to choose between otherwise identical brown and white dolls in response to such instructions as these:

Give me the doll that you like to play with.
Give me the doll that is the nice doll.
Give me the doll that looks bad.
Give me the doll that is a nice color.

The Clarks reported that the majority of the children "indicated an unmistakable preference for the white doll and a rejection of the brown doll." They concluded, "The fact that young Negro children would prefer to be white reflects their knowledge that society prefers white people."

In 1950 Clark wrote a monograph for the Midcentury White House Conference on Children and Youth, in which he summarized not only his and his wife's research but also the rest of the existing literature on the effects of racial segregation on black children. The monograph came to the attention of Robert Carter, a young lawyer with the National Association for the Advancement of Colored People.

An NAACP legal team, headed by Thurgood Marshall, had decided to make an all-out attack on the constitutionality of state laws mandating or permitting segregation of the schools. Such statutes, the NAACP claimed, violated the equal-protection clause of the Fourteenth Amendment ("No state shall . . . deny to any person within its jurisdiction the equal protection of the laws"). Carter thought that Clark might be a useful witness in some of the pending cases; he also wanted to explore with Clark the possibility of enlisting other social scientists to buttress the NAACP argument that "separate but equal" schooling not only was inherently unequal but also inflicted psychological damage on the segregated black children.

The "separate but equal" doctrine had been established by the Supreme Court in *Plessy v. Ferguson* (1896). During a train trip in Louisiana, Homer Plessy, a "seven-eighths Caucasian"—he had had one Negro great-grandparent—refused to move to a car for "colored" passengers, as a recently passed state law required. A New Orleans judge ruled that, contrary to Plessy's argument, the segregation statute did not violate the Fourteenth Amendment. On appeal, the Supreme Court, by a seven-to-one vote, affirmed the lower court's decision. Justice Henry Billings Brown, speaking for the majority, declared that laws requiring racial separation "do not necessarily imply the inferiority of either race to the other." Indeed, he said, "we consider the underlying fallacy of the plaintiff's argument to consist in the assumption that the enforced separation of the two races stamps the colored race with a badge of inferiority."

He continued, "If this be so, it is not by reason of anything found in the act, but solely because the colored race chooses to put that construction upon it." As long as they were equal, separate facilities, based on "the established usages, customs, and traditions of the people," were constitutional. And to give further support to that conclusion, Justice Brown noted that "the most common instance" of lawful segregation "is connected with the establishment of separate schools for white and colored children, which have been held to be a valid exercise of the legislative power even by courts of states where the political rights of the colored race have been longest and most earnestly enforced."

In 1951, when the NAACP was organizing its legal strategy for getting *Plessy* overturned, racial segregation of children was in force in more than eleven thousand school districts in the United States. (Seventeen states and the District of Columbia had passed laws establishing school segregation, and four other states allowed school segregation where it was the wish of a local community.)

The year before, NAACP lawyers had scored partial victories in two cases dealing with segregation at the state-university level. One, *Sweatt v. Painter,* concerned a black student who had tried to enroll in the University of Texas Law School, whereupon state authorities created a separate black law school. Here the Supreme Court ruled in favor of the black plaintiff, Herman Sweatt, but not on the ground that separate but equal facilities were unconstitutional. In this case, the Court said, the State of Texas had manifestly not made the separate facilities equal, and so it was ordered that Herman Sweatt be admitted to the white law school to which he had applied. It was not necessary, said Chief Justice Fred M. Vinson, that "we reach petitioner's contention that *Plessy v. Ferguson* should be re-examined in the light of contemporary knowledge respecting the purposes of the Fourteenth Amendment and the effects of racial segregation."

The other case, *McLaurin v. Oklahoma State Regents,* which was decided on the same day as *Sweatt,* was more difficult for the Court to resolve without considering the validity of *Plessy.* Under federal court order, George McLaurin had been admitted to the Graduate School of Education at the University of Oklahoma, because the courses he wanted to take were not available in the state's Negro college. But within the university McLaurin had been segregated from his class-mates. His desk was separated from all the others by a rail, to which a sign reading RESERVED FOR COLORED was attached. He also had a seg-regated desk in the library, and he was compelled to eat by himself in the cafeteria. Everything else was "equal"—professors, books, and physical facilities.

The Supreme Court, deciding unanimously for McLaurin, said that "the conditions under which this appellant is required to receive his education deprive him of his personal and present right to the equal protection of the laws," because "such restrictions impair and inhibit his ability to study, to engage in discussion and exchange of views with other students." What particularly encouraged the NAACP's legal team was the Court's further judgment:

"We hold that under these circumstances, the Fourteenth Amendment precludes differences in treatment by the state based upon race." Nonetheless, *Plessy v. Ferguson* had not been struck down. Had the state of Oklahoma provided a separate graduate school for McLaurin with truly equal facilities, that maneuver would conceiv-ably have been lawful, according to the decision reached in *Sweatt* the same day. But once McLaurin had been enrolled in the University of Oklahoma, there could be no "differences in treatment . . . based on race" in that newly biracial environment.

This ruling appeared to mean that certain forms of segregation were unconstitutional, but not all. Furthermore, these two cases were restricted to graduate education. For millions of young black children, the NAACP maintained, the harm done by segregated schools begins in the first grade.

One approach to combating racial separation in elementary and sec-ondary schools was to keep bringing lawsuits on the basis that a particu-lar black educational facility was unequal to its white counterpart. Because this was indeed the case in most segregated school districts, the NAACP figured that it could win discrete victories on these grounds; however, to break down the racial walls on a case-by-case basis might take a half century or more. The alternative was to launch a direct assault on the *Plessy* doctrine by arguing that even if all facilities were "equal," the very nature of segregation made separate education profoundly unequal for black children and profoundly damaging to their sense of self-worth.

In February 1951, Kenneth Clark began to work with NAACP lawyers on the preparation of three of the four cases—from Kansas, South Carolina, Virginia, and Delaware—that, three years later, were to be grouped by the Supreme Court in its *Brown v. Board of Education* decision. In all but the Kansas suit (the title case), Clark testified and helped recruit other social scientists as witnesses.

The NAACP had used social-science testimony before. In *Sweatt,* for instance, an anthropologist had testified on scientific interpretation of racial differences. But now the legal strategy was to include a systematic analysis—by psychologists, sociologists, anthropologists, and a variety of experts on education—of the nature of segregation itself and of its effects on children.

As a witness in one of the four test cases, *Briggs v. Elliott,* Clark testified before the federal district court in Charleston, South Carolina, in May 1951, saying the following:

> I have reached the conclusion from the examination of my own results and from an examination of the literature in the entire field that discrimination, prejudice, and segregation have definitely detrimental effects on the personality development of the Negro child. The essence of this detrimental effect is a confusion in the child's concept of his own self-esteem—basic feelings of inferiority, conflict, confusion in his self-image, resentment, hostility toward himself, hostility toward whites, intensification of . . . a desire to resolve his basic conflict by sometimes escaping or withdrawing.

In February 1952, testifying in Richmond, Virginia, in another of the cases, *Davis v. County School Board,* Clark was asked on cross-examination by T. Justin Moore, chief counsel for the Prince Edward County School Board, if it was not true that the Negroes of Virginia, as long as they were provided with equal facilities and equipment, could indeed get an equal education. "Why can't the Negro have pride of race?" Moore asked. "Why does he want, I suggest, to be in the category of what I believe someone has described as a 'sun-tanned white man'?"

Clark answered coolly, "I don't think it is the desire of a Negro to be a 'sun-tanned white man.' I think it is the desire of a Negro to be a human being and to be treated as a human being without regard to skin color. He can only have pride in race—and a healthy and mature pride in race—when his own government does not constantly and continuously tell him, 'Have no pride in race,' by constantly segregating him, constantly relegating him to a second-class status."

In three of the four NAACP cases, the lower courts held firm to *Plessy*. In the fourth, *Gebhart v. Belton,* Judge Collins J. Seitz, of the Delaware Court of Chancery, said that although he himself believed that "the 'separate but equal' doctrine of education should be rejected," it was up to the Supreme Court, rather than to him, to make that decision.

As part of the appeal of the four cases to the Supreme Court, the NAACP legal strategists decided to present all the social-science data for the Court's consideration in a special appendix to the formal briefs. This appendix was prepared by Kenneth Clark; Stuart Cook, chairman of the graduate psychology department of New York University; and Isidor Chein, director of research for the Commission on Community Interrelations of the American Jewish Congress. Titled "The Effects of Segregation and the Consequences of De-segregation: A Social Science Statement," the appendix summarized and documented the testimony that had been presented at the trial by the NAACP's expert witnesses. It was signed by thirty-two prominent social scientists and psychiatrists who had done extensive research in race relations. Dr. Clark has since noted that "while there was some precedent for inclusion of social-science data in legal briefs, this was probably the first time that a separate nonlegal brief dealing with the social and psychological aspects of a constitutional issue was submitted to and accepted by the United States Supreme Court."

On May 17, 1954, the Court, in a unanimous decision delivered by Chief Justice Earl Warren, overturned *Plessy v. Ferguson.* To separate black children "from others of similar age and qualifications solely because of their race generates a feeling of inferiority as to their status in the community that may affect their hearts and minds in a way unlikely ever to be undone," the Court declared. "Whatever may have been the extent of psychological knowledge at the time of *Plessy v. Ferguson,* this finding is amply supported by modern authority."

At that point in the decision, there was a footnote, No. 11, consisting of a list of sources exemplifying "modern authority," the first of which was "K. B. Clark, 'Effect of Prejudice and Discrimination on

Personality Development' (Midcentury White House Conference on Children and Youth, 1950)." The Court continued: "We conclude that in the field of public education the doctrine of 'separate but equal' has no place. Separate educational facilities are inherently unequal. Therefore, we hold that the plaintiffs and others similarly situated for whom the actions have been brought are, by reason of the segregation complained of, deprived of the equal protection of the laws guaranteed by the Fourteenth Amendment."

Kenneth Clark was, of course, jubilant—the more so because it appeared that the Supreme Court had taken "judicial notice," as he put it, of that unusual social-science appendix. As his professors at Howard University had taught him, disciplined intelligence *could* achieve social justice, and the social sciences were surely going to be as effective in their fields as the biological sciences were in theirs.

Despite the unanimity of the Supreme Court in *Brown,* and despite its acknowledgment of "modern authority," racism has, of course, proved much more intransigent than Clark anticipated in the immediate aftermath of the striking down of *Plessy.* But long after it had become clear that the expectations of that May day might not be fulfilled until the end of the century—if then—Dr. Clark was still emphasizing the historic impact of the 1954 decision.

In 1976, delivering a speech in Munich titled "The Status of American Minorities in the Bicentennial Year of the American Revolution," he noted:

> Within three years after the *Brown* decision, Martin Luther King, Jr., Roy Wilkins, Whitney Young, and Malcolm X emerged as the significant leaders of the modern civil-rights movement, which then became in effect a mass movement. American . . . blacks who seemed to have accepted compliantly racial segregation since the latter part of the nineteenth century now openly defied institutionalized racism. They refused to sit in the back of the bus. They boycotted all public accommodations that sought to impose racial humiliation upon them.

And in the wake of *Brown,* Clark added, Congress passed the Civil Rights Act of 1964 and the Voting Rights Act of 1965.

That said, Clark, in his bicentennial lecture, turned to the "distinction between appearance and substance." After all the marches, demonstrations, and new laws, the majority of blacks "are still to be found in menial positions, are underemployed, or are unemployed," he pointed out. "Most black children, twenty-two years after the *Brown* decision, are still required by various evasive devices to attend racially segregated and inferior schools." He continued:

> This problem is particularly exacerbated in northern urban communities, such as Boston, New York, Chicago, Philadelphia, Los Angeles. These so-called cosmopolitan centers of America are now the bastions of sustained resistance to . . . the desegregation of their schools. Racially segregated communities remain the norm in American cities. White suburbs remain predominantly white *Bantustans,* with only occasional Negroes being permitted to purchase homes within these compounds of privilege. Urban ghettos are expanding and proliferating, and the pathologies of the ghettos—crime, drugs, defeatism of the young, reinforced by inferior education—remain unsolved problems which threaten the viability if not the survival of major American cities.

Brown had indeed made history, but not enough.

In the decades since *Brown,* Kenneth Clark has become more and more firmly convinced that the primary way to regenerate the hopes and energies ignited by the *Brown* decision is to transform the schools. In speeches and seminars, he has repeated this theme: "One cannot expect a group to attain the full status of equality of citizenship if the masses of the children of that group are being denied adequate education in their elementary and secondary schools, if the abilities of these children are not being developed to the maximum at these crucial stages of their development, and if these children are being subjected to educational experiences which deprive them of the ability to compete successfully with others."

7

DR. KENNETH CLARK, PART II:
SIMPLE JUSTICE AND HOW IT GOT LOST

"I saw this white kid, and he was saying, 'Look, this segregation is increasing bigotry.'"

*E*ven before the *Brown* decision, Dr. Clark had been pressing for change in the New York City school system, and throughout the 1950s he continued to accuse the New York Board of Education of permitting significant increases in de facto segregated education that was decidedly unequal. His indictments were rejected, and in the late 1950s, to document further the damage done to black children in the city's public schools, Clark assigned a number of his white students at City College to interview white elementary and secondary school teachers.

In *Dark Ghetto*, Clark reported that many of the teachers told the interviewers "that Negro children are inherently inferior in intelligence and therefore cannot be expected to learn as much or as readily as white children; and that all one would do, if one tried to teach them as if they could learn, would be to develop in them serious emotional disturbances, frustrations and anxieties."

Obviously, Clark continued, "children who are treated as if they are uneducable almost invariably become uneducable." Furthermore, it is the "negative influence" of such teachers, he said, more than the influence of home and community, that causes the negative self-image of so many minority schoolchildren.

To any who asked, and to the many who did not ask, Clark provided his own solution to teaching "the disadvantaged." It is "embarrassingly simple," he wrote. "Teach them with the same expectations, the same acceptance of their humanity and their educability and, therefore, with the same effectiveness as one would teach the more privileged child. In other words, teach them the way you would the kids in Scarsdale, or in any other upper-middle-class community."

In 1955, to prove that this embarrassingly simple approach would work, Kenneth and Mamie Clark began a "crash program" in remedial reading at the Northside Center. It had long been evident to the Clarks that, as he put it, "the most frequently stated concern of the parents of Northside children is not their economic status, not their housing, not their family problems, but the inefficient education of their children." For four or five weeks in the summer, therefore, one-hour classes in reading were given five days a week at the center. Each summer, over a period of five years, the average gain in reading level for each child who took the course turned out to be about a year. "These children were woefully retarded academically," Clark pointed out. "So much so that their schools had said they couldn't do anything with them, because they could not learn. And they were poor. Their parents suffered from all the disadvantages that are supposed to cripple the learning abilities of children from such homes. Most were on welfare.

"But in this place these children were being taught to read by people who believed they could learn to read and who related to them with warmth and acceptance. Under these conditions, they learned. And, what's more, they sustained what they had learned during the regular school year. But they did not increase those gains during the regular school year. In the public schools, their progress stopped. But their home environment had remained constant. They had been just as poor in the summer, with us, as they were for the rest of the year in school. The difference was in the learning environment."

Despite what Northside kept proving about black children's ability to learn, achievement levels in the ghetto classrooms of the city continued to fall; indeed, the longer most poor children stayed in school, the more steeply their rate of learning declined.

In 1962, Kenneth Clark thought he might finally have the chance to demonstrate, in a much, much larger setting than Northside, that black children are as educable as any others. The Kennedy Administration had set up the interdepartmental President's Committee on Juvenile Delinquency and Youth Crime, with Attorney General Robert Kennedy as chairman. The committee provided funds to Harlem Youth Opportunities Unlimited (HARYOU) for a two-year study of how best to control juvenile delinquency in central Harlem. The study was also to include a specific plan that, if it was approved, would get large-scale funding for its realization. Clark was appointed acting chairman of HARYOU.

"From the beginning," Clark told me, "we recognized that we could not deal seriously with the problem of delinquency in Harlem without identifying and remedying those pervasive problems in the community which stunted and dehumanized Harlem's youth." One of those problems was education. Accordingly, the eventual plan, which was presented in a 620-page report titled "Youth in the Ghetto: A Study of the Consequences of Powerlessness and a Blueprint for Change," included a carefully detailed design for "thorough reorganization of the schools." Along with rezoning, open enrollment, and other strategies to increase the number of racially heterogeneous schools, Clark called for the selection of teachers and administrators solely on the basis of their "special competence," with "extra pay tied to superior skill." The promotion of these educators would depend on how well the children in their classrooms learned.

On the basis of the Northside experience in intensive summer reading, Clark, in a written proposal, recommended a Reading Mobilization Year. Because "all studies of the problem of education in deprived communities agree on the fact that the central pathology in these schools is the fact that the children in these schools are woefully deficient in reading," he wrote, the central board of education would drop its normal curriculum in the Harlem area for half a year or a year, and during that time "the total school program . . . would be geared toward the improvement of reading." (There would be a different curriculum during that year for children who were not retarded in reading.)

This vast "crash program in reading," Clark declared, "would significantly decrease juvenile delinquency by reducing the dropout rate and giving thousands of children some realistic hope for their future.

In addition, Clark's plan included extensive preschool education. To start with, at least four thousand children between the ages of three and five would be enrolled in "Pre-School Academies," in which parents also would be instructed in how to "participate fully in the education of their children." As might have been expected from Clark, the focus in these early classes would not be on "the conventional play approach of most day-care-center and nursery-school programs" but on "linguistic and conceptual skills," because such skills "are necessary preparation for learning to read, write, and handle numerical relationships."

Still another part of the HARYOU plan envisaged "After-School Study Centers," which would "compensate for the past failures of the public schools." And along with a variety of continually monitored job-training programs, there was to be a counseling service for high school dropouts, which would either get the youths back into school or train them in work skills. Furthermore, Clark had devised a plan for a "Community Service Corps," for those "so severely damaged" that they were not yet ready for advanced job training.

Pervading the entire "Youth in the Ghetto" report was an insistence on the continuing participation of the residents of Harlem, including the young, in the development of each part of the design. They would act as recruiters, research aides, and teaching aides, among other capacities. This, Clark pointed out, was to be a break with "the traditional social service, welfare, dole approach" to the poor, an approach that continually increased the dependency and stigmatization of "the clients." If Harlem was not to continue to be "a powerless colony," its citizens would have to learn the skills, including those of confrontation, if necessary, to bring about lasting social change on their own. HARYOU, if it worked, was to be Harlem's declaration of independence. "The program must work," said Clark in his proposal. "It is the city's last hope to save these children from a wasted life."

"Youth in the Ghetto" was presented to the review panel of the President's Committee on Juvenile Delinquency in April 1964 (the committee was continuing its work under President Lyndon Johnson), and the panel recommended an initial allocation of $1 million to begin to make the blueprint real. An additional $3.5 million was provided by the city of New York, and the Department of Labor made a grant of $500,000 to begin the job-training and job-placement programs. Over a period of three years, there would be a total of some $110 million in federal funds for all the intersecting programs.

At this point, as the two years of research and planning appeared to be moving toward realization, Clark resigned from HARYOU. There was a struggle between him and Representative Adam Clayton Powell Jr. over its independence, and Clark lost. Clark later explained, "Powell was the first major political figure to understand the political dynamite inherent in the community-action components of the HARYOU planning document. Seeing this, he insisted that if it was going to operate in his district, it would have to be under his control." Powell already controlled an existing "action program," Associated Community Teams (ACT), which provided work for Harlem youths and was financed in part by the President's Committee on Juvenile Delinquency. Under pressure from Powell, HARYOU and ACT were merged, and a former Powell assistant became the executive director of the new organization. Powell controlled the board of directors.

Clark resisted the merger, knowing that if his plan became subject to Powell's political patronage and political direction, it would surely fail. For a time, feeling that all the moral weight was on his side, he believed he could successfully force Powell to back off. "Adam kept trying to win me over," Clark recalled. "He'd say, 'Kenneth, don't be such a baby.' I must admit I liked him very much. He was a charming man. And he was honest. That is, he was honestly corrupt. He had undertaken the most difficult civil rights challenge, the integration of corruption. He knew exactly what he was doing, and he enjoyed doing it. Adam had no sense of guilt that I was ever aware of, and he was very shrewd.

"He had read the HARYOU report carefully, and he knew that, for him to survive, the ghetto must survive, the ghetto must survive as it was. If the ghetto were transformed so that its residents took power for themselves, his power would be destroyed. Adam kept telling me that I couldn't win this battle, because he had too much power. But I was naïve and refused to believe him. Until the very end, moreover, I was trying to persuade Adam that if he did not contaminate

HARYOU, if he insulated it from pork-barrel politics, it would become a monument to him."

Clark finally realized that he had been defeated when he went to see Powell in his Washington office in the summer of 1964. "I was in the city for a board meeting at Howard University, and I wanted to try once more to convince Adam that he should leave us alone," Clark told me. "I still did not believe I was entirely powerless, because Robert Kennedy agreed with me, and he still chaired President Johnson's Committee on Juvenile Delinquency, the chief funding source."

Powell, Clark recalled, began by saying amiably, "You know, you have nobody on your side, Kenneth. I am chairman of the House Education and Labor Committee, through which all antipoverty legislation must go, and so Lyndon has to keep me satisfied. So does Bob Wagner, because, as mayor of New York, he needs Lyndon. As for Bobby Kennedy, he's going to run for the Senate in New York, so he can't afford to antagonize me, either. He needs the votes I can deliver."

The telephone rang at that point. It was not an ordinary phone but an instrument that allowed Powell to carry on a conversation without having to speak directly into a receiver. He could move freely about the room as he talked, and the amplified voice of the caller could be heard throughout the room. Powell had first seen such a telephone on Lyndon Johnson's desk, and when he expressed admiration for it, the president had given one to him. On the phone was a close associate of Robert Kennedy. The associate was on the staff of the President's Committee on Juvenile Delinquency. During the previous weeks, he had been assuring Clark that he was right to continue battling Powell and that the committee would support him.

"But here was the man's voice floating in the room," Clark recalled. "'Mr. Congressman,' he said, 'I want you to know that I've got the Puerto Ricans lined up behind us, and they will attack Clark on this HARYOU thing.' Adam was smiling, winking at me. He ended the phone conversation by saying, 'Keep up the good work. And tell the attorney general I sent my best.' Adam hung up and said, 'See, that's politics. You've got to grow up, Kenneth.'"

Clark resigned from HARYOU immediately after this postgraduate lesson in politics. "I really was naïve," he said. "Roy Wilkins had tried to warn me. He had told me that a tough-minded, competent, independent HARYOU would not be permitted by Adam. As for Bobby Kennedy, when reports began to appear in the press that Adam was about to exploit HARYOU, Bobby was quoted as saying, 'I have no fault to find with Adam Clayton Powell.' So Adam won, and his victory effectively blocked any systematic and serious realization of the plan.

"Once more, the poor had been fought *about*, not for. They remained hostages, instruments of other people's profit and power. As it turned out, all we did at HARYOU was to produce a document. Oh, it had some influence. When President Johnson appointed Sargent Shriver the director of his War on Poverty, Shriver talked with me a number of times, and it was clear that he and his staff had read 'Youth in the Ghetto.' That's where they got the idea for their 'community-action programs' and for having the 'maximum feasible participation' of the poor in the planning stages."

"But despite those slogans, the actual takeover pattern set by Adam Powell was repeated throughout the country. The poor just didn't have the training, let alone the power, to cope with the established political bureaucracy in terms of who was to control the so-called community-action programs. Middle-class bureaucrats took them over, and while some of the indigenous poor did learn to become antipoverty hustlers, the masses pretty much remained as they were, except that their frustrations grew deeper because of what these antipoverty programs had promised. It is probably not coincidental that the urban riots of the middle and late 1960s came in the wake of all the false talk about 'maximum feasible participation' of the poor."

Clark added that mistakes were also made by the planners who were not part of the old political apparatus but earnestly regarded themselves as allies of the poor. "The most important mistake," he said, "was that we did not take into sufficient account the debilitating, inhibiting effect of the most persistent and stark factor in American poverty, the quality of education in the public schools in the low-income areas of our cities."

With so much damage being created by those schools, Clark said, it was difficult to find enough people with the analytic skills; the disciplined, sustained energy; and the hope required to engage in the long, complex battles necessary to overcome white political power, on the one hand, and the Adam Clayton Powells, on the other. Nonetheless, Clark does not believe the War on Poverty was a total failure. "For all the pork-barreling," he said, "many individuals in the ghettos did get a sense that they have certain rights and that community action *is* the way to proceed—if they could ever become strong enough politically to control that action."

After losing the HARYOU battle, Dr. Clark continued teaching at City College and, in 1967, also became the president of a nonprofit corporation known as MARC—the Metropolitan Applied Research Center. Staffed by specialists in the social sciences, law, and municipal affairs, MARC described its work as "an attempt to determine by systematic exploration whether trained intelligence can be mobilized as an effective form of power for positive social change." Through research, to be followed sometimes by intervention, MARC intended to address itself to specific problems of the poor, and through fellowships and student-internship programs it would create cadres of experienced, disciplined activists who could function anywhere in the country.

MARC was housed near Fifth Avenue in an attractive three-story building on East 86th Street. The rooms were airy; the furnishings were imaginative and crisply coordinated; and Clark himself occupied a spacious third-floor office that opened onto a plant-lined terrace. "If the Ford Foundation can have a place with class and taste, why shouldn't a black think tank?" he said at the time. Actually, the staff was integrated, as all of Clark's research teams have been. "Racial separatism is a blind alley," he has said. "It means the abandonment of hope. Furthermore, just as there are white idiots, so there are black idiots."

Although MARC explored a considerable range of urban issues, Clark, characteristically, was most concerned with finding ways to make the public schools work for the poor. In 1970, it looked as if he, MARC, and the public would finally get a chance to demonstrate in the school system of an entire city what he had been prevented from demonstrating through HARYOU: that low-income black children are as educable as any other children.

In Washington, D.C., a newly elected school board, headed by Anita Ford Allen, a graduate of Howard University who had become an administrator in the United States Office of Education, invited Dr. Clark to design an educational program for the hundred and fifty thousand children then attending school in the District of Columbia. More than 90 percent were black, and many were poor. (Many middle-class residents of Washington, black and white, were sending their children to private schools.)

Mrs. Allen had come to Clark because for years District of Columbia students had been scoring considerably below national norms in reading and mathematics, and the longer they stayed in school the further they fell behind. By the end of the sixth grade, a majority of the children were at least two years behind their peers in other school systems, and many of those who finally graduated from high school were clearly deficient in basic skills.

Dr. Clark accepted the challenge, saying at the time, "This is an opportunity to show that it is possible to raise the academic achievement of minority-group children by accepting them, by respecting them, and by teaching them with the same efficiency as one would educate more privileged children. These educationally retarded children are human beings. They are not expendable. We simply cannot allow another generation of black youngsters to be sentenced to lives of failure and futility."

Clark and his associates at MARC designed what they called an Academic Achievement Project for Washington. (Their work appeared as a book in 1972, with the title *A Possible Reality: A Design for the Attainment of High Academic Achievement for Inner-City Students*. In his design, Clark called for a Reading Mobilization Year, as he had in Harlem, for all the students in the first through the ninth grade in the District of Columbia school system. Intensive instruction by teams of teachers would raise the reading levels of all children to their grade level and higher. Teachers and administrators would be held accountable for the success or failure of their students. Their rank and salary level would depend on the achievement of the children in their charge. And to find out just how much, or how little, was being achieved, standardized testing and other assessments of reading progress would take place throughout the year.

Clark's "possible reality" did not have a chance to prove or disprove itself. From the beginning, as an academic observer of the experiment has explained, "Clark and his plan were seen as a threat by the educational professionals. Hugh Scott, a new superintendent of schools—and the first black to hold that post in the District—felt that Clark, as an outsider, would weaken his own control of the system. And the largely black teachers' union, led by William Simons, objected strenuously to the idea of having teachers monitored and evaluated on the basis of the academic progress of their students. Implicit in such a plan, the union felt, was the eventual erosion of tenure protections. If the students of a particular teacher consistently failed, the time might come when the teacher could be fired, tenure or not. Simons said at one point, "What is good for children is not going to be purchased at the price of dignity for adults."

Furthermore, there was much disagreement about whether the Clark plan was realistic, considering the nature and quality of the District's students. Dr. Clark had said that normal children, of whatever color, could learn, but both the superintendent of schools and the head of the teachers' union questioned whether the term *normal* could be applied to the black children of Washington. "Let's face the facts," Scott said in a speech to a group of Young Republicans. "A goodly number of the black kids in this district were not raised in a normal social, political, and economic environment, and it may not be an accurate thing to use that terminology—normal—without taking in the full consequences of these other factors."

In sum, his position was that the District's black children, though they were born with the potential to participate effectively in society, might have been so handicapped in their intellectual growth and development by "the historic grievances and limitations of an abnormal environment" that they could not function normally in school. If this were so, Scott said in subsequent statements, it would be unfair to hold schools and teachers responsible for the failure of students, because it was the society that had stunted their development.

Clark responded sharply to Scott's line of reasoning. "I used to think that a man could only talk that way because he is not black," he said. "These are the same things I've heard from white segregationists and white liberals and condescending whites. It's crossed the color line." He went on to say, "The fact that Dr. Scott is black does not grant him immunity from assessment of his performance. I believe Dr. Scott cannot be an effective implementer of any academic design."

Another black man attacked the "possible reality" in a different way, Clark recalled. "On television one night, a teachers' union official said that if my plan turned out to be successful, it would merely store up frustrations for black youth, because once they are able to read and compete they would still be discriminated against on account of their color and would become even more bitter. When I heard it, I did not believe that a teachers' union official could really be saying such a thing."

Scott and Simons joined forces against Clark and his reading plan, and it failed. It had been stripped of a crucial element: the ranking of teachers according to the progress of their students. This concession by the board of education came after the union had threatened that its members would simply refuse to administer the standardized tests—and some *had* refused. To avoid further confrontations, the board agreed that under no circumstances would test results be used to evaluate teachers. In 1971, Clark's firmest supporter, Anita Ford Allen, was defeated in her attempt to be reelected president of the board of education, and the Academic Achievement Project essentially came to an end.

"The most terrible thing about the Washington experience was the passivity of the community," Clark said. "Once the teachers' union, the superintendent, and the rest of the educational hierarchy had decided to dismantle the plan, we couldn't get any significant number of parents to fight for their own children. Nor did such community organizations as the local chapter of the NAACP and the Washington Urban League publicly support us. Certain officials in those groups cheered us on privately, but they did not want to become involved in the politics of the conflict. The politics of adult power. In this case, black adult power. The children did not count."

One day in early July of 1970, as Clark was outlining his Academic Achievement Project to the District of Columbia Board of Education, one of its members heatedly objected to the proposal that standard

English be used exclusively in the teaching of the almost entirely black school population. Arguing for an emphasis on what had come to be called Black English, the dialect used by many of the children at home and on the streets, the critic insisted that rejecting a child's speech patterns was equivalent to rejecting the child. "Here was this black man, speaking impeccable English—he was a graduate of Harvard, I believe, and he really used the language impressively," Clark recalled. "I could not resist saying to him, 'Look, I would like these youngsters to speak the way you do, so that people will pay attention to them, even when they're speaking nonsense, as you are now.' And while this was going on, I remembered reading that Harold Laski once said, 'You know, the class system in England will never really be improved until someone finds a way of teaching the Cockneys to speak middle-class English.'" Clark won his point at that meeting, but not before his antagonist on the school board had called him a racist for insisting that black children be held to the same standards of language as white children.

Racial separatism of any kind, whether in the teaching of English or in the setting up of exclusively black departments or facilities on a college campus, has always been vehemently opposed by Dr. Clark. "I do not believe that the purpose of education is to reinforce parochialism," he has said. "What I try to help my own students understand is the commonality of man. As for the supposed justifications for black separatism in any form, I do not believe that genuine pride in oneself can be based on anything as external as color. I do not accept the pride argument from Black Power people any more than I do from white supremacists. In both cases, it's racism."

In 1968 Edward H. Levi, then provost of the University of Chicago, asked Dr. Clark for advice when a group of black students demanded an all-black dormitory on campus. Clark responded in a letter. "The university's involvement in the setting up of an all-black or an all-white dormitory for its students would be a profound violation of academic freedom," he wrote Levi. "It would be a mockery of the goals of education and could only occur in a society which was so severely ill with the disease of racism and its symptoms of guilt, hostility, and ambivalence as to be in severe crises of survival." Although he was not an expert in constitutional law, Clark added that he was convinced that "any university or college which sets up an all-Negro dormitory violates the letter and the spirit of the *McLaurin* decision and also the *Brown* decision of the United States Supreme Court."

He explained: "In the *McLaurin* decision, the Court was quite clear that the University of Oklahoma and its governing board could not segregate or isolate Negro students on the arbitrary basis of race without violating the equal-protection clause of the United States Constitution. I do not believe that this basic principle is inoperative merely because the victims ask for the segregated facilities."

He went on to say this: "For all of the above reasons—and others which are much too visceral for me to express with any pretense of coherence—I am personally unalterably opposed to any educational or other public or quasi-public institution classifying, or in any way categorizing, its students or personnel on the basis of the irrelevant and arbitrary factor of race or color. I am opposed to all-Negro or all-white classes, dormitories, schools or colleges."

Clark ended the letter by saying, "Those of us who still believe in the positive potential of human beings, and that educational institutions must reinforce these positives, cannot contribute to the disease but must try to cure the patient even when such cure might require the painful remedies of courage and clarity."

The year before, Clark had antagonized some of the Black Power advocates at his own alma mater by proposing that Howard University become a nonracial institution. "I had tended to idealize my all-black college experience," he said then. "But as I grew older I came to believe that the very fact of a segregated college is an abomination. It's institutionalized psychosis, and is possible only in a crazy society."

In 1969, Clark was attacked as a "moderate," and even as an "Uncle Tom," by a number of black militants around the country when he resigned from the board of directors of Antioch College because the college had supported the creation on its campus of a racially exclusive Afro-American Institute. In his letter of resignation, after citing the arguments against all forms of segregation, which were based on psychology and constitutional law, Clark said, "I do not believe that Antioch, in permitting some of the more hostile Negro students to coerce and intimidate other Negroes and whites . . . has showed the courage necessary to maintain that type of academic climate which permits man that freedom of inquiry, freedom of thought, and freedom of dissent which are essential to the life of the intellect." He also made the rather mordant point that precisely those "who need a black studies program most of all"—the whites—were, with the full cooperation of the college, being barred from this Afro-American Institute.

The vogue for black separatism intensified in the early 1970s. During that period, Dr. Clark was sometimes confronted personally by its advocates. "I was once stopped on my way to class at City College by a well-dressed black man in his late thirties," he recalled recently. "'You're Dr. Clark?' this man asked. I nodded, thinking he was going to compliment me, and he said, 'We're going to get you, you son of a bitch!' I just looked at him and asked when this was going to happen. He walked away, and that turned out to be the end of it. But that was the climate of those years."

Not long after that encounter, Clark was walking to class during a time when some black and Puerto Rican students were trying to close down City College by way of enforcing their demands for more Third World courses and faculty members. "I saw a group of those on strike physically keeping one of my students from going to class," he told me. "I was so furious I walked over and yelled, 'Damn it! Leave him alone!' They were so shocked at the spontaneous force of my rage that they let the student go. We went in to class, and there were only a couple of others there. But I would have conducted that class if there had been only one student. A class is sacred. It should never be interfered with."

Mamie Clark thoroughly understood her husband's uncharacteristically loud public rage at the assault on his classroom. "His first love is teaching," she said not long ago. "It always has been. He has given a great deal to his students, not only by teaching them how to think but also by impressing on them the possibilities of using their education to affect the society they live in. And, of course, his impact as a teacher has reached far beyond those who have actually been in a classroom with him. Most well-known black people are not in the academic field—they're in the theater or in sports or, increasingly, in politics—and so the renown and the great amount of respect that

Kenneth has achieved have been of a rather rare kind. And I think that by achieving them he has given psychic sustenance to many blacks, whether or not they themselves have gone into teaching on the college level."

Dr. Clark retired from City College in 1975, intending to concentrate on research and writing. He couldn't bear to give up teaching entirely, however, so he had a weekly seminar for adult students at Mercy College, in Dobbs Ferry, New York, some two miles from where he lives—in a Tudor-style house in Hastings-on-Hudson. He described the seminar as dealing with "contemporary social issues from the perspective of a psychologist." Although the seminar was his only regular academic commitment, Dr. Clark more than filled the hours he used to spend as a professor at City College: He still complains that he can't find enough time for writing. But he recognizes that this chronic conflict is of his own making.

"Kenneth is more restless than ever," his wife said. "He feels there's so much to be done, and there's not enough time in which to do it all. I keep saying, 'Why don't you rest a little bit and be an elder statesman, which is such a nice comfortable thing to be?'" She adds, smiling, "But that's only my opinion."

"I came to realize that I just couldn't devote myself solely to a life of leisurely scholarship and writing," Clark said. "And Mamie, for all that she talks about the comforts of my becoming an elder statesman, knew that before I did. A year or so before I retired from City College, she said very calmly one day, 'Kenneth, do you realize that you've never been able to write anything without competing commitments?' Well, she's a psychologist, you know, and I said, 'I'd like to try. I'd like to see what it's like to have nothing to do but write.' Even more calmly, she said, 'I hope you succeed.' I kept thinking of that conversation, and it bothered me increasingly as the retirement date came closer. It might well be that if all my time were free for writing, I wouldn't write at all."

Dr. Clark's primary focus is still on education. "I continue to be an extremist," he said. "An extremist in persisting in believing that black kids can learn, and that segregation is one way in which they are prevented from learning. I remain an incorrigible integrationist. Or, if you prefer, I remain a rigid, hard-line integrationist. Some of my black friends urge me to be more 'realistic,' more 'pragmatic'—to accept the fact that the *Brown* decision has just not worked in the big cities, especially those outside the South, and that we should therefore go for separate but 'quality' schools."

This is the position reluctantly adopted by Robert Carter, the NAACP lawyer who initially recruited Clark to the research team that helped bring about the victory in the *Brown* decision. In the *Harvard Civil Rights–Civil Liberties Law Review,* Carter, a longtime battler for school integration (he is now a federal district judge in New York), wrote that the main requirement of the *Brown* decision was "equal educational opportunity." The Court, in 1954, equated that goal with integration. Carter now maintains that if equal educational opportunity can be achieved without integration, "*Brown* has been satisfied."

Carter wrote, "I am certain that a racially integrated America is best for all of us, but I also know that quality education is essential to the survival of hundreds of thousands of black children who now seem destined for the dunghill in our society. There are solutions, I believe, which can readily achieve integration and deliver equal education at the same time: state systems, metropolitan school districts combining the central city and suburbs, or clusters of schools outside districts on large campuses (much like colleges). The hope of getting approval of such remedies today through litigation or legislation is, I think you will agree, minimal."

Therefore, Carter wrote, although it would be a "disaster" to abandon integration "as the ultimate solution," to focus on it for the present "is a luxury only the black middle class can afford." He concluded, "The immediate and urgent need of the black urban poor is the attainment, in real terms and in settings of virtually total black-white school separation, of at least some of the benefits and protection of the constitutional guarantee of equal educational opportunity that *Brown* requires. The only way to insure that thousands of the black urban poor will have even a remote chance of obtaining the tools needed to compete in the marketplace for a decent job and its accompanying benefits is to concentrate on having quality education delivered to the schools these blacks are attending, and in all likelihood will be attending for at least another generation."

Clark's response to Carter and to others who have come to this conclusion is, "I don't doubt they now find this position more practical, but what they are advocating will intensify and further rigidify segregation." He said, in addition, "Under the guise of what they call realism, they are willing to concede defeat, as they mask that defeat with various euphemisms. Those who propose to raise the achievement level in segregated schools instead of renewing their efforts to integrate those schools are actually renewing the myth of 'separate but equal.' They are resurrecting *Plessy versus Ferguson*. And, even aside from the fact that their proposal is unconstitutional, they provide no evidence that 'separate but equal' will work educational wonders in any school, in any system, when it has not done so anywhere in these United States for over a hundred years.

"As Robert Carter says, there *are* ways to achieve integration. And, yes, one approach is to form metropolitan school districts, combining the central city and the suburbs. Another is for states to finance regional schools that would cut across urban-suburban boundaries. There could also be prestige regional schools, financed by the federal government, that could cut through *state* boundaries and provide facilities for resident students.

"There is indeed enormous opposition to any workable attempts to integrate the public schools, but there always has been. I remain convinced that there is no choice but to keep fighting for integration. The accuracy of the Supreme Court's language in *Brown* has not changed: 'To separate [children] from others of similar age and qualifications solely because of their race generates a feeling of inferiority as to their status in the community that may affect their hearts and minds in a way unlikely ever to be undone.' The act of segregation itself damages the personality. This is as true now as it has ever been.

"If necessary, I am prepared to stand alone as an integrationist. Oh, attempts have been made to move me backward. Some years ago, Barbara Jordan, who was then in Congress, called a meeting of some black legislators and educators to gain recruits to her position that the best way to get more federal aid for all the public schools was to lessen the pressure to integrate all the public schools. I raised hell. I told her, 'This is "separate but equal." You're trying to equalize the separateness, and I will not be a party to that.' She looked at me and said,

'Your unrealism is passé.' So there I was, my old-fashioned extremism once more supposedly getting in the way of progress."

Mamie Clark spoke to me about the schools as they are and about the children who are not learning in those schools. "If children don't learn, teachers and administrators should be fired," she said softly. "At least, if a sizable number of them were fired, the rest might start doing what they're paid to do. There has to be a war. A war with the teachers' unions. A war with the whole system. A war for the children. But you have to get the parents to fight that war, and there has not been any force to move them, to help them develop strategies."

She paused, and her voice was even softer when she resumed. "You know, things are *worse* than they were when we started Northside. They really are worse. More people are without hope now. But thirty years ago there *was* hope. People got excited when things happened to their children. They tried harder to change things for their children. And they tried harder still in the 1960s. But now—well, now they know that nothing has changed. I'm depressed about it. So is Kenneth. We talk about it all the time." She laughed—a short, dry laugh. "We say the same things over and over. I don't know what the answer is."

Her voice now was barely audible. "I really don't know." There was another silence, and she smiled. "But he won't stop looking for the answer. Oh, sometimes Kenneth is very down, but he bounces back. He always bounces back. It's quite marvelous to watch, because, when you consider the issues he's always dealing with, he could become so depressed he'd commit suicide. But there are always new battles."

"That's it," another voice said. Kate Clark Harris, the Clarks' daughter, a woman of vibrant energy and an easy, informal manner, had come into the room. "It's all those challenges, all those battles, that keep him continuing. My father has a lot of anger. He's often angrier than he'll say, or show. But this way, battling all the time, he's found a way to express that anger so that it's constructive for him and—if people would listen—for society. For all the despair, he really enjoys his life."

"We have a place on the Cape," Mamie Clark said. "In West

Hyannisport. He has never spent a whole lot of time there. Oh, he always announces that he's going to take the whole summer, but at best he manages three or four long weekends, because there's always a new project or problem here. Just about all he does when he's there is read and sleep. He has nothing to do with any physical activity. Kenneth has no aptitude for any sport. He even had a hard time getting out of physical education in college. But he does have one avocation." She smiled. "He's very fond of raising cactuses. They're tough plants, and somehow survive against all odds."

A few days later, I paid another visit to Dr. Clark's office. He was wearing a pin-striped gray suit, a button-down blue shirt, and a gray-and red-striped tie. It occurred to me that although I had known him for more than twenty years, I had never seen him without a tie—or, for that matter, without a button-down shirt. His office held shelves of books and reports, pictures of his grandchildren, and a portrait of W. E. B. Du Bois. "One of my heroes," Clark said. "Such a tough mind. Such courage, clarity, and persistence." In a *New York Times* Op-Ed article written two years ago with Lawrence Plotkin, Clark quoted from Du Bois's *The Souls of Black Folk:* "One ever feels his two-ness—an American, a Negro; two souls, two thoughts, two unreconciled strivings; two warring ideals in one dark body, whose dogged strength keeps it from being torn asunder."

I spoke of what his wife had said about the worsening state of children in Harlem, in all the Harlems.

"Things *are* worse," Dr. Clark said. "In the schools, although scores are going up in some places, more black kids are being put on the dung heap every year. But it's not just the schools. Residential segregation is worse. Not only the increase and proliferation of ghettos but the pathology of ghetto life. The closest I can find to something positive is that more blacks are now in positions in the private sector from which they were previously excluded. Also, there is the fact that more blacks are being elected to office. There are more black mayors, for example. But I'm stymied when I try to tie that to observable positive changes in the lives of black people who live where there are black mayors. Maybe it's too early for a connection to be made, or maybe this development will just contribute to further political disillusionment among blacks. Yet there must be options that will work.

My job is to keep looking for those options. Honest options. That's what I've had to do all my life—differentiate between the evidence and my wishes.

"There are times when I feel that all I've done with my life is produce documents—reports, memorandums, books—and that as for actually helping produce social change, my life has been one big failure. It's as if I were a physician, and the disease has metastasized."

"Then what keeps you going?" I asked.

"When I was in high school, my biology teacher made his subject real by having us look at living cells through a microscope. And what I took out of that ninth-grade class was that the cell is constantly in a state of struggle. Looking at the amoeba and the paramecium, I saw they were continually active. The irritability of protoplasm, as it's called, is the essential difference between protoplasm and other forms of matter. As I grew up and went through college and graduate school, and later, when I was teaching, it became all the more evident to me that, while there are gradations of intensity, life really is a continuous struggle. And when the irritability of protoplasm stops, life stops.

"On our level of the biogenetic scale, that struggle takes on different forms—struggle for comfort, struggle for status. But the highest form of life, in terms of evolutionary development, involves struggling for such abstractions as justice and decency. And always there has been a minority of human beings engaged in that kind of struggle— people who insist on being unrealistic, people who won't give up when everything seems to indicate that they should. If you're one of those people, it's just something you have to keep on doing. You have no more choice than an amoeba has in whether to be active or not. In other words, I can't stop.

"There's so much that needs doing, and, like everywhere else, it's getting much harder to do. In the 1960s, the struggle was so much more clear-cut. You could see the dogs and the horses on television. It was not unlike the newsreels from Germany showing the Storm Troopers forcing Jews to scrub the sidewalks. And the *Times* would put pictures of the civil rights demonstrators in the South on the front page. They'd also be on the network news. So people got immediate, visceral reactions to visible atrocities. But that's not what we're dealing with now. These years, children are being destroyed silently, in the first and second grades."

As I was about to leave the building, I saw Russia Hughes, Clark's longtime associate. Before coming to work for Dr. Clark, she had been a teacher, and, indeed, she had taught his daughter at the Horace Mann–Lincoln School. Russia and I talked about Dr. Clark's unwavering focus on education, and Russia said, "My very first memory of him has to do with a classroom. He and Mamie brought Kate to school on her first day in the first grade. Mamie made the more striking impression on me. She had on a little many-colored knit hat, with bits of metal dangling from it. She looked terribly elegant, terribly beautiful. And there, also, was her husband. From that day on, he came all the time, to observe the class. I'm a terribly involved kind of person, who doesn't really notice things going on outside of what I'm doing, and all of a sudden—I didn't even know *when* he first came in—I'd see Dr. Clark standing quietly in the corner. He'd stay there quite a long time. He was utterly absorbed. Not only in what Kate was doing but in the other children, too. He wanted to see children learning."

As the years went on, Dr. Clark often seemed depressed. The promise of *Brown v. Board of Education* seemed to be ever more deferred. Hopeful auguries were decreasing. One afternoon, after seeing Dr. Clark, I looked up a draft memorandum that had been circulated to the other justices deliberating on the *Brown* case. The author was Justice Robert Jackson:

> Since the close of the Civil War the United States has been "hesitating between two worlds—one dead, the other powerless to be born." War brought an old order to an end, but as usual, forces proved unequal to founding a new one. Neither North nor South has been willing really to adapt its racial practices to its professions. The race problem would be quickly solved if some way could be found to make us all live up to our hypocrisies.

Our hypocrisies were still in charge despite the glorious beginnings. For years, May 17, 1954, had appeared to me to have been one of the most liberating days in our history. At 12:52 P.M., Chief Justice Earl Warren read from the bench the Supreme Court's unanimous decision in *Brown v. Board of Education*. It looked as if the deadly world of legal racism was finally to be interred, and a new world had at last been born. "Separate educational facilities," the chief justice said, "are inherently unequal." And therefore unconstitutional.

That day, Warren said the following about another school segregation case, *Bolling v. Sharp,* in the District of Columbia: "Segregation in public education is not reasonably related to any proper government objective, and thus it imposes on Negro children of the District of Columbia a burden that constitutes an arbitrary deprivation of their liberty in violation of the Due Process clause."

In his indispensable book, *Simple Justice: The History of Brown v. Board of Education and Black America's Struggle for Equality* (Knopf, 1976), Richard Kluger quotes the reaction on that day in 1954 of Ernest Rubinstein, a clerk for Justice Tom Clark. "I felt good and clean," Rubinstein recalled. "It was so right." Also exhilarated—as I've noted—by the decision on that day was Dr. Kenneth Clark.

In all the years since, however, Kenneth Clark has been trying to transform *Brown v. Board of Education* from a notation in the law books into a presence in the lives of black and white schoolchildren. It has been a bruising, sometimes bitter battle.

Clark has faced down separatists, black as well as white. He believes that voluntarily segregated education is damaging to children, just as forced segregated education is. He is one of the last true integrationists, black or white.

In 1992, the day after the United States Supreme Court ruled in *Freeman v. Pitts* that *segregated schools* are constitutional if they result from residential patterns—and not from specific laws—I called Kenneth Clark. I asked him his reaction to the unanimous opinion of the Court that school districts are "under no duty to remedy imbalance that is caused by demographic factors."

Clark answered, "We are now not only whittling down *Brown versus Board of Education,* but we are moving back to the 'separate but equal doctrine' of *Plessy versus Ferguson.* What the Court is saying is 'forget *Brown versus Board of Education.* Let's put all that stuff about desegregation aside.' What really bothers me is there doesn't seem to be any concern about the children—white or black."

He was depressed, except when he saw on television, the night before, a reaction to the *Freeman v. Pitts* decision from DeKalb

County, Georgia, where the case originated and where the school system was predominantly segregated. "I saw this white kid," Clark said. "He was around eleven or twelve. And he was saying, 'Look, this segregation is increasing bigotry.'"

There is an interview with Kenneth Clark in Studs Terkel's book *Race* (New Press, 1992). "I thought," Clark said, "that the *Brown* decision and the civil rights movement would liberate the whites as well. But if they were liberated, you'd have to liberate blacks, too. They [the whites] didn't want that sort of liberation. . . . I am not sanguine about any kind of solid decency and justice in the era of race in America. The best we can settle for is appearance."

Talking about *Brown,* Clark also noted, "In New York City and other cities today, there is a much higher percentage of segregated schools than there was before *Brown.*"

Dr. Clark is right. Most white Americans see no reason to combat the continued segregation in the public schools. This seems to them the logical order of separation of their children from "inferior" children. And an increasing number of black parents have lost hope that the Supreme Court's ruling in *Brown v. Board of Education* (1954) has any real meaning in the lives of their children. Despite *Brown,* a majority of black students still attend predominantly black public schools, where they are badly prepared for higher education and a decent economic future.

Accordingly, there are indications that a growing number of black parents are giving up on integrating public schools. They speak of all-black schools in their own neighborhoods, schools under black control that will ensure that black students achieve at least as well—and better—than white youngsters. However separate but equal schools have not worked for black kids before and there are few signs that there would be sufficient economic—and political—resources to enable all-black schools to make that much of a difference in the achievement of the students attending.

Insofar as there remains a chance of ending deeply structured segregated education in America—segregation that leads to economic and residential isolation when many of these children grow up—there is an outline for a possible future of authentic change in Dr. Jean Anyon's *Ghetto Schooling: A Political Economy of Urban Educational Reform* (Teachers College Press, 1997).

Anyon is chairperson of the Department of Education at the Newark campus of Rutgers University, but she also has worked in Newark schools. She boldly presented an analysis of what has to be done: "Attempting to fix inner-city schools without fixing the city in which they are embedded is like trying to clean the air on one side of a screen door."

Ultimately, she said, we have to "redress the effects of destructive ghettoization of cities and their poorer residents—and to reduce or eliminate the political and economic isolation that produces such ghettoization. . . .

"Academic achievement in U.S. schools is closely correlated with student socioeconomic status. To really improve ghetto children's chances, then, in school and out, we must (in addition to pursuing school-based reforms) increase their social well-being and status before and while they are students."

This sounds like pie-in-the-sky, but the early labor union organizers and other creators of coalitions among the powerless faced even worse odds than in the current America, where the social gospel is largely limited to Sunday references to Jesus's Sermon on the Mount.

Anyon's vision is not necessarily a distant one: "We are beginning to see a resurgence of grassroots movements in this country. Rooted in labor unions, inner-city neighborhoods, religious communities, and consumer activity, [this coming together reflects] a burgeoning concern about safety, housing, jobs, the economy, and the environment. This spirit is abroad in the land. Education reformers need to work with people active in these movements—as well as with relevant established institutions, agencies, and nongovernmental institutions."

She has another proposal, one that has been advanced by others, notably former New York congressman Herman Badillo:

> I envision making the school a community center where the economic and political disenfranchisement of parents is addressed through a wide variety of services that include housing assistance, job training and career opportunities, preparation [for high school equivalency degrees], and college assistance.
>
> Parents may be considerably more likely to participate in school reform activities, and be more involved in their children's

education, *if they see meaningful results for themselves from involvement at the school* (emphasis added).

Something that can be done at any school right away is a resurrection of Dr. Kenneth Clark's saturation reading program starting in the first grade. (I know a public school principal in a low-income neighborhood who had his kindergarten pupils reading by the time they entered the first grade.)

Mary Leonhardt, in a letter to the *New York Times* (November 14, 1997), noted that "in Norfolk, Virginia, in the 1950's, we put freshmen at Norfolk Catholic High School—who were reading below a seventh-grade level—into a classroom filled with books, magazines and comic books. We asked them to read for 45 minutes every day. For every six months in this program, students gained an average of 18 months in reading scores. . . .

"As a high school English teacher who has taught for 27 years across the country, I can testify that few administrators or teachers have the courage to open up their curriculums and make developing avid readers the priority." (Dr. Kenneth Clark certainly found this to be true.).

Harvard professor William Julius Wilson, in an introduction to Jean Anyon's *Ghetto Schooling,* pointed out the following: "Job prospects for workers who lack skills in reading, writing, performing arithmetic calculations, and operating a computer are very slim indeed. . . . Changes in skill-based technology have made a basic education indispensable. It has also enhanced the importance of—and increased the urgency for—effective urban public school reform."

We shall see.

In New York City, the principal of Brandeis High School, Marlene Lazar, focuses on the most necessary, immediate education reform: the need to help failing students before they get to high school. She is quoted in the *New York Times* of October 26, 1997, describing the freshman class at Brandeis: "Only 20 percent arrived able to read or solve math problems at their grade level. We need to do a lot differently. We don't want to set children up to fail."

That's what Kenneth Clark has been saying for many years.

8

Color Coding:
She Had to Leave the Room Because
the Class Was Reserved for
African American Students

*T*he stigma of color continues, sometimes in intentionally benign—but hurtful—ways. For example, in the selection of homecoming queens in Montgomery, Alabama, young black women of courage finally ended a rule that said one had to declare oneself either black or white to enter the competition. These students brought the mandate of the Fourteenth Amendment—"equal protection under the laws"—into their lives and those of the other public school students in the city.

The stigma of race can cut the other way, as Janice Camarena Ingraham discovered at public San Bernardino Community College in California. As a white student—and only because of her color—she was excluded from a class. And, like the black students in Montgomery, she refused to be a second-class citizen.

First, I tell the story of the black students in that Alabama city.

I was last in Montgomery, Alabama, during what A. Philip Randolph called the "unfinished revolution." E. D. Nixon—a Pullman porter, head of the local NAACP, and the man who persuaded Martin Luther King Jr. to lead the Montgomery bus boycott—met me at the airport.

Neither of us was aware that an unmarked police car was tailing me and taking note of everyone I interviewed in that segregated city. The day after my story appeared in the *New Yorker,* an editorial in the

Montgomery Advertiser excoriated this outside agitator and named people I had talked to—much to their concern.

The *Advertiser* has changed; some very able reporters cover the news without conspiratorial spins. But there has still been segregation in the city's high schools and junior high schools, although not of the usual kind. This form is "benign" in intent, but it winds up separating kids because of their color.

In a number of junior high and high schools, there have been racial quotas in homecoming elections at the end of the football season. The homecoming court must be half white and half black, and the girls who run for the court—and for queen—have to declare whether they are white or black. The intent is to give kids of both races a fairer chance to be on the court.

At the start of a recent *NBC News* story on this attempt to bring the races together by putting tags on them, reporter Bob Dotson was at homecoming night at Prattville High. The football team and the band were resplendent, but Shanda Davis was not. She had wanted to run for homecoming queen, but her homeroom teacher told her she could not be on the ballot unless she declared herself as either white or black. She refused and dropped out of the race.

"I'm black and white," Shanda Davis told the NBC camera. "My mother's white and my father's black." She added that she was going to gather signatures on a petition to change the policy.

Crystal Ransom, her white friend, said, "It's a whole personality thing. It's not your color." And Crystal Maylin added, "They make you vote on people by the color of their skin. And if you're going to do that, then you're not really saying that they're equal."

The last NBC shot was of black and white girls hugging, as Shanda looked on, grinning.

Not everyone in the Montgomery school system agreed there was a need for change. In a Montgomery *Advertiser* series by reporter Holly Kurtz, Madelyn Taylor, organizer of Lanier High School's homecoming elections, declared: "Everybody seems to agree that what we're doing is perfectly fine." Among the high schools that preserved racial quotas for homecoming elections were the Robert E. Lee and Jefferson Davis schools.

Quotas remained in place regardless of the demographics at the schools. Holly Kurtz wrote that "in the 1995–96 school year, Cloverdale [Junior High School] was 91 percent black and 9 percent nonblack. Yet half the slots on the homecoming court were for whites. A student there, Bethany Godby—who is black and white—pointed out, "In the past, a lot of white students have won homecoming elections just because they were white."

A sort of reverse affirmative action.

But at Prattville High School, the times they are a-changing. Shanda Davis and another girl have collected 171 signatures on a petition to end the racial quotas. And the principal, Roy Johnson, told the Montgomery *Advertiser,* "We will make a change next year. We want to make it as fair as we can."

The principal first had some learning to do. Earlier in October, he talked to eight girls who are neither black nor white but belong to other races. "They felt like they were excluded," the principal said. "And strictly speaking they are."

Even nonstrictly speaking. That's how quotas work.

But Holly Kurtz reported that she interviewed a number of parents in Montgomery—black and white—"who see nothing wrong with electing a half-black, half-white homecoming court in a school that is 90 percent black."

"I guess it keeps the peace," said one mother.

Suddenly, however, at the end of October, the Montgomery school board, very much aware of press attention to racial quotas in its schools, voted to end all racial quotas for school offices, including homecoming queens and their courts. The school board finally was compelled to realize that labeling does not make for peace or equality or fairness.

On January 19, 1994, Janice Camarena Ingraham, a student at San Bernardino Community College in California, began her first day of English 101. A widowed mother of three small children, she was eager for education, because she expected to have to support her family for a long time to come. She was twenty-four.

In front of the class, the instructor told Ingraham that she had to leave the room because the class was reserved for African American students. As she went out the door, the laughter of the students followed her.

The class was part of the Black Bridge Program, which is geared to enabling black students to go on to four-year colleges. And it is largely successful in that goal. Students in the program receive special academic counseling and seminars, advice on career development from black mentors, and other targeted services.

The Black Bridge Program exists on several dozen campuses in the community college system, as does the Puente Project, which provides Latinos with special academic support. Ingraham also tried to enter the Puente Project, but she was informed that because she is white, there was no place for her.

Ingraham told me that the double rejection made her realize that although one of her three children could in time enter the Puente Project, the other two would, like their mother, be excluded. Her eligible child is half Mexican American. As she said to the Crestline *Courier-News* at the time, "I have told my daughters they'd be treated fairly, regardless of race, but now they couldn't even attend the same college class together."

Furthermore, Ingraham discovered that there were black students in the Black Bridge Program whose backgrounds were more economically advantaged than her own. By contrast to those students, she could be defined as disadvantaged.

Janice Ingraham decided to break down the racial and ethnic barriers in the California community colleges. She found the right lawyer, Robert Corry, who is on the staff of the Pacific Legal Foundation, a conservative outfit. Corry is particularly interested in free-speech cases and in countering the separation of college students "into ethnic enclaves and telling them they can only succeed in an atmosphere restricted to other members of their race and mentors of their race."

I first knew Corry when, as a recent graduate of Stanford Law School, he succeeded in having its speech code overturned even though he was faced in court by the university's high-priced attorneys. It was like Paul Newman versus James Mason in *The Verdict,* a movie about a single lawyer's battle against powerful political and religious forces to get justice for his client.

Ingraham's lawsuit wound up in U.S. District Court for the eastern district of California. It resulted in a settlement that affects the nation's largest community college system, with its 106 campuses, and may influence colleges in other states.

Ingraham did not ask for compensatory damages. She wanted all students to be treated fairly. This is what she won, as summarized by the *Chronicle of Higher Education:* "Course catalogues and other marketing tools produced by the system may no longer describe certain offerings as 'designed' for black or Hispanic students. The system also cannot choose mentors or counselors for students on the basis of race." Although the system cannot mandate that students of one race choose mentors or counselors of the same race, the students themselves can choose the mentors they want.

At the core of the settlement is the precept that "all academic and educational programs at the California community colleges shall be open equally to students regardless of race, color, national origin, or ethnicity."

Programs to help black and Mexican American students move on to four-year colleges will continue, and those students will be able to identify courses in the program from the descriptions of the course content. But now, no students will be told to leave the room because of their color.

A considerable number of signatures were collected on a petition supporting Janice Ingraham, circulated by students. The petition said: "We do not feel that anyone has the right to tell students that we do not belong together because we are of different races. In 1954, the Supreme Court outlawed racial segregation in public schools. We feel that it is time that the public education system acknowledge the laws of the United States of America." Among the signers were a number of black and Mexican American students.

Recently, Janice Ingraham enrolled her children at a school in Lake Arrowhead, where she lives. A clerk reminded her she had neglected to check the box that declared the race of her children.

"I told her," said Ingraham, "that they're human."

9

INDIVIDUALS OF CONSCIENCE AGAINST THE STATE

"Those who won our independence by revolution were not cowards."

One of our most insistent and lucid champions of American liberties was Supreme Court justice Louis Brandeis. Before he was confirmed as the first Jewish justice on the Supreme Court, Brandeis suffered a four-month-long confirmation process in the Senate that was marked by blatant anti-Semitism.

When he arrived at the Court, Brandeis found more prejudice. The custom, then and now, is for the justices to shake hands with one another before they begin their initial deliberations on the cases they have just heard. One of the justices, James McReynolds, would never shake hands with Brandeis because he was a Jew.

Brandeis ignored the insult. He just did his work on the Court, producing some of the most powerful opinions concerning free speech, privacy, and other civil liberties in the Court's history. For example, the following words are from *Whitney v. California* (1927): "Those who won our independence . . . valued liberty both as an end and as a means. They believed liberty to be the secret of happiness, and courage to be the secret of liberty. . . . They believed that it is hazardous to discourage thought, hope and imagination; that fear breeds repression; that repression breeds hate. . . . Those who won our independence by revolution were not cowards. They did not fear political change. They did not exalt order at the cost of liberty."

The Americans portrayed in this chapter had views that were decidedly unpopular in their communities, which ranged from Grand Saline, a small town in Texas, to the national community of basketball fans in the case of Mahmoud Abdul-Rauf, a star of the game. What happened to them illustrates the fear of James Madison, the architect of our Bill of Rights, that the majority in any community is often willing to violate individual rights and liberties—and often does.

Sometimes a dissenter ultimately triumphs, but others are defeated, at least temporarily. Rarely, a member of Congress—Nancy Pelosi here—has the courage to speak publicly against her party and her president. And it is not often that a college or university president—such as Belinda Wilson in California, who figures in this chapter—resists strong pressures from the left and the right to bar an incendiary speaker from appearing at the university.

In their diverse ways, everyone featured in this chapter lives the Bill of Rights and has been attacked for being faithful to the Constitution. Two resounding illustrations are the stories of a Georgia high school teacher, Sherry Hearn, and of a high school student in a small Tennessee town, Kathryn Sinclar.

At the June graduation exercises of Riverdale High School in Murfreesboro, Tennessee, eighteen-year-old Kathryn Sinclair was one of four valedictorians. In addition to her 4.0 average, she had been accepted in the honors program in premed studies at East Tennessee State University with a full scholarship.

Yet when she finished her speech, there was silence—in contrast to the applause for the other valedictorians. Indeed, some of the students had planned to turn their backs on her and sing the school's alma mater while she spoke, but a degree of reluctant civility had prevailed. In case of a disturbance, however, two teachers and a plainclothes county policeman were assigned to keep an eye on Kathryn and her family.

In her speech, Sinclair quoted from the First Amendment and from one of her favorite songs: "You've Got to Stand for Something or You'll Fall for Anything" by country singer Aaron Tippin. To her mostly sullen classmates, she said, "My challenge to you is not to be afraid to stand up for what you believe. If no one else supports you, know that you can support yourself."

In recent months, Kathryn Sinclair had shown how to do that. In April, she was told that as a valedictorian, she would have to submit her speech to school officials for approval. It had to meet their standards. (No other public schools in the immediate area have such a policy.)

The other three valedictorians dutifully obeyed the rule, but Sinclair objected. She had no intention, she said, of saying anything negative, but she had a First Amendment right not to subject herself to prior restraint of the content of her speech. The principal, Hulon Watson, told reporter Amy Sutton of the Murfreesboro *Daily News Journal* that his standards did not call for changing the content. But he insisted that he had a right to "make sure it's not vulgar, racist, or derogatory to other people." In addition, he said, "we would certainly not allow things in bad taste to be done." The latter term was not defined, nor was the principal's definition of censorship.

Kathryn Sinclair eventually did read her speech to the principal beforehand, but she told him that she would not permit any change in its content if he found anything "negative" in it. Supporting her was an unexpected ecumenical alliance of the Tennessee ACLU and the Virginia-based American Center for Law and Justice, founded by Pat Robertson. Both groups said they would defend her if she took legal action.

The principal finally decided that despite Sinclair's defiance of his stated power to change the speech if he wanted to, she would be permitted to deliver it as written. Meanwhile, Sinclair was so ostracized in school for her rebellion that she finished her senior year at home. Before she left the school, some students had worn armbands reading K.K.O. (for "Kick Kathryn Out").

"They don't realize," she told me, "that they're doing exactly what I'm fighting for. They are utilizing their freedom of speech."

At her home, there were hostile letters—at one point, five or six in a day. One afternoon, reporter Amy Sutton told me over the phone that Dan Sinclair, Kathryn's father, had just told her he had received a threat to firebomb their home. Kathryn heard from students that someone might stab her at the graduation.

The students were angry at her particularly because they were afraid she would spoil their graduation by saying something negative about the school. "And no one on the faculty," Kathryn Sinclair said, "has come out in my support." A number of faculty members said she was making the school look bad.

"There were threats that I'd be beaten up if I went back to school," Kathryn said. "When I did [go back] for an awards ceremony, before graduation, I was kicked during the assembly."

At graduation, after her speech, one brave student broke the silence. He rose and applauded Kathryn Sinclair.

Afterward, she tried to get at the root of what had happened: "One of the main things they should be teaching is who we are as Americans. In four years, we had to memorize the preamble of the Constitution for extra credit, but a study of the Bill of Rights was never required. We did not cover the First Amendment or any of the other amendments."

It was not surprising, she added, that the principal of Riverdale High School never told the students during the furor that they—and Kathryn—have First Amendment rights. But in his way of teaching Americanism, this principal is far from alone among the nation's educators.

The following is a true story about a teacher accused of satanism in Grand Saline, a town of twenty-six hundred in northwest Texas. In addition to the eerie light it sheds on ideological terrorism, the story is valuable because it shows that the involvement of a Christian Right *organization* is not necessary to "expose an infectious sinner." No one can be sure of the extent to which these purely local autos-da-fé take place, because many are unreported. I first found out about the pursuit of evil in Grand Saline as a result of People for the American Way's annual state-by-state report, *Attacks on the Freedom to Learn.*

The credo of most parents of schoolchildren in town is, as one of them put it, "We don't like our children being separated from the values we've given them."

At the center of the story is a teacher, Jackie Haskew, who refused to hand over her integrity. A fourth-grade teacher with a child of her own, she began to be accused of assigning books containing satanic imagery. (For example, someone might point to the goat head in an African folktale called "Brother to the Wind.")

It was no wonder, then, that her "true reason" for being a teacher was found out at Christmastime. There, on her classroom door, was a large drawing of Santa Claus with a big bag of gift books. That drawing, once some parents saw its significance, had to be taken off the classroom door. Why? Look carefully at the letters in Santa, they, said. Could it be an anagram hiding its actual meaning? Could it stand for—SATAN?

At home, Jackie Haskew began receiving anonymous calls from people accusing her of teaching devil worship and of being an atheist. As it happens, for all the good it did her in Grand Saline, Jackie Haskew is a Christian, a churchgoing Methodist.

A town meeting was held to discuss this strange woman. (Cotton Mather did not attend.) As Jackie Haskew sat there, amazed that this was happening to her, a woman came over and took her hand. At last, a comforter. The woman told the teacher to be of cheer because something good would come of all this.

You see, the woman said, these recent events had awakened many people in Grand Saline to realize that the Antichrist is present in the town, and to realize that the Antichrist must be destroyed. The comforter then said to Jackie Haskew with a knowing nod that she, the teacher, was the Antichrist.

I doubt that there is a course in any teachers college that tells a teacher how to respond to that.

Haskew was getting very angry. Her seven-year-old daughter, who also attended the eventful Grand Saline elementary school, asked her mother one day what a devil worshiper is. When one hears one's mother called that, it helps to know what it means. To add to Jackie Haskew's frustration as a teacher, a parent firmly informed her that it is not safe for children to read fairy tales.

At last, Haskew fought back. She filed a defamation suit against a number of her more wildly imaginative critics. And she told the *Houston Chronicle,* "I don't know how it's going to come out, but I'm not going to give up. I think the children are worth it. I think all children are worth it."

But she did give up. When Jackie Haskew heard that the school board was going to fire her, she and her daughter left town. I called people in Grand Saline and in Houston who knew her, but they have no idea where she is now.

While she was still teaching in the Athens of Texas, Jackie Haskew heard some parents tell her point-blank, "Don't teach my child to think." And one day she was confronted by a parent who sternly lectured her that she did not want her child to read anything concerned with "death, abuse, divorce, religion—or any other issue."

Jackie Haskew is a classic example of a teacher who believes that one of her responsibilities is to nurture the imagination of her students and to create a classroom that is as wide as the world, enabling kids to learn about cultures and ideas they never dreamed of.

The parents of Grand Saline haven't the slightest idea of how much their children have lost. Nor will the children themselves know, except for those who may eventually leave Grand Saline and discover how much there is to know and dream of.

A couple of months after I tried—and failed—to reach Jackie Haskew, I was watching *CBS Evening News* and saw a segment about, of all places, Grand Saline.

There was no mention of Jackie Haskew or the bearded, red-suited fat man from Hell. The focus of the reporting piece was on the fact that Grand Saline is all white. Not a person of color lived within the town limits. Moreover, as several proud citizens emphasized, Grand Saline always has been free of blacks and always will be.

Said one contented woman, "We're not used to being around black people. If any of them moved here, I don't know that they would stay."

After sundown.

While I was looking into the Jackie Haskew story, I talked to one of the journalists in Grand Saline. The town has only one paper, a weekly. The journalist wasn't all that eager to speak to me. Outside reporters, she said, kept distorting what went on in Grand Saline, blowing things out of proportion or making things up, like that story about Santa Claus being taken off the classroom door. I told her that Ann Tartelton of the International Reading Association verified that story for me, as she did for People for the American Way.

There was no response. "Bad press," the journalist in Grand Saline said. "We always get bad press."

For a very long time, Satan has had the same complaint.

★   ★   ★

During the national firestorm over the refusal of Mahmoud Abdul-Rauf to stand for the national anthem, I remembered an incident from when I was in the fifth grade of the William Lloyd Garrison public school in Boston. For several weeks before Christmas, all of us had to sing Christmas carols, including those citing Jesus as our Savior.

He was not my savior, but it never occurred to me to ask to be excused. My immigrant parents had sent me to public school to be assimilated, to become an American. Anyway, students had no rights then. The Supreme Court was otherwise occupied.

When lyrics affronted my conscience, I inserted, mumbling irreverent Yiddish substitutes. I didn't have the courage to declare my protest so it could be heard. The principal, who could have posed for an illustration in a Dickens novel, had a rattan in her office that she applied vigorously to the hands of any child who needed civilizing. I had felt the sting and didn't want to return.

Abdul-Rauf, a Muslim, did not hide his dissent, and some patriotic sportswriters and talk-show hosts told him he could either love this country or leave it. The state commander of the American Legion in Colorado characterized this member of the Denver Nuggets as having committed "treason." Rooting for Abdul-Rauf, I agreed with the admirably lucid statement of Alex English of the Players Association: "We support Mahmoud Abdul-Rauf, and we support the American flag, which symbolizes Mahmoud's right to precisely the action he is taking."

Years before, Supreme Court justice Jackson had emphasized that a free society means the freedom to differ. He added that "freedom to differ is not limited to things that do not matter much. That would be a mere shadow of freedom. The test of its substance is the right to differ as to things that touch the heart of the existing order."

During the uproar over Abdul-Rauf's exercise of *his* right to differ, I wondered if any public school teacher in the land dared to bring the words of Justice Jackson into a class discussion of the controversy, if there was any class discussion at all.

Abdul-Rauf's objections to taking part in compulsory patriotism were not a First Amendment issue. That arises only where there is action by the government—federal, state, or local. But there is also, or should be, the spirit of the First Amendment: a respect for the freedom to differ even when the rules are imposed by a private organization such as the National Basketball Association. I suggest that in a future contract, the Players Association include an "act of conscience" clause.

Abdul-Rauf finally compromised, although he says he hasn't. Now, as the anthem of liberty reverberates, he stands and prays, but not to the Stars and Stripes. He used to say he would not stand for "any nationalist ideology" or a flag that is "a symbol of oppression." However, as noted by Steven Shapiro, the legal director of the American Civil Liberties Union, this accommodation shows "the enormous pressure people come under when they stand up for their personal beliefs in the face of enormous public opposition."

At least Abdul-Rauf did openly hold to his beliefs for a while, which is more than I did in the fifth grade. This "Star-Spangled Coercion," as the *New York Times* called it in an editorial, is quite a civics lesson for America's schoolchildren.

Ron Rappoport, National Public Radio's sports reporter, said: "A man stands up for his beliefs! What's this country coming to?"

Diogenes searched with a lantern, in daylight, for an honest man. He figured he needed the extra illumination even before dark because honest folk would be so hard to find.

For some thirty years, I have been searching, around the country, for teachers who have the knowledge and passion to make the words of the Constitution, including the Bill of Rights, leap off the page and into the lives of their students.

I have found very few of those teachers. Most of the kids I've talked to—in middle schools and high schools and, for that matter, colleges—are as ignorant of the Constitution as are the majority of voters and Bill Clinton. In the last presidential election, the most fundamental issue—Bill Clinton's dangerous weakening of constitutional rights—was utterly ignored by nearly all newspapers and the broadcast press. This evisceration of basic liberties included limiting habeas corpus to one year, thus condemning prisoners on death row who will not have time to prove their innocence. Clinton also pushed for limiting the Internet to material suitable only for children. In addition, he enabled people to be deported without their—or their lawyers'—ability to see the evidence against them.

The voters, having been deprived during their schooling of the most vital information an American should have, were as ignorant of Clinton's betrayal of their rights as were the journalists "covering" the election. And they were kept ignorant by these journalists. Moreover, Jim Lehrer, host of the only news hour on public television, failed even to mention the subject during the presidential debates he moderated.

Undaunted, I keep searching for educators who help at least some youngsters to understand what their liberties and rights are. One of the most impressive reachers of constitutional freedoms I've found is Sherry Hearn in Savannah, Georgia. I first talked to her after she was fired last year for her knowledge of—and dedication to—the Constitution.

The story of her termination begins with one of the frequent, massive random raids on students at Windsor Forest High School, where she had been teaching for more than twenty years. The raids were described as follows by Bill Osinski in the *Atlanta Constitution:* "Without warning, teams of armed county and school-system officers would periodically come into the schools, order everyone into the hallways, use dogs to sniff the students' book bags and purses, and scan the students' bodies with metal detectors." The students were imprisoned in their classrooms for two to three hours.

Although the Supreme Court has set a lower standard for searching students in schools than when they are stopped on the street, the Court has not approved random searches of *all* students in a school without reasonable suspicion that *any* of them may have violated the law. The way it comes down in Savannah and a number of other cities and counties, every student during these dragnet raids is presumed guilty of possessing drugs or weapons—unless exonerated by a drug dog.

A massive police detention and search of students, without any particularized information about anyone's possession or use of drugs, is a serious invasion of constitutional rights. It is in contempt of the Fourth Amendment of the Bill of Rights, which presumably secures us all against limitless invasion of our privacy by law-enforcement officers.

Sherry Hearn had taught the Fourth Amendment for years. She was outraged by these unconstitutional SWAT team invasions of her classroom—and the whole school. Accordingly, whenever there was a random police search, Sherry Hearn protested—to the principal, to the school board, and to cops she accused of being unduly rough with students during the sweep searches.

During a November 1995 lockdown, as the cops called these raids, one of her students asked Hearn why she was so angry. Said Hearn, "Because I teach the Constitution!"

She is much admired by students who have been in her classes over the years, and she has turned some of them away from drugs. In April 1994, she was named Teacher of the Year in Chatham County.

One of Hearn's caustic comments about the lockdown was overheard by a cop. He reported her to the principal, thereby showing his respect for Hearn's freedom of speech. The cop also told the principal that because Hearn had an "attitude" problem, she ought to be detained or restrained during the next surprise raid.

The police had now marked Hearn—and her family. During a subsequent sweep, her son was the only student out of fifteen hundred to be searched with special care.

In April 1996 there was another lockdown at Windsor Forest High School, and in addition to searching students in the classroom, the cops and canine brigades were assigned to search the cars in the parking lot. Under school policy, however, no teacher's car could be searched without the teacher's consent.

Sherry Hearn's car had a large white faculty identification card on the dashboard. Nobody asked her consent to the search, but the police dog jumped in and found—what do you know?—half a hand-rolled marijuana cigarette.

School authorities later conceded that Sherry Hearn had absolutely no record of drug use. So how did that marijuana cigarette get into her car? Surely no cop would have planted it?

For months in Georgia, particularly in Atlanta and Savannah, the letters columns in the newspapers were filled with praise or scorn for a teacher, Sherry Hearn. She was fired because she had, at first, refused to take a drug test after the half of a marijuana cigarette had been found.

The school administration and the school board said they had initially suspended her because her refusal to take the test violated school policy. She, on the other hand, pointed out that as a passionate teacher of the Constitution she had told her students that they did not have to go along with unconstitutional orders. In recent years, she had particularly criticized the kind of SWAT team search—with drug dogs—that reached into all the classrooms and the parking lot, without even reasonable suspicion that *any* student had drugs.

When she was ordered to take the drug test, she said, although she was only three years short of retirement, "How could I face my students? To do what I genuinely believed to be an unconstitutional act out of fear was a kind of public shaming I could not face."

Moreover, ever since she had complained about the unconstitutional drug searches, the police had marked her as a possible troublemaker. It was noted that she had left open the doors and windows of her car, an old Oldsmobile, when she parked it. Also, the school board and the superintendent stated unequivocally that she had no previous record of drug use. So who could have put the marijuana cigarette in her car? Satan?

After she refused to go for the drug test, Sherry Hearn, with great reluctance, decided to take one the next day. Her lawyer had persuaded her that she might need that test as medical evidence if she ever had to sue the school board. She passed the test, but the school superintendent refused even to look at the results because she had not taken the test *he* had ordered.

After a long hearing by the school board, Sherry Hearn was fired. It was not because of any suspicion of drug use but for insubordination—for not taking the test when she was ordered to.

After she was fired, I called the superintendent of schools, Patrick Russo, who is the very model of an unyielding bureaucrat. I had found out, beforehand, that he did not have to fire her. He had the options of reprimanding or suspending Sherry Hearn. So why fire her, especially because Russo regards her as "a wonderful teacher"?

Russo answered, without hesitation, "Because she failed to uphold the integrity of the school system's drug policy." She didn't jump when he told her to jump into the test.

Because of the school district policy that no teacher's car can be searched without his or her permission and because the search dog, and its uniformed companion, did not have Sherry Hearn's permission to search her car, I asked Patrick Russo if any action had been taken against the officer who prowled through her car without asking her first and therefore violated the school's drug policy.

"No action has been taken," Russo said.

The *Atlanta Constitution* made this comment in an editorial: "This is not about drugs. This is about the fundamental freedoms guaranteed by the U.S. Constitution."

Since being fired in the spring of 1966, Hearn has not been able to find a full-time teaching job; she told me that "most public systems are fearful of anyone involved in a lawsuit." Our right to file a lawsuit for redress of injustice can keep us unemployed.

On the other hand, Sherry Hearn was honored by the Georgia Civil Liberties Union. She was pleased to get the award, but she would be more delighted to be back in school enabling kids to discover their liberties and rights under the Constitution.

Her ordeal—beginning with her protest against the warrantless SWAT team's contempt for the Fourth Amendment—climaxed with the violation of her own privacy rights. This brought to mind a fiery eighteenth-century Boston lawyer, James Otis, whose fierce arguments before the king's judges in Massachusetts set the stage for the eventual inclusion of the Fourth Amendment in the Constitution.

Like the SWAT teams in the public schools now, British troops in the colonies were ransacking places and people at will, searching for contraband goods. The colonists had no protections against these brazen invasions of their privacy.

In 1761, in a Boston courtroom, Otis established the American case against British tyranny. As Justice William O. Douglas admiringly summarized Otis's speech, Otis reminded the judges that "the freedom of one's house is an essential liberty and that any law which violates that privacy is an instrument of slavery and villainy."

Otis also delivered a not too subtle warning to the king of England, recalling that it wasn't so long ago that a recent king of England had lost his head and another his throne because he authorized the kind of arbitrary power that now, in the colonies, encouraged the king's troops to search without restraint the properties and bodies of the colonists.

Listening intently in the courtroom was a young lawyer, John Adams, who was to become the second president of the United States. "Then and there," he wrote in his notebook that night, "was the first scene of the first act of opposition to the arbitrary claims of Great Britain. Then and there the child Independence was born."

But not yet in the Georgia public school system.

It was a landmark Supreme Court decision. In *West Virginia Board of Education v. Barnette*, Justice Robert Jackson, writing for the Court, ruled that no public school student can be suspended, expelled, or otherwise punished for refusing to salute the flag for reasons of conscience, religious or secular.

The West Virginia Board of Education had expelled the children of Jehovah's Witnesses, forbidden by their religion to bow to any "images," and refused to let them return to school until they obeyed the state's command to be properly patriotic. If they did not, their parents could then be prosecuted for complicity in that delinquency.

Justice Jackson, in the most illuminating definition of Americanism in the history of the Court—or anywhere else—said this: "If there is any fixed star in our constitutional constellation, it is that no official, high or petty, can prescribe what shall be orthodox politics, nationalism, religion, or any other matters of opinion, or *force citizens to confess by word or act their faith therein*" (emphasis added).

Justice Jackson's decision came down in 1943, and since then there has been a series of utterly clear federal court rulings that no public school student can be punished in any way for refusing to salute the flag or refusing to stand for the Pledge of Allegiance. It has been further ruled that if a student remains in his or her seat during the Pledge of Allegiance, he or she cannot be removed from that room and exiled in the principal's office. This is wholly settled law.

One would think that in public schools, the principal would know Supreme Court law as it affects his or her responsibilities. However, throughout the country there are principals who know— but ignore—certain Supreme Court decisions and instead bow to the desires of conservative religious parents. For example, official prayers in a public school are unconstitutional—being a violation of the separation of church and state—yet in some public schools the day begins with a prayer, often recited over the public address system.

It takes a brave parent, willing to be ostracized in her community, to go to court and have the principal overruled In some towns, no parents are that brave.

I was surprised to learn that in Connecticut—a state not known to be backward in these matters—Waterbury school officials have for years been penalizing Tisha Byars, a black student. She has never participated in the Pledge of Allegiance because she does not believe there is "liberty and justice" for African Americans in this country.

Tisha Byars went to federal court through the Connecticut Civil Liberties Union (*Byars v. City of Waterbury*). As the record shows, from the first grade on, she remained seated during the Pledge. Initially, her refusal was on the instruction of her father, Dennis, who is convinced that the wording of the Pledge is unconnected with black reality in the United States.

Predictably, this First Amendment lawsuit, based on her First Amendment freedom of belief, has been condemned by some war veterans and others to whom the flag is more sacred than someone's freedom of conscience. One angry protester couldn't resist a touch of bigotry, urging that the Byars family move to Africa. When Tisha's picture appeared on the front page of a local newspaper, several business owners threatened to remove their ads. Joe McCarthy is not quite dead.

Part of Tisha Byars's court action concerned school officials' refusal to qualify her for the National Honor Society, although she had the credentials. Their ostensible reason was an incident of misconduct: Tisha once was eating corn chips in class and wouldn't stop right away when told to by the teacher.

Her case was heard in New Haven by Chief Federal Judge Peter Dorsey. During oral arguments he told one of the school officials, "I think you're dead wrong." As his ultimate ruling showed, the judge didn't believe any of the alleged educators, principals or faculty.

Judge Dorsey declared flatly that it was a violation of the First Amendment to banish Tisha Byars from her homeroom and segregate her in the principal's office during the Pledge of Allegiance. It must stop, he said.

As for her crime of eating corn chips in class, Judge Dorsey noted there was no other misconduct on her record. She had, moreover, apologized to the teacher, and no further action had been taken. The judge added pointedly that the school officials' decision to keep her out of the National Honor Society had nothing to do with corn chips but rather with her refusal to stand for the Pledge of Allegiance.

In his ruling, the judge mentioned another instance of misconduct by the school officials. Another student, Ira Sykes had also been denied admission to the National Honor Society because of what school officials called an "intemperate" essay he had written while serving an in-school suspension for refusing to stand for the Pledge of Allegiance. That "intemperate" essay, Judge Dorsey noted sardonically, was the young man's analysis of his constitutional right to stay seated while refusing to give the Pledge of Allegiance.

In his decision, Judge Dorsey, of course, cited Justice Robert Jackson's decision in *West Virginia School Board of Education v. Barnette*. And his own decision mirrored Jackson's declaration: "To believe that patriotism will not flourish if patriotic ceremonies are voluntary and spontaneous instead of a compulsory routine is to make an unflattering estimate of the appeal of our institutions to free minds."

Waterbury's school authorities—anticipating Judge Dorsey's ruling, decided that students would no longer be removed from their homerooms if they refused to pledge allegiance to the flag. Indeed, Waterbury students will no longer be required to pledge allegiance at all.

Tisha Byars should be honored by the Waterbury school system—and the state department of education—for being Connecticut's leading educator of the year. Meanwhile, the court has awarded her $60,000 in damages plus legal costs.

The faculty of California State University at Northridge was divided about whether former Ku Klux Klan grand wizard David Duke should come to the campus for a debate on affirmative action. Journalism professor Cynthia Rawitch, a member of the faculty senate, pointed out during debate that "we'd look foolish if we were the only part of the university that failed to support free speech, since the students and the university president have already supported Duke's coming."

When she sat down, a young professor leaned forward and instructed her, "There is such a thing as too much free speech, you know."

"As a matter of fact," Rawitch told him, "there isn't. That's the point."

Rawitch's point was largely lost during preparations for the debate. A good many newspaper editors and columnists deplored the university's decision to have Duke come. (Duke is "beyond the pale of legitimate political discussion," said an editorial in the *San Francisco Examiner*.) However, the *Los Angeles Times,* in an editorial, noted that "free speech is not the exclusive province of excellent messengers or even decent ones."

The subject of the debate was Proposition 209, which was on the state's ballot in November 1997. It would prevent California from granting "preferential treatment to any individual or group on the basis of race, sex, color, ethnicity or national origin in the operation of public employment, public education, or public contracting."

Ward Connerly, chairman of the Proposition 209 campaign and a member of the state's board of regents, wrote to Blenda Wilson, president of Northridge, saying he would accept a previous invitation to participate in the debate provided she instructed Duke not to come "unless it is your choice to dishonor your university."

Wilson, former chancellor of the University of Michigan, Dearborn, and Northridge's first black president, made it clear she finds Duke's views repellent. She told Connerly that it was up to the students who invited Duke, not her, to rescind the invitation. But she emphasized that since Northridge is "a public, taxpayer-supported institution, it must always be an open place where all ideas are explored. If only one view is heard, there is no learning."

Later, Wilson said to me, "This debate about the debate is what I call 'a teaching moment.' I think the students will learn a lot about free speech."

California governor Pete Wilson emphatically disagreed. He insisted, as did Ward Connerly, that bringing Duke was a setup to discredit Proposition 209. Meanwhile, opponents of 209 were just as furious, predicting Duke would arouse the kinds of racial prejudices that might militate for Proposition 209.

Blenda Wilson remained calm and firm. "You know," she told me, "there is a twenty-two-year-old black student who says he wants Duke to come because 'I've never heard a white racist out loud.' Also wanting to hear and challenge Duke were leaders of some of the minority groups on campus, including the Black Student Union and the American Indian Student Association.

At last, on September 25, the debate took place despite efforts of Proposition 209 officials to get a court to stop the dread arrival of David Duke. Opposing Duke in the debate was Joe Hicks, director of the Los Angeles Multicultural Collaborative. Some eight hundred diverse spectators peacefully listened to, and some participated in, the exchange of views. Outside, however, there were confrontations, some briefly violent but controlled by the police.

Prominent among the two hundred fifty protesters outside were members of a Berkeley-based group, BAMN, who are dedicated to opposing Proposition 209 "by any means necessary." They were at Northridge to disrupt the debate, but they failed, and few Northridge students joined them.

Also on hand, as reported by Sarah Lubman of the *San Jose Mercury News,* was Susan Scheer, "one of 15 self-proclaimed communists." She shouted, "No free speech for racists!"—and presumably felt good. Ward Connerly, exercising his own free speech, held a counterrally nearby.

During the melee in front of the student union while the debate was going on, an aging member of the Jewish Defense League was dressed in Klan-like white robes to express his acute distaste for David Duke. It had not occurred to him that others who shared his view would not recognize that he was in disguise. As he was being attacked by haters of the former grand wizard, the Jewish protester was rescued by members of the Nation of Islam, who had come to observe the goings-on. That was a true multicultural teaching moment.

In 1989 the world watched in horror as Chinese troops massacred large numbers of unarmed pro-democracy students in Tiananmen Square. Some of the students held up, as long as they could, a replica of the Statue of Liberty. The chief of staff of the People's Liberation Army at the time was General Chi Haotian. It was under his orders that the brutal, bloody suppression of dissent was carried out. Since then, he has been promoted to defense minister.

On December 9, 1996, Chi Haotian and his entourage arrived in Washington on an official visit, the highest-level Chinese military delegation ever to be welcomed by the Defense Department—and to meet the president of the United States.

As Vicky O'Hara reported on National Public Radio, General Chi was received "with flags flying, anthems playing, and cannon firing over the Potomac." It was a disgusting, disgraceful spectacle, all the more repellent because it bore the approval of the president of the United States. Clinton's imprimatur was not surprising. He has no democratic principles to betray because he has no principles to start with.

Neither do the loyalists around him. In November of 1996 Secretary of State Warren Christopher, soon to depart, said in Shanghai about the monster of Tiananmen Square that his government and ours have "common hopes and interests."

The following is from the *Human Rights Watch World Report 1997*: "Torture of China's detainees and prisoners continues. . . . Medical treatment continued to be denied to political and religious prisoners. . . . [Chinese] security forces in Tibet used forms of torture which leave no marks against those suspected of major pro-independence activism."

I wonder if Bill Clinton, after just a month in a Chinese prison, would still consider trade with China more important than the broken bodies of its political prisoners. The protesting Chinese students once hoped that the United States, the fount of democracy, would at least publicly condemn a government that so viciously and persistently violates the most basic human rights. Instead, General Chi Haotian is a highly honored guest in this cradle of democracy. An old-fashioned political cartoonist might have shown the Statue of Liberty with a tear in her eye.

There was some concern among Washington apparatchiks that the general's visit might be marred by vigorous demonstrations that could sour relationships between China and the United States, thereby causing loss of trade. But there was little protest against the presence of the general. Chris Smith, the conservative, pro-life New Jersey Republican, did attack Clinton for honoring "the butcher of Beijing" and for giving a "stamp of approval to the continuing reign of terror in China."

Where, however, were the liberal Democrats in Congress? A breakfast reception for the general on Capitol Hill was boycotted by all Republicans but one. Democrats loyally attended. Nancy Pelosi was the only publicly dissenting congressional Democrat. She *is* a Democrat, but she considers human rights in China a far greater priority than loyalty to the president, the alleged leader of the free world.. *Human Rights Watch* called her "the conscience of the Congress on China and human rights."

Pelosi, who also continually attacked George Bush's dismaying record on human rights in China, including Tiananmen Square, gives no quarter to Clinton. On the day the butcher of Beijing arrived to the flying flags and cannonades, Pelosi expressed her vehement objection "to our country giving full military honors to the person who was in operational command over the Tiananmen Square massacre. . . . Those civilians honored our ideals, and now we honor those who crushed them.

"At the same time that President Clinton will not meet with any of the Chinese dissidents or have an official meeting with . . . the Dalai Lama of Tibet, he has an official meeting with the person who continues to crush dissent in China and Tibet. With its actions, the Clinton administration has given great face to the hardliners in the Chinese regime."

Pelosi angrily called attention to the October 25, 1996, "unclassified biography of General Chi Haotian prepared by the CIA for members of Congress and other officials. It makes no mention of the 1989 Tiananmen Square massacre. . . . This is indicative of the policy of the Clinton administration to make this visit appear as benign as possible."

The most grotesque event during this "benign" visit was a statement by General Chi at the National Defense University. A navy officer asked the general if he had any regrets about the use of military force against civilians in Tiananmen Square. Said Chi: "Here I can tell you in a responsible and serious manner that at the time *not a single person lost his life in Tiananmen Square*" (emphasis added).

In his report on that astonishing piece of revisionist history, John Diamond of the *Washington Post* pointed out that "hundreds, perhaps thousands of student demonstrators and civilian bystanders were killed by forces of the People's Liberation Army sent into Beijing by Chi to quell the demonstration."

If there were a Joseph Goebbels Big Lie Prize, General Chi would win it hands down. It should be noted that the general made his speech washing all the blood from Tiananmen Square on International Human Rights Day.

In the *Washington Times,* Bill Gertz reported that Marc Theissen, a spokesperson for Senate Foreign Relations Committee chairman Jesse Helms, said that General Chi's remarks about Tiananmen were appalling and compared them to Joseph Stalin's denials of killing millions of people under Soviet rule.

Why was no member of Congress as appalled as Nancy Pelosi? Bill Clinton has turned the Democratic Party into a mirror image of his slippery self—and Al Gore will be no better.

This celebratory visit by General Chi is one of the low points in American history, and there have been more than a few. William Triplett, a specialist on China and former chief Republican counsel to the Senate Foreign Relations Committee, said of Chi's pretending there was no massacre of the Chinese students: "He is an unreconstructed killer."

This killer of Chinese students who so desired democracy has been honored by the president of the United States—as the torture continues in Chinese prisons of others guilty of wanting to be free.

I asked Pelosi about her reaction to a dismaying, disheartening Oval Office photograph of a smiling Clinton and the smug general. "Oh, my God," she said. "I thought I would never see the day. The president won't see the Dalai Lama, he won't see the pro-democracy dissidents, he won't see Harry Wu, but he did see this thug. It's absolutely appalling."

Pelosi criticized Clinton "with great regret because I think he is capable of some good things." She did not enumerate what these are. But Clinton's policy of placing trade with China over criticism of its abysmal human rights record has, said Pelosi, "led to crackdowns in China. You would be hard put to find a dissident to talk to in China. They're all in prison, in labor camps, or in exile. Their families have been silenced. It's heartbreaking."

She told me of a characteristic Clinton turnaround: In 1995, at the United Nations anniversary session in San Francisco, he actually said in his speech, "We will not limit our enthusiasm for human rights just because of the almighty dollar."

"I was sitting in the box with Tony Lake (then the National Security Adviser), and I said, 'How can he possibly say that?'"

I asked her what Lake said. "Nothing," said Nancy Pelosi.

It is not only Clinton and his administration that anger Pelosi. She spoke of the "huge amounts of money" being spent to legitimize the trade-over-human-rights policy. "Corporations allowed to do business in China make presentations in Washington, lobby and schmooze with members of Congress and journalists. Money is the biggest enemy of those of us on the other side. All we have been asking is that the Clinton administration does for human beings in China what it does for American intellectual property rights."

A corollary obstacle to helping China's prisoners of conscience is, as Pelosi put it, the revolving door by which lobbyists become administration policymakers. "Sandy Berger," she noted, "was the point person at the Hogan & Hartson law firm for the trade office of the Chinese government. He was a lawyer-lobbyist. When he went into the Clinton administration he was second to Tony Lake, and now he is Clinton's National Security Adviser."

When the president of China, Jiang Zemin, came to Washington on a state visit in October 1997, Nancy Pelosi was protesting at a rally outside the White House: "It is shameful for the United States to give a state dinner and a twenty-one-gun salute to the leader of a regime that crushed Tiananmen Square. It's the best welcome money can buy for a regime that tortures political prisoners, uses prison labor, forces women to have abortions, and restricts freedom of speech and religion."

10

BANNING THE BILL OF RIGHTS AND THE REST OF THE CONSTITUTION FROM OUR PRISONS

*A*mericans who have the most difficulty in exercising their fundamental rights under the Constitution are prisoners and defendants in court who are charged with capital crimes. Popular opinion is so enraged against those being prosecuted—and particularly against those already convicted—that the state is under no significant pressure to try to be fair.

The opening story about a maximum security prison in California demonstrates that prisoners—including those on death row—are human beings and are persons under the Constitution. Also, in Georgia and other states of the South, there are lawyers who keep hope alive when otherwise there is no reason for hope.

In 1842 Charles Dickens visited the Eastern Penitentiary on the outskirts of Philadelphia. "The system here," he wrote, "is rigid, strict and hopeless solitary confinement." The prisoner "sees the prison officers, but with that exception he never looks upon a human countenance, or hears a human voice. He is a man buried alive; to be dug out in the slow round of years."

Dickens had seen cruel prison conditions before, but he found this American model utterly depressing and frightening: "I hold this slow and daily tampering with the mysteries of the brain to be immeasurably worse than any torture of the body." And because no outside attention was being paid, Dickens denounced this "secret punishment which slumbering humanity is not roused up to stay."

There are now, in America, more such remote prisons where inmates are being buried alive. The keepers of all our prisons no longer waste much time in attempts at rehabilitation. Their mission is punishment. And when prisoners are violent or otherwise difficult, they must be controlled in separate, even more rigid institutions that markedly resemble the prison Dickens was chilled by in 1842.

It was pointed out in the journal of the American Civil Liberties Union's National Prison Project that "there is an accelerating movement" to build "supermax" facilities where these prisoners "are locked in their cells approximately 23 hours a day."

One such unit in particular—Pelican Bay in Northern California near the Oregon border—is often visited by prison officials from other states and countries. They see it as a state-of-the-art paradigm of how totally to control and break the spirit of even the toughest convicts. When former California governor George Deukmejian dedicated Pelican Bay in 1989, he proudly predicted that "it will serve as a model for the rest of the nation."

In Pelican Bay there are some 3,250 prisoners of whom 1,056— those requiring the most control—are in the inner prison, the Security Housing Unit (SHU). There, nothing has been left unplanned. No sunlight enters the SHU. The prisoners are locked in their eight-by-ten cells twenty-two and one-half hours a day and, as Jan Elvin wrote in the *National Prison Project Journal,* "officers communicate with prisoners through disembodied speakers in the walls.... Every move is monitored by a closed-circuit camera." Furthermore, the cells are so designed that the prisoners cannot see out.

When the prisoners leave their cells, for the hour and a half of exercise in a small, concrete room or to go to the law library, they "never emerge without being handcuffed and in chains."

As described in the prison Charles Dickens visited, prisoners get their food from a slot in the cell door. The convicts in that nineteenth-century Pennsylvania prison could at least distract themselves from the awful solitude during hours of work in their cells—at a loom, a bench, or a wheel. (Dickens told of a new prisoner who begged, "Give me some work to do, or I shall go raving mad.")

At Pelican Bay, however, the hours are flat and empty. "Activity is strictly limited," Jan Elvin noted. "There are no training programs for prisoners, no correspondence courses, and no vocational training. . . .

No personal calls are permitted unless there is a verifiable emergency such as a death in the family."

After his time at the Eastern Penitentiary, Charles Dickens predicted that "those who have undergone this punishment must pass into society again morally unhealthy and diseased."

Speaking of Pelican Bay, James Park, a former assistant warden at San Quentin, told the *San Jose Mercury News:* "The amount of isolation and limited sensory input isn't a good thing. . . . I'd say that when people are released into the community, they're not prepared to adjust."

Charles Dickens was a superb journalist as well as, of course, a world-class novelist. He was not, however, a lawyer. Accordingly, he could observe and write about dreadful injustices, but he could not bring justice to the particular prisoners he observed.

> *Capital punishment is for them who have no capital.*
> —AN OLD PRISON ADAGE

> *After the execution of Washington Goode, a black man sentenced to be hanged for murder in Massachusetts in 1848, the* Boston Herald *observed that if a "white man who had money had committed the same crime, he would not have been executed."*
> —STEPHEN BRIGHT

> *Despite the fact that indigent defendants are [now] entitled to court-appointed attorneys, there are currently at least 100 death row inmates in Alabama, California, and Texas—some with execution dates—who are not represented by an attorney. In short, there is a death row counsel crisis in this country.*
> —NEW YORK STATE COURT OF APPEALS JUDGE
> JOSEPH BELLACOSA

Steven Bright is director of the Southern Center for Human Rights in Atlanta, where the salary for every employee—whether the director, other attorneys, or secretaries—is $23,000 a year. Supported by foundations, churches, and individuals hooked on justice, the center receives no government funds. It is thereby insulated from the get-tough-on justice vows of members of Congress—both Democrats and Republicans.

Following is a description of the kind of case the Southern Center for Human Rights takes, as described in its report *Discrimination and Death:*

> Center attorneys are representing 27-year-old Levi Pace in challenging his conviction and death sentence in the state courts of Alabama. Mr. Pace, an African American, was sentenced to die in Morgan County, the site of the notorious trials of the "Scottsboro Boys" more than 50 years ago. He was convicted largely on the testimony of a police informer who was a convicted murderer—yet was released from jail in return for her cooperation.
>
> Since entering the case, Center attorneys have uncovered and presented to the appellate courts proof that the district attorney at Mr. Pace's trial deceived the jury into believing that the gun used in this killing had been used by Mr. Pace in a robbery in another county, when in fact as the prosecutor knew, the gun had actually been tied to another individual and not Mr. Pace.

Steve Bright and others at the center have also become all too knowledgeable about the rampant incompetency of many inexperienced trial attorneys in the "defense" of those charged with murder. (Not the O. J. Simpsons, but people without resources, who have no choice but to accept incompetent court-appointed attorneys.) In the appellate courts, Bright and his colleagues try to remedy the life-endangering errors of these less than amateur lawyers in the lower courts.

If indigent defendants get screwed at trial—by their own lawyers as well as by the prosecutor—their lives may depend on whether they can get lawyers of the quality and determination of Steve Bright and those like him, for whom the law is a calling, not a passport to big bucks. To say the least, there aren't enough such lawyers, and that's why, on some death rows, the condemned have no lawyers at all.

(Keep in mind that there is no federal constitutional *right to counsel* for inmates on postconviction appeals.)

Steve Bright has described—in law-review articles, in legislative testimony, and in conversations with me—what it's like to be charged with a capital crime and then be defended by a lawyer who can barely find the courtroom:

"In Mississippi, a person was represented at a capital trial by a public defender and a third-year law student. Over half of the witnesses at the trial were examined by the third-year law student, who told the judge at one point that she needed some time, because she had never been in court before. There have been other cases in which the lawyer's first trial after law school was a capital trial.

"A lawyer who has tried a number of death penalty cases in Georgia was . . . asked to name any criminal-law decisions from any court—the Supreme Court of the United States, the Georgia Supreme Court, any court in the country—that he knew. He answered, 'Well, we've got the *Miranda* case. Everybody knows the *Miranda* case [1966]. Asked to recall any others, he could only name the case in which he was involved and the *Dred Scott* case [1857]. Those were the only criminal cases that he could name."

In an Op-Ed piece for the *New York Daily News,* Bright pointed out that "people have been sent to death rows in Alabama, Georgia, Texas and other states after trials in which they were represented by attorneys who were sleeping through part of the trial, were intoxicated or were unaware of the law and of the procedures governing capital trials.

"A judge in Houston responding to a capital defendant's complaints about his lawyer sleeping during the trial at which death was imposed, remarked, 'The Constitution does not say that the lawyer has to be awake.'"

Bright and his associates do most of their work in what is called the Death Belt—Louisiana, Georgia, Texas, and Florida—where two-thirds of all executions are carried out. Although the lethal attorney incompetence detailed by Bright takes place in every state, the South is the pits.

New York State Court of Appeals judge Joseph Bellacosa tells in a *Pace Law Review* article that "in 1990, the *National Law Journal* conducted a six-month investigation into the quality of representation afforded capital defendants in the South:

> The results were appalling. More than half the attorneys inter-viewed said they were handling their first capital murder case when their client was convicted. Even more disturbing, the *Journal* found that in the six states they studied, attorneys repre-senting indigent death row inmates were disbarred, disciplined or suspended at rates ranging from three to forty-six times the overall rates for those states. About twenty-five percent of the inmates on death row in Kentucky were represented by attorneys who were subsequently disbarred, suspended or convicted of crimes themselves.

As often as Steve Bright rings the changes on the chronic injustice of the justice system, his sense of astonishment and anger and disgust never diminishes. For example, he told me the following:

"The failure of defense counsel to present critical information is one reason that Horace Dunkins was sentenced to death in Alabama. Before his execution in 1989, when newspapers (after the trial) reported that Dunkins was mentally retarded, at least one juror came forward and said she would not have voted for the death sentence if she had known of his condition. [His lawyer hadn't mentioned it.]

"This same failure of the defense counsel to present critical infor-mation also helps account for the death sentences imposed on Jerome Holloway—who has an IQ of 49 and the intellectual capacity of a seven-year-old—in Byron County, Georgia, and on William Alvin Smith—who has an IQ of 65—in Oglethorpe, Georgia."

Ah, but a sophisticated state like New York isn't like Alabama or Georgia? Judge Joseph Bellacosa responds in the *Pace Law Review:* While the death penalty was in force, "New York appear[ed] to hold the dubious distinction of having executed more innocent individuals than any other state—up to now," and "at least eight men have been wrongfully executed in New York."

Then, as now, even competent defense attorneys have had nowhere near the resources of those dedicated to putting defendants to death. As Judge Bellacosa noted, "The prosecution has virtually no limits. It operates with virtually unlimited resources, with budgets a little like that of the CIA—secret, hidden, fungible, protected by 'official' smoke and mirrors." Said attorney Stuart Melkejohn: "In most of the [death penalty] cases I've seen . . . it's almost like the defendant hasn't had a lawyer."

Before the graduates of Yale Law School received their degrees in 1994, they were confronted by the insistent challenge of Justice Hugo Black: "Under our constitutional system, courts stand—against any winds that blow—as havens for those who might otherwise suffer because they are helpless, weak, outnumbered, or because they are nonconforming victims of prejudice and public excitement."

Quoting and underlining Black's words—at a time when the legal profession was being charged with pursuing Mammon more enthusiastically than justice—was commencement speaker Stephen Bright. Appointed as a J. Skelly Wright Fellow and visiting lecturer in law at Yale, Bright's course is titled "Capital Punishment: Race and Poverty."

Bright teaches from experience. His Southern Center for Human Rights has won a number of significant Supreme Court decisions setting aside capital convictions or sentences as well as lower-court orders obtaining equal educational and vocational opportunities for women imprisoned in Louisiana and Alabama.

Also, as Bright notes, the center secured "an order correcting numerous unconstitutional conditions and setting standards for virtually every aspect of life in all of South Carolina's twenty-seven prisons."

When not trying to bring the radical news of due process and equal protection of the laws to Southern judges and prison wardens, Bright lectures at law schools. His aim is to show law students how badly their skills are needed beyond corporate boardrooms.

During his commencement address at Yale Law School, Bright looked at the graduates and said these words: "There are seventy-two people languishing on Texas's death row who do not have a lawyer— even though they have legal avenues of review of their cases.

"Think of it. They cannot even confer with a lawyer to find out the status of the cases in which they were condemned to die. How can a system that claims to be one of justice allow such a thing? And year after year, many others with urgent legal needs in both civil and criminal matters have no access to an attorney at all."

Bright realizes that some of the law students he tries to enlist may worry about how much money they will make. Virtue is not necessarily negotiable. At the Yale Law School graduation, Bright addressed this concern: "Remember that it is no sacrifice to receive the same income as that received by teachers, farmers, workers on the assembly line, and other good, decent working men and women who raise families and contribute to their communities."

The Pied Piper has harvested a fair number of souls. "This summer," he tells me, "four students from Yale Law School will be with us here in Atlanta at the Center for Human Rights. Other Yale students from my class will be doing capital punishment work at public defender offices or programs in Charleston, Chicago, Montgomery, New York [NAACP Legal Defense Fund], Houston, and New Orleans. . . . One of the graduates from the class last year is now doing death penalty defense work full-time in South Carolina."

In 1987 Justice William Brennan was the commencement speaker at Ohio State's law school. He told those graduates the following: "Over too many years, we as lawyers and as citizens stood idly by while minority citizens were deprived of their most basic legal rights. How can we expect much respect for the law in those who have seen how readily even lawyer-citizens have tolerated such legal inequities?"

Consider the respect for the law that Stephen Bright could create if he were on the Supreme Court—even as a lone dissenter to the Rehnquist Court's decisions diminishing constitutional standards of decency and fairness. But could a Pied Piper of the Bill of Rights be nominated and confirmed? Fat chance.

A Supreme Court case that seems to stay in the minds of many schoolchildren is *Gideon v. Wainwright.* Those I have talked to are impressed that this convict—without any money, without a lawyer— sent a handwritten petition, in pencil, to the Supreme Court, and it was actually read by those distant, mysterious figures. More than that, the court said he was right, and his name from then on became part of American constitutional law.

Charged in Florida, with thievery, Gideon had asked a Florida state court judge to appoint a lawyer for him. The judge said he couldn't under previous Supreme Court rulings. In 1963 Justice Hugo Black, speaking for a unanimous Supreme Court, said that Gideon and other indigent defendants are indeed entitled to a lawyer in felony cases. (This right has since been expanded to include misdemeanor cases that involve imprisonment.)

Hugo Black noted in his opinion that "any person hauled into court, who is too poor to hire a lawyer, cannot be assured a fair trial unless counsel is provided for him. This seems to us to be an obvious truth."

Yet it is also obvious that *Gideon* isn't working for more and more defendants with no other resources than an old Supreme Court decision. For instance, I have seen enormously overburdened public defenders meeting their clients for the first time only fifteen minutes before a hearing. The January/February 1993 issue of the *American Lawyer* detailed, in a series of appalling case histories from throughout the country, that a great deal needs to be done "to finish the job that . . . a ne'er-do-well drifter from the backwaters of Florida set in motion . . . more than 30 years ago."

The need is particularly pressing now; the article in the *American Lawyer* pointed out that, "nationwide, approximately 80 percent of all felony defendants are represented by [publicly paid defenders], compared to 48 percent in 1982."

Not only are more funds needed to share the caseload but also more lawyers who, as Stephen Bright keeps saying when he's asked to speak at law schools, "will commit not just a few years to learn at the expense of the poor, but who will commit a lifetime to legal services, public defender and other programs."

Bright has done just that. After working as a last-chance lawyer in Appalachia and Washington, he became director of the Southern Center for Human Rights in Atlanta. Bright is familiar with death rows throughout the South, and he has sometimes had death sentences reversed. Because movies are hardly ever made anymore of the order of *Mr. Smith Goes to Washington* or *High Noon,* a television documentary on Steve Bright's journeys and campaigns could be powerfully revealing. Especially interesting would be his collection of stories of the rampant incompetence of many court-appointed lawyers in states that do not consider public defender work important enough to pay these lawyers decently or to insist that the courts examine their qualifications.

In a talk at the University of Missouri–Columbia, Bright told of a Georgia case in which the court-appointed defense lawyer "did not put on evidence to seek to avoid the death penalty. The jury that sentenced the youth to die was not even told that he suffered from schizophrenia."

In another Georgia case, the convicted defendant, John Young, who was waiting to be executed, "met his defense lawyer in the yard at the jail. The lawyer [who was also imprisoned] said he was under considerable distress during John Young's trial. He was on drugs. He was breaking up with his wife. He was breaking with his gay lover. He really was not focused on the trial. But this was close enough attention for government work. John Young was executed in 1985."

Bright keeps asking, "Why would any conscientious judge, why would any bar association, why would any system that is supposed to dispense justice ever allow these kinds of things to happen?"

In 1995 Steve Bright came to Washington as part of a nationwide series of events to promote law in the public interest. This call to conscience for lawyers was put together by the Alliance for Justice, which works for the survival of public interest law.

In the auditorium of the National Education Association, Bright spoke to an audience of more than five hundred law students, lawyers, and members of the Justice Department. Attorney General Janet Reno was the opening speaker, but she left before Bright spoke truth to power. She should have stayed because he specifically had her, among other mandarins of the law, in mind.

Bright told the audience that three days before his talk he had been in a Georgia courtroom trying to keep a black defendant from being added to the death penalty statistics. Sitting there, he had thought of the Olympic Games coming to Georgia and how Georgia, like South Africa, "has a long history of apartheid and racial oppression. Yet now South Africa has moved ahead, joining the rest of the civilized world in abandoning capital punishment. But we in Georgia are still burning people up in electric chairs while other people celebrate their deaths outside."

Are we actually less civilized than South Africa? "Already," Steve Bright said, "the president is running reelection television ads proclaiming his support for the death penalty. Last year he signed into law a crime bill providing for the death penalty for fifty more crimes."

Bright spoke of the attacks by Congress on due process, which is the supposedly fundamental fairness guarantee of our justice system. For example, habeas corpus—federal judicial review of state verdicts in capital cases—is becoming dangerously diminished, as is the number of qualified lawyers available to represent the inhabitants of death row.

Revealingly, he added, when the funding for the death penalty resource centers around the country—staffed by young lawyers who have developed expertise in that complex field of law—was killed by Congress, "not a word of protest was heard from the White House or the Department of Justice." And he told of men on the verge of being executed who have until now been released because lawyers from the resource centers have proved them to be innocent.

"Our country," Bright continued, "could have benefited from a lesson on due process from the president or the attorney general." But in these times, "there is no commitment to fairness on the part of our national leadership in either party."

Bright urged the law students in the audience to think of going into public interest law: "A law firm may pay one partner $600,000. At our office in Atlanta, that is the entire operating budget for a year for nine lawyers, three investigators, one paralegal, three administrative people, and a number of law students."

With the intensity of a preacher trying to save souls, he asked people from big law firms to come forward after his speech and pledge money for fellowships in public interest law and to volunteer themselves for capital cases. "We have people in a number of states who are facing the executioner alone."

Steve Bright was vigorously applauded after his speech. But on that day of celebration of public interest law, no one from a law firm came forward to pledge some help to bring fairness, however incrementally, to the American system of justice.

★ ★ ★

Contrary to the real-life experiences and knowledge of Steve Bright and other activists for fairness in prison cells, a rising chorus has been heard in state legislatures and on television shows saying that American prisoners are being "coddled." It is commonplace, for instance, to rail at frivolous lawsuits being filed by inmates.

There *are* frivolous lawsuits, but the emphasis on them adds to the general impression that our prisons are not nearly punitive enough. Instead of having access to law libraries, some say prisoners should do the hardest time possible.

But Steve Bright has continued to illuminate the actual conditions under which many prisoners try to survive. One of his decidedly non-frivolous lawsuits concerned a jail in Muskogee County, Georgia. Keith Porter, a mentally ill prisoner, was placed in an isolation cell after the correctional staff saw him barking like a dog. Within a day of the isolation, Porter hanged himself. The jail, with almost one thousand inmates, had one doctor who worked there four hours a week.

Then there are the conditions of confinement at the Julia Tutwiler Prison for Women in Alabama. As noted by Steve Bright, "the segregation unit holds women on death row, along with maximum security and protective custody women, and those being held for initial 90-day evaluations." Locked in their cells for twenty-three hours a day, they are joined by women with serious mental illnesses.

"These mentally ill women," said Bright, "scream and curse at all hours; spit at, threaten, and assault other inmates; and regularly throw feces, urine, and other unsanitary objects at guards and other inmates."

A magistrate judge ruled that the prison was violating the United States Constitution, but he also found that the present officials are not "subjectively culpable" in that they were not "deliberately indifferent" to conditions there. He refused to issue an injunction, and so the daily terror at Tutwiler remained unconstitutional, to say the least.

Steve Bright told me of the freewheeling style of Georgia's corrections commissioner, Wayne Garner, a former undertaker and state senator with no experience in prison management. In the *Atlanta Constitution,* reporter Rhonda Cook told of the suit that Bright brought against Garner, who sometimes accompanied tactical squads on sweep searches of inmates and cells: "The lawsuit, which lists 10 inmates as plaintiffs, claims inmates were abused during a sweep of Scott State Prison. According to the suit, handcuffed inmates were beaten, prisoners' heads were slammed into cinder-block walls or onto concrete floors, convicts were kicked and punched, and Garner watched much of the abuse." During a deposition in the suit, a guard testified that Commissioner Garner praised his law-enforcement officers that day for "kicking ass."

In response to a successful suit by Steve Bright, Georgia's Department of Corrections decided that the prisons can somehow function without putting inmates in "five point restraints." This practice is also known, among inmates as "the motorcycle." With his hands and feet shackled and a belt tightly fixed around his waist, the prisoner is then fully prepared for his ordeal by having a football helmet placed on his head. "Inmates were restrained for days at a time," the suit declared, "during which they frequently defecated and urinated on themselves, were unable to sleep, and experienced psychological trauma."

In an article in the British *Economist* about prisons throughout America, it was noted that "in general, the United States is not content with depriving criminals of their freedom which [deprivation] they generally deserve; it also seems bent on doing all it can to make their lives miserable."

In recent years, television watching for prisoners has been limited; exercise and educational courses have been cut in a number of prisons, as have visiting hours; press access to prisoners has been banned; and chain gangs are back in vogue in some states, as are "stun belts," which by remote control can electrically shock a prisoner through 50,000 volts into losing control of his bladder, bowels, and balance.

When Charles Dickens visited American prisons in the last century, he wrote of the inmates' "depth of terrible endurance." That has not changed—except for those frivolous lawsuits.

11

Nowhere in the Constitution Is There a Mention of God: The Continuing Battles for Freedom of Religion—and Freedom from Religion

*I*n the First Amendment, the only words concerning religion are as follows: "Congress shall make no law respecting an establishment of religion, or prohibiting the free exercise thereof." (Later, the First Amendment came to apply as well to the individual states and localities.) Yet these sixteen words have caused some of the most bitter battles inside and outside courtrooms. To some, what is called the Establishment Clause means strict separation of church and state. The government must not prefer any or all religion. "A union of government and religion," wrote Justice Hugo Black in *Engel v. Vitale* (1962), "tends to destroy government and to degrade religion."

"In Colonial America," Black emphasized, "Catholics found themselves hunted and proscribed because of their faith; Quakers who followed their conscience went to jail; Baptists were particularly obnoxious to certain dominant sects; men and women of varied faiths who happened to be in a minority in a particular locality were persecuted because they steadfastly persisted in worshiping God only as their consciences dictated. And all of these dissenters were compelled to pay tithes and taxes to support government-sponsored churches whose ministers preached inflammatory sermons designed to consolidate the established faith by generating a burning hatred against dissenters."

Government and religion, therefore, must not intermingle.

Everyone has the right to worship in his or her own home or church or synagogue or mosque, but without any form of governmental imprimatur anywhere.

Indignant members of the clergy and laypersons, on the other hand, have claimed that the courts—very much including the Supreme Court—have discriminated against religion, banishing it to the margins of public life. Some of them insist that Creationism be taught in the public schools as a counterforce to the study of evolution. There is also a demand that prayer be admitted into public schools and that such religious symbols as crèches and crosses take their rightful places in the public square.

A number of well-known preachers go farther and insist the United States is a Christian nation. According to Pat Robertson, the separation of church and state "is a lie of the Left."

Yet the Constitution states plainly: "No religious Test shall ever be required as Qualification to any Office of public Trust under the United States." And nowhere in the Constitution is there a mention of God.

Moreover, Thomas Jefferson said this: "Millions of innocent men, women and children, since the introduction of Christianity, have been burnt, tortured, fined, imprisoned; yet we have not advanced one inch toward uniformity. What has been the effect of coercion? To make one half the world fools, and the other half hypocrites. To support roguery and error all over the earth."

One story in this chapter tells of a Supreme Court case vigorously affirming the separation of church and state. Another is an account of a young woman of religious faith fighting for her right to express that faith personally in a school assignment. Finally, as previously cited, children of Jehovah's Witnesses in West Virginia refuse to abandon the principles of their religion even at the price of being expelled from school.

Daniel Weisman is chair of the Social Work Department at Rhode Island College. He is Jewish. In 1986 his eldest daughter, Meredith, graduated from the Nathan Bishop Middle School, a public school in Providence, Rhode Island.

At the graduation ceremony there appeared, invited by the school, a fundamentalist Baptist minister. He delivered a prayer, all about the power of Jesus Christ and the salvation he can bring if one only lets him into one's heart. And it was Jesus, of course, who deserved the credit for the accomplishments of these scholars before him, including Meredith Weisman.

"As a Jew," Daniel Weisman recalled, "I had a deep personal reaction to this imposition on my beliefs at an important event. I felt isolated and vulnerable. A letter I wrote to the school expressing my concerns about this went unanswered."

That act of callousness was eventually going to cost the school a lot of money in legal fees.

In 1989 Weisman's second daughter, Deborah, was to be graduated from the same school. For this ceremony, a rabbi was invited to participate. A smart move. However, it didn't work out that way.

"I still feel," Weisman said, "it is inappropriate for one's religious beliefs to be foisted on those of other faiths at any government-sponsored activity.

"I am embarrassed to be the imposer as much as I am uncomfortable to be imposed upon. As a citizen in a pluralistic society, I find it both wrong and dangerous to mix public business and private faith.

"Even something as seemingly innocent and trivial as a minute of invocation and benediction at a public school graduation reinforces the mistaken notion that religion and public education are interconnected."

The rabbi's invitation was not withdrawn, and Daniel Weisman went to the Rhode Island affiliate of the American Civil Liberties Union. The ACLU sued to bar the rabbi's invocation and benediction at the event, but the chief federal district judge, Francis J. Boyle, refused the request. This is an important church-state case, he said, and he needed more time to study it.

School officials, meanwhile, carefully instructed Rabbi Leslie Gutterman to stay within proper bounds during his performance. They gave him a pamphlet, "Guidelines for Civic Occasions," put together by the National Conference of Christians and Jews. And they drilled into the rabbi that his prayers had to be nonsectarian.

Nevertheless, the rabbi blew it. At least the Weismans thought so. The words of Rabbi Gutterman at the graduation ceremony now have

a place in American constitutional history, for they figured promi-
nently in the Supreme Court case *Lee v. Weisman* (1992). Said the
rabbi at the historic graduation ceremony:

"God of the free, hope of the brave, for the legacy of America,
where diversity is celebrated and the rights of minorities are protected,
we thank You. . . . For its court system, where all can seek justice, we
thank You."

So what was wrong with that?

In reporting the event for the *Providence Journal-Bulletin*, Joan
Castelluci wrote that Deborah Weisman "noted that Rabbi
Gutterman had invoked the name of God in the benediction, and her
mother said he ended both the invocation and the benediction with
the word, 'amen.'"

The mother added that "Rabbi Gutterman made it very clear that
both the invocation and the benediction were prayers."

The lawsuit was joined. The federal district court found for the
Weismans. The rabbi had certainly prayed, and those prayers created
"an identification of school with a deity, and therefore [with] religion." The rabbi, then, had advanced religion during this graduation
ceremony at a public school. "It is the union of prayer, school, and an
important occasion that creates an identification of religion with a
school function," said the court.

The First District Court of Appeals agreed with the lower court.
The school authorities filed a petition asking the Supreme Court of
the United States to review the case. Significantly, the United States
solicitor general at the time, Kenneth Starr, filed an amicus brief asking the Court to take the case and to come to a conclusion that would
markedly diminish the wall between church and state beyond this
case.

Clearly, the Bush administration had taken a particular interest in
Lee v. Weisman, apparently believing that God resents being treated as
if He or She does not belong in a public school. And that a lot of voters agree with God.

This was the case that could begin to open the schoolhouse doors
for God. In 1989 Justice Anthony Kennedy—speaking also for Chief
Justice William Rehnquist, Justice Antonin Scalia, and Justice Byron
White—had declared war on what Kennedy had called the "callous

indifference to religion" on the part of the other members of the Court.

Kennedy wanted a new test. Government could sponsor expressions of religious belief provided government involvement did not coerce anyone into participating in that religion. By 1991 Thurgood Marshall and William Brennan had left the Court. Now was the time to strike.

An ACLU volunteer attorney from a Rhode Island firm, Sandra Blanding, appeared before the Supreme Court for the Weismans. Her brief laid out the bare bones of the violation of church-state separation in this case: "[This] is about prayer in a public school . . . delivered by a member of the clergy chosen by a public school official and both planned and supervised by school officials as the culmination of a child's progress through the public school system."

To the kids and their parents, this was a very important event, but it was not supposed to be a religious event—not in a public school.

The Providence school committee had selected a well-known Washington lawyer, Charles "Chuck" Cooper, who had been head of the Justice Department's Office of Legal Counsel under then attorney general Edwin Meese.

I had suspected that Cooper might win this case, given the present composition of the Supreme Court, by arguing the need for government to accommodate religion more generously, including at public school graduations. But it may be that, like the Baptist minister and the rabbi at the Nathan Bishop Middle School, Chuck Cooper got carried away during oral argument.

For one thing, Cooper argued that having a prayer at a public school graduation is not at all coercive. Kids who object don't have to come. This bothered Justice Kennedy:

> I find it very difficult to accept that a prayer given at the start of graduation is non-coercive, or that objecting students could leave or sit out the prayer. . . .
>
> I find it very difficult to accept the proposition that it is not a substantial imposition on a young graduate to say you have your choice of . . . hearing this prayer or absenting yourself from graduation. In our culture, graduation is a key event in a young

person's life . . . and I think it is a very, very substantial burden
[to place this choice on a young graduate].

There was more. Sandra Day O'Connor asked Cooper if a state
legislature, assuming no coercion was involved, could adopt a particular religion as the state religion—the way, she said, a state can adopt a
bolo tie as the state tie.

Cooper, to the seeming astonishment of some of the justices, said
that a state *could* adopt a religion for itself, provided people in that
state were not forced to be part of that religion.

(Imagine how a Protestant would feel if the New York legislature
were to adopt Judaism as the official state religion. Like an outsider,
right?)

Said O'Connor sternly to Cooper, "That certainly is not the holding of our cases."

Justice Antonin Scalia also had a turn at Charles Cooper.
"Coercion isn't the only test," Scalia said. What about sectarianism
and the Constitution? The Supreme Court, Scalia went on, does not
open its session with "Jesus Christ Save the United States and This
Honorable Court." Nor, he added, do our coins say, "In Jesus Christ
We Trust."

Cooper answered that the reason Jesus's name is not used in these
areas is that it "would not be politically possible."

Scalia was close to bursting with frustration: "If we could get the
votes for it, that would be constitutional? That's what you're saying?
You do not see anything in our constitutional tradition that says you
cannot be sectarian?"

It may be that Cooper startled Kennedy, Scalia, and some of the
others into seeing way down the slippery slope—what might occur if
they were able to break down most of the wall between church and
state.

Linda Greenhouse noted the following in the *New York Times* of
November 22, 1992: "Providence might still win its appeal, of course.
But it was less clear after the argument that it would."

Inadvertently, Chuck Cooper had kept the Establishment Clause
of the First Amendment from being eroded. Jefferson and Madison,
among others back then, insisted on keeping government out of reli-

gion because they knew, from history and their own experiences, that, as Hugo Black said, "a union of government and religion tends to destroy government and degrade religion."

In a five-to-four decision, the Supreme Court decided for the Weismans. Justice Anthony Kennedy spoke for the majority:

> The injury caused by the government's action, and the reason why Daniel and Deborah Weisman object to it, is that the State, in a school setting, in effect required participation in a religious exercise. It is, we concede, a brief exercise during which the individual can concentrate on joining its message, meditate on her own religion, or let her mind wander. But the embarrassment and the intrusion of the religious exercise cannot be refuted by arguing that these prayers, and similar ones to be said in the future, are of a *de minimis* character. To do so would be an affront to the Rabbi who offered them and to all those for whom the prayers were an essential and profound recognition of divine authority. And for the same reason, we think that the intrusion is greater than the two minutes or so of time consumed for prayers like these. Assuming, as we must, that the prayers were offensive to the student and the parent who now object, the intrusion was both real and, in the context of a secondary school, a violation of the objectors' rights.
>
> And to say a teenage student has a real choice not to attend her school graduation is formalistic in the extreme. True, Deborah could elect not to attend commencement without renouncing her diploma; but we shall not allow the case to turn on this point. Everyone knows that in our society and in our culture school graduation is one of life's most significant occasions. A school rule which excuses attendance is beside the point. Attendance may not be required by official decree, yet it is apparent that a student is not free to absent herself from the graduation exercise in any real sense of the term "voluntary," for absence would require forfeiture of those intangible benefits which have motivated the student through youth and all her school years. Graduation is a time for family and those closest to the student to celebrate success and express mutual wishes of

gratitude and respect, all to the end of impressing upon the young person the role that it is his or her right and duty to assume in the community and all of its diverse parts.

The importance of the event is the point the school district and the United States rely upon to argue that a formal prayer ought to be permitted, but it becomes one of the principal reasons why their argument must fail.

Their contention, one of considerable force were it not for the constitutional constraints applied to state action, is that the prayers are an essential part of these ceremonies because for many persons an occasion of this significance lacks meaning if there is no recognition, however brief, that human achievements cannot be understood apart from their spiritual essence.

While in some societies the wishes of the majority might prevail, the Establishment Clause of the First Amendment is addressed to this contingency and rejects the balance urged upon us. The Constitution forbids the State to exact religious conformity from a student as the price of attending her own school graduation. This is the calculus the Constitution commands.

A consortium of civil liberties and religious organizations—including, among others, the ACLU, the American Jewish Congress, the Baptist Joint Committee, and the American Muslim Council—has issued a parental guide to religion and the law in the public schools.

One section states: "Teachers may not require students to modify, include, or excise religious views in their assignments, if germane. These assignments should be judged by ordinary academic standards of substance, relevance, appearance and grammar."

In March 1991 Dana Ramsey, a teacher in the Dickson County, Tennessee, School District, gave a research assignment to her ninth-grade English class. Students could choose any topic they wanted provided they could show four secondary sources for their research. Among the topics the teacher approved were witchcraft, black magic, the occult, and spiritualism (supernatural meetings with dead people).

Brittney Settle, then fifteen, decided to write a paper titled "The

Life of Jesus Christ," for which there were decidedly more than four secondary sources. The teacher rejected the topic, telling Brittney it was "not an appropriate thing to do in a public school." Moreover, it was all the more inappropriate, the teacher added, because Brittney was a Christian and already knew a lot about the subject, in which she was intensely involved; therefore, it would be hard for her to research and write the paper in a properly scholarly way. Brittney wrote and submitted the paper anyway, and she was given a grade of zero.

When a lawsuit was filed charging discrimination against religious speech under the First Amendment, the teacher said, during a deposition, that "we don't deal with personal religious beliefs in a public school."

Dana Ramsey was supported by her principal, the school board, the federal district court, and the Sixth Circuit Court of Appeals. This unequivocal rejection of the student's claim that she was being punished for her religious viewpoint was in odd contrast to the Dickson County School District's written policy concerning compositions, which permitted "Student-initiated expressions in assignments which reflect their beliefs or non-beliefs about a religious theme."

School boards often tend to be shamelessly contradictory in defending their violations of student speech rights. For instance, this school board said that Brittney's zero grade did not conflict with its stated policy on protected religious expression in school assignments. After all, said the board, Brittney Settle's paper was not a "composition."

Adding to this educational obfuscation was the teacher's response when she was asked about having given her imprimatur to the topics of reincarnation, spiritualism, and the occult. Those were not, she said, religious topics.

The Sixth Circuit Court of Appeals declared that "Learning is more vital in the classroom than free speech," as if the two had nothing to do with each other. And does that mean that refusing to give the Pledge of Allegiance is now prohibited? Or the right, affirmed by the Supreme Court, to have a student-initiated religious club before or after classes?

Speaking for the Sixth Circuit, Chief Judge Gilbert Merritt dealt with the teacher's convoluted—and constitutionally specious—reasons for rejecting Brittney's research paper on the life of Jesus. Those reasons, he said, "fall within the broad leeway of teachers' rights to determine the nature of the curriculum and the grades to be awarded students—even [teachers'] reasons that may be mistaken."

On the other hand, Michael McConnell, a law professor at the University of Chicago, pointed out the following: "When a research paper is otherwise appropriate, as this one was, the fact that it involves religion is not a legitimate basis for exclusion."

In November 1996 the U.S. Supreme Court refused to review *Settle v. Dickson County School Board.* No reasons were given. The court may have considered the case moot, because Brittney had graduated. This discriminatory Sixth Circuit approach to religious speech in a public school is now the rule only in that circuit (Kentucky, Michigan, Ohio, and Tennessee), but the decision may be cited by courts elsewhere.

The merits of this particular constitutional classroom issue, therefore, have not yet been decided on by the Supreme Court. The refusal to renew does not preclude a similar case's coming up.

It is not surprising that the American Civil Liberties Union was not moved to protect Brittney's speech rights. The ACLU is also sometimes confused about students' religious speech rights in public schools. The state must not compel religious speech in its schools, but students do not shed their personal religious viewpoints at the schoolhouse gate.

In *Minersville School District v. Gobitis* (1940), the Supreme Court heard a case in which two Jehovah's Witnesses children had refused to salute the flag on the ground that doing so would violate their religious beliefs. To exercise their religion freely the students and their parents said, they must be allowed to reject the flag salute because they considered the flag "an image" within the meaning of God's command in the Old Testament: "Thou shalt not make unto thee any graven image . . . thou shalt not bow down thyself to them, nor serve them."

I described the case and its aftermath in *The First Freedom* in 1980. Lillian Gobitis, age twelve, and her brother William, ten, were expelled from the public schools of Minersville, Pennsylvania, for their refusal to salute the national flag as part of a daily school exercise for teachers and students. By an eight-to-one vote the High Court declared that the Gobitis children *could* constitutionally be expelled.

In delivering the opinion of the Court, Justice Felix Frankfurter maintained that there are certain laws that a legislature considers essential to secure "that orderly, tranquil, and free society without which religious toleration itself is unattainable." The Pennsylvania flag-salute law is such a statute, he maintained, for it recognizes that "the ultimate foundation of a free society is the binding tie of cohesive sentiment. . . . We live by symbols. The flag is the symbol of our national unity, transcending all internal differences, however large, within the framework of the Constitution."

It may be, Frankfurter conceded, that a compulsory flag salute is not the best way of "training children in patriotic impulses." Perhaps the deepest patriotism is engendered by giving all beliefs "unfettered scope" and leaving their adherents free to salute the flag or not. But this is a matter of educational policy.

The High Court's decision had an immediate effect, as Leo Pfeffer pointed out in *God, Caesar, and the Constitution* (Beacon Press, 1975):

The Court's decision was announced on June 3, 1940. Between June 12 and June 20, hundreds of physical attacks upon the Jehovah's Witnesses were reported in the United States Department of Justice. At Kennebunk, Maine, their Kingdom Hall was burned. At Rockville, Maryland, the police assisted a mob in dispersing a Jehovah's Witnesses Bible meeting. At Litchfield, Illinois, practically the entire town mobbed a company of some sixty Witnesses who were canvassing it. At Connersville, Indiana, several Witnesses were charged with riotous conspiracy, their attorney beaten, and all driven out of town. At Jackson, Mississippi, members of a veterans' organization forcibly removed a number of Witnesses and their trailer homes from the town. In Nebraska, a Witness was lured from his house, abducted, and castrated. In Richwood, West Virginia, the chief of police and deputy sheriff forced a group of Witnesses to drink large doses of castor oil, and paraded the victims through the streets, tied together with police department rope. In the two years following the *Gobitis* decision there was an uninterrupted record of violence and persecution of the Witnesses. Almost without exception, the flag and flag salute were the causes.

A quite different reaction to the *Gobitis* decision was expressed by the *Christian Century:* "It is bitterly ironical that a free government should inflict a penalty for refusal to salute a symbol of freedom."

Three years after *Gobitis,* the Court reversed itself. The case, *West Virginia State Board of Education* v. *Barnette,* also involving Jehovah's Witnesses, resulted from a ruling by the West Virginia Board of Education, after the *Gobitis* decision, that all teachers and pupils were required to salute the flag. A refusal would be "regarded as an Act of insubordination, and . . . dealt with accordingly." For the student, this meant expulsion from school with no readmittance until the student had yielded and saluted the flag. Meanwhile, the student would be listed as "unlawfully absent" and could be proceeded against as a delinquent. In addition, his parents or guardians were liable to prosecution.

In his opinion for the Court (which was divided six to three), Justice Robert H. Jackson said that Jehovah's Witnesses' children "have been expelled from school and are threatened with exclusion for no other cause [than refusing to salute the flag]. Officials threaten to send them to reformatories maintained for criminally inclined juveniles. Parents of such children have been prosecuted and are threatened with prosecutions for causing delinquency."

Jackson recalled that in the *Gobitis* case one basis on which the Court had justified the expulsion of children refusing to salute the flag was its view that it did not have the competence to interfere with school boards and legislators in matters of educational policy. (If the Court were to act otherwise, Justice Frankfurter had said in *Gobitis,* it would become "the school board for the country.") Jackson, speaking for a new majority, rejected that argument. He emphasized that each citizen is protected by the Bill of Rights against the state itself and all of its creatures, "Boards of Education not excepted." Furthermore, the fact that boards of education *"are educating the young for citizenship is reason for scrupulous protection of Constitutional freedoms of the individual, if we are not to strangle the free mind at its source and teach youth to discount principles of our government as mere platitudes"* (emphasis added).

In the same decision, Jackson made another point that is fundamental to a full understanding not only of the First Amendment but of everything else in the Bill of Rights: "The very purpose of a Bill of Rights was to withdraw certain subjects from the vicissitudes of political controversy, to place them beyond the reach of majorities and officials and to establish them as legal principles to be applied by the courts. *One's right to life, liberty, and property, to free speech, a free press, freedom of worship and assembly, and other fundamental rights may not be submitted to vote; they depend on the outcome of no elections*" (emphasis added).

Jackson went on to what he considered "the very heart" of the *Gobitis* decision, which the Court was now overturning. In that previous ruling the Court had held that "national unity is the basis of national security" and that the authorities therefore have "the right to select appropriate compulsory means for its attainment."

Does the state have the right to go beyond persuasion and example in its desire to attain national unity? Does the state have the right to try to achieve national unity by such means as *compulsory* flag salutes?

No, said Jackson: "Those who begin coercive elimination of dissent soon find themselves exterminating dissenters. Compulsory unification of opinion achieves only the unanimity of the graveyard."

In this country, on the other hand, "the First Amendment to our Constitution was designed to avoid these ends by avoiding these beginnings. . . . We set up government by the consent of the governed, and the Bill of Rights denies those in power any legal opportunity to coerce that consent. Authority here is to be controlled by public opinion, not public opinion by authority."

Accordingly, the West Virginia State Board of Education had acted unconstitutionally in compelling the flag salute because it thereby invaded "the sphere of intellect and spirit which it is the purpose of the First Amendment to our Constitution to reserve from all official control."

Lower courts have used the *West Virginia State Board of Education v. Barnette* decision to support rulings that schools cannot force students to stand during the Pledge of Allegiance because refusing to stand is an expression of political or religious belief and therefore protected by the First Amendment.

In one New York case, a student who did not want to participate in the flag salute on political grounds was ordered by school authorities to leave the room if she refused to stand during the salute; the court said she did not have to stand *or* leave the room. In Arizona, when school officials insisted that students stand during the singing of the national anthem—even when certain pupils claimed that doing so would violate their religious beliefs—the court ruled the order unconstitutional because it interfered with the protesting students' "free exercise" of religion.

The New York case was *Frain* v. *Barron* (1969). Mary Frain, a student at Jamaica High School, had refused to recite the Pledge of Allegiance because she said that to do so would indicate her approval of the government's policies, and she disagreed with some of them. Moreover, for her to stand during the Pledge would imply that she agreed with the words "liberty and justice for all," and she did not agree that all Americans had equal justice. Then why did she not at least leave the room, as ordered, during the Pledge? Because being sent from the classroom was a way of punishing students and stigmatizing them as troublemakers, and she did not believe she should be punished for following her conscience.

The federal district court agreed with Mary Frain, ruling that a student cannot be stigmatized for obeying her conscience rather than obeying school authorities. Accordingly, Mary Frain was allowed to remain seated in the classroom during the Pledge of Allegiance.

In 1977 Deborah Lipp, a sixteen-year-old sophomore at Mountain Lakes High School in New Jersey, became a figure of fierce controversy because of her attitude toward the Pledge of Allegiance. In all other respects, she was a model student, receiving straight A's and working part-time as a teacher's aide, helping eight- and ten-year-olds with perceptual problems.

One day in May, however, a teacher, noting that Deborah was not standing for the Pledge, told her that she must stand and show respect if she wanted to remain at Mountain Lakes High School. The principal backed up the teacher, threatening Deborah with expulsion.

New Jersey State law supported the principal and the teacher. The law stated that students with "conscientious scruples" against saluting the flag or making the Pledge of Allegiance would not have to do either but were required to stand at attention while the Pledge is given "to show full respect to the flag."

Deborah Lipp refused to be intimidated, believing the requirement that she stand was an "absolutely absurd denial of the 'liberty'" promised to everyone by the Pledge of Allegiance. And she quoted Supreme Court Justice William O. Douglas: "The right to dissent is the only thing that makes life tolerable. . . . The affairs of government could not be conducted by democratic standards without it."

With the help of the American Civil Liberties Union, Deborah Lipp went into federal district court to challenge the New Jersey law requiring every student to stand during the Pledge. Her lawyer, Constance Hepburn, cited during her argument a 1973 federal court of appeals decision in a similar case, which held that "the act of standing is itself part of the pledge" and therefore could not be commanded by the state if a student had conscientious objections to reciting the Pledge itself. Said that court in 1973: "Standing in silence is an act that cannot be compelled."

Meanwhile, editorials sharply criticizing Deborah appeared in the local newspapers along with hostile letters to the editor about her and her case. Deborah herself received some supportive mail and phone calls but also many abusive letters and calls that abounded in foul language. There were also bomb threats. Many of these ferocious critics, Deborah noted, "describe themselves as patriots and call me un-American, Communist, and other names. Do they consider harassment and threats of violence more American than lawful use of the U.S. judicial system? I suggest these people reassess their values."

"I've been told I should go to Russia," Deborah wrote in an article for the *New York Daily News.* "Perhaps the people who feel this way—people who don't like to hear different opinions expressed—would feel more at home there. Certainly in Russia I wouldn't have the right to do what I've done here. I have no intention of leaving my country."

But why did she keep refusing at least to stand at attention during the flag salute and Pledge of Allegiance? "The Pledge," wrote Deborah, "states that I am standing for a country of 'liberty and justice for all.' I don't believe that the country exists. I look around me and see every day that blacks, poor people, women, American Indians, atheists, and countless other minorities do not have equal rights under the law. I can't bring myself to believe that 'my standing [during the Pledge] will change the injustice that exists, nor can I close my eyes to that injustice and salute a 'dream' and not do anything to further that dream, as so many people would have me do." Furthermore, she said, forcing her to stand during the Pledge would be an unconstitutional denial of her freedom of expression.

At home, her father, a management official of a computer company, criticized her stand. "He tries to tell me about patriotism," Deborah said. "I don't know how to define that word. If it means love of the Constitution, then I'm patriotic. But if it means love for the country for what it is today—with the ugliness, the poverty, and the government corruption—then I'm not patriotic. But I do love the freedom I have in this country to do what I'm doing right now. I love the freedom to fight a law I don't like. In other countries, I'd have to keep my mouth shut."

In August 1977 a federal judge in Newark overturned the "compulsory standing" New Jersey law because, he said, it compelled Deborah Lipp—and any other student who refused to make the Pledge—to commit an act of "symbolic speech." That is, because the act of standing is itself part of the Pledge, the state, by forcing Deborah to stand, was making her affirm a belief she did not in fact hold. (Among the cases the judge cited was *West Virginia State Board of Education v. Barnette*.) From then on, New Jersey students opposed to the Pledge of Allegiance could remain seated while their classmates recited it and saluted the flag, so long as the seated dissidents did not "whistle, drum, tap dance or otherwise be disruptive."

Deborah was delighted that her faith in the Constitution, "a marvelous, magnificent document," had been redeemed. Looking back at the furor that had attended her exercising her First Amendment rights, Deborah recalled the bumper stickers—SEND THE LIPPS BACK TO SIBERIA—that had appeared around the state. "Well," she said, "I am standing up for my personal beliefs. If I can't do that in New Jersey, then this state isn't as good as Siberia."

Years later, Tisha Byars, whose story I have told, also stood up, in conscience, for *her* belief, and she was vindicated by a federal judge. The late Justice Robert Jackson's language in *West Virginia Board of Education v. Barnette* has become a permanent and vital part of our heritage.

12

FURTHER BOLD ADVENTURES OF MEN
AND WOMEN OF CONSCIENCE

The ordinary man is passive. Within a narrow circle (home life, and perhaps, the trade unions or local politics), he feels himself master of his fate . . . but [otherwise] he simply lies down and lets things happen to him.

GEORGE ORWELL, *INSIDE THE WHALE,* 1940

*A*s has been evident throughout this book, it takes courage—sometimes a lot of courage and fortitude—to act on a matter of conscience. In the case of Vera Katz, a white professor at predominantly black Howard University in Washington, D.C., it required dealing with deeply offensive speech, not by trying to suppress it, but rather by responding to it with more speech—truthful speech.

In addition to Vera Katz, this chapter is about Enrique Oppenheimer, who worked eighteen years for the city of New York and suddenly had to face risking his job—and his reputation—if he refused to attend a mandated sexual harassment prevention training course. Because his religious beliefs prevented him from taking part in such a course, Oppenheimer, despite great pressure, stood his ground.

There are times when *no!* is the most satisfying and strengthening word in the language. Several years ago, as it grew dark on lower Fifth Avenue, I saw a young woman stalked by a creep who began to mutter what must have been some particularly disgusting invitation.

The woman turned around, and in a voice that may have carried well beyond Washington Square, she roared, "No!" We passersby all looked up, but our help wasn't needed. The man scuttled away, and she strode on.

Readers of a certain age may remember C. Wright Mills's saying "no" in the 1950s to any support whatever for the concept and practice of nuclear deterrence. And he went further. He urged the rest of us, especially scientists and intellectuals, to refuse to be "good soldiers" for our country: "If you do not protest, you at least are not responsible for it being done. If you refuse to do so out loud, others may refrain quietly from doing it, and those who still do it may then do it only with hesitation and guilt. . . . To refuse to do it is an act affirming yourself as a moral center of responsible decisions. . . . It reveals the resolution of one human being to take at least his own fate into his own hands."

A. J. Muste, the radical pacifist who became the key strategist of the anti–Vietnam War movement, used to remind his colleagues— and anyone else who wanted to hear—that "this naked human being is the one *real* thing in the face of the machines and the mechanized institutions of our age."

A. J. was a minister who once, leaving the faith for a time, was asked by Leon Trotsky to be his main man in the United States. Although I think A. J. and Enrique Oppenheimer might have had profound differences on the nature of a just society and a just Christianity, they both refused to bend to the "mechanized institutions of our age."

Enrique Oppenheimer is an accountant at New York City's Department of Housing Preservation and Development. I first heard of his refusal to hand over his conscience to his bosses from Ray Kerrison, writing in the *New York Post*. Everyone in the department was ordered to attend a sexual harassment prevention training course. These courses are becoming standard at more and more organizations, particularly law firms, which have taken big financial hits on losing sexual harassment cases.

Oppenheimer is a Pentecostal Christian, and he maintained from the beginning that the government had no right to force him to be immersed in a sexual harassment prevention course: "My religion instructs me as to my moral behavior code. As a practicing Christian,

I take from the Bible the mandate from God as to how to behave with my fellow humans." The state, he added, was trying to force him to participate in indoctrination, but this kind of instruction, he said, "I reserve exclusively for private religious life instruction."

During my conversation with him, I felt Enrique Oppenheimer made an especially telling point, considering his background and the fact that during his eighteen years in government, he had never been accused of sexual harassment or any other untoward behavior.

In view of that personal history, Oppenheimer emphasized, "If I go to that sexual harassment course, I will be contaminated by it." It's as if a group of federal employees were mandated to take a course in sexual harassment from Bill Clinton.

The penalties at the Department of Housing Preservation and Development for refusing to take the sexual harassment course were charges of insubordination; a resultant fine; and reprimand, demotion, or termination.

Oppenheimer was not daunted by these prospects. Indeed, he hoped to convince others to commit civil disobedience as acts of conscience. He wanted to "embolden other people" to resist illegitimate authority. That last phrase had considerable currency during the antiwar movement, but it can apply widely, including in private and public workplaces.

The case raised interesting constitutional issues. Because Oppenheimer worked for a public agency, the First Amendment could come into play concerning its protection of beliefs and therefore of conscience. In this case, Oppenheimer's belief is religious in nature and could bring in the free-exercise-of-religion clause of the First Amendment. In the 1972 case *Wisconsin v. Yoder,* the Supreme Court affirmed the right of the Amish to refuse, under the free-exercise clause, to put their children in state secondary schools. This was a matter of their conscientious beliefs.

On the other hand, the state has a right to show a compelling need that trumps someone's right to say "no!"—even on the basis of conscience. In Oppenheimer's case, the City of New York could claim that in view of the extent of sexual harassment in the workplace—and the harm it does—all employees in a public agency must attend these sessions designed to so sensitize them that they will henceforth abjure

186 ★ NAT HENTOFF

any such behavior. But if a worker has a record entirely free of the merest traces of sexual harassment on the job and outside, does the state have the right to ignore that record and, in this case, ignore Oppenheimer's religious beliefs?

Meanwhile, ten of Oppenheimer's co-workers said they, too, would not attend the course, but eventually they wound up as dutiful students. According to Oppenheimer, "they were intimidated into attending."

Oppenheimer began to go through the disciplinary procedures of the Department of Housing Preservation and Development. He was summoned to a conference and then to another hearing where the department seemed to be willing to make some concessions to this stubborn employee.

Oppenheimer was told that he would be excused from the course if he agreed to having a letter of reprimand placed in his file and if he would read, at his leisure, some material on sexual harassment.

The defendant did not have to ponder the offer. Using the kind of logic with which people of conscience madden their judges, Oppenheimer asked, "Why should I be reprimanded when I have done nothing wrong?"

A pretrial hearing followed. There, this heretic was assured by the head of the tribunal that he was making a big deal out of what really was a minor issue. Oppenheimer hardly ever lets a euphemism go by. "If this isn't a big deal, why am I here?" Why, he added, had he had to go through a continuing series of confrontations? His secular religion being truth and logic, Oppenheimer tried again to make his case: "I didn't have to wait eighteen years for the government to tell me how to behave toward women. I conduct my life according to my religious beliefs. It is not a part-time thing. It is everything in my life. I explained this at every hearing, but it did not matter to them."

There was, of course, yet another hearing. Franz Kafka knew the drill. This time, an administrative law judge was in charge, and he was somewhat embarrassed. He admitted that he also, as an administrative judge was an employee of the department. But he never—no, never— attended the training course on sexual harassment prevention.

The department's case against Oppenheimer began to unravel. It was disclosed that not only the administrative judge but also a sizable number of other employees had silently escaped, one way or another, the training sessions.

As this was being revealed, Enrique Oppenheimer sat in the hearing room, Bible in hand. Also sitting there were his witnesses, among them his pastor and a woman who had worked with him for years and was ready and willing to testify as to his character.

Robert Lashaw, Oppenheimer's diligent attorney, took up the narrative: "After an hour so of testimony and cross-examination, the lawyer for the department announced that the Department of Housing Preservation and Development did not want to prosecute this person anymore." How could the department make a conviction stick when others had, with impunity, also not taken this mandatory course?

Still, they had to do something to this heretic. The deal was that he would be free of all penalties if he agreed to receive some written materials on sexual harassment. But—and here is the bureaucratic mind in full spin—Oppenheimer did not have to take any tests on the material. Obviously, then, he did not have to read it.

Enrique Oppenheimer accepted the department's sword of surrender. There is no charge of insubordination on his record. His record is as pure as ever.

In 1952 A. J. Muste, in the essay "Of Holy Disobedience," spoke of Georges Bernanos, the novelist, who refused to stay in France under the Nazis. One of the Bernanos passages quoted by A. J. is not without contemporary relevance: "The moment, perhaps, is not far off when it will seem as natural for us to leave the front-door key in the lock at night so the police may enter, at any hour of the day or night." (Remember the Bill Clinton–endorsed proposal that people who live in public housing projects should sign an agreement allowing the police, *without a warrant,* to enter at any time to seize drugs and perpetrators? Our irrelevant attorney general, Janet Reno, did not object.)

There is another Bernanos warning that I quoted for years at the end of every lecture I gave. It comes from his book, published here in 1952, *Tradition of Freedom:*

I have thought for a long time now that if, some day, the increasing efficiency of the technique of destruction finally causes our species to disappear from the earth, it will not be cruelty that will be responsible . . . but the docility, the lack of responsibility of the modern man—his base, subservient acceptance of every common decree.

The horrors which we have seen, the still greater horrors we shall presently see, are not signs that rebels—insubordinate, untameable men—are increasing in numbers throughout the world, but rather that there is a constant increase, a stupendously rapid increase, in the number of obedient docile men.

"Who caught and killed Nat Turner?"

"Jews!"

"Who controls the Federal Reserve?"

"Jews!"

"You're not afraid to say it, are you?"

"Jews! Jews!"

"Who controls the media and Hollywood?"

"Jews!"

"Who has our entertainers, our athletes, in a vise grip?"

"Jews!"

"Am I lying?"

"No!"

—LAW STUDENT MALIK ZULU SHABAZZ, LEADING A CROWD
OF A THOUSAND—AT LEAST HALF OF THEM STUDENTS—
AT HOWARD UNIVERSITY, FEBRUARY 23, 1994

When I was a kid, I lost a couple of teeth one night when a blunt object crashed into my face. It was the fist of an Irish anti-Semite. It seemed I had killed Christ.

So I hated the Irish, except for James Joyce, and he was dead. But then, at Boston Public Latin School, I became friendly with an Irish classmate, and we stayed friends the six years we were both there.

That friendship taught me something about stereotypes. I learned even more about how stupid they are when Frances Sweeney, the contagiously independent editor of a muckraking newspaper in Boston that exposed and denounced anti-Semites, gave me my first job as a reporter. There was no pay, except for the glory of working for her. She was not only Irish, but a devout Roman Catholic—another stereotype dismantled.

The preceding litany of poisonous stereotypes of Jews is not a rehearsal of a play based on a Nazi Nuremberg rally of the 1930s. Malik Zulu Shabazz, the law student who led the call-and-response rhythms of hatred, was a warm-up speaker that evening at Howard University for the Nation of Islam's most notorious messenger, Khallid Abdul Muhammad, who, in his public appearances, parades his anti-Semitism, anti-Catholicism, homophobia, and racist views of whites. And that night at Howard University he kept on stoking his bigotry.

Although a number of the students cheered on Khallid Abdul Muhammad, not all of the students agreed with the Goebbels-like display of anti-Semitism. In a report in the *Chronicle of Higher Education* on free speech at Howard, Maurice Dolberry, a junior majoring in biology, wrote the following: "One of the things the Nation of Islam says is that a white person wouldn't be mistreated by blacks because it is not a black person's nature to mistreat someone. But in the next breath, they'll be calling white people 'crackers' and 'devils.' I know Jewish people I like, and Jewish people I don't like. I let people's actions speak for them."

Still, on that night at Howard University, those Roman candles of pure anti-Semitism were traumatic for many Jews around the country who became aware of them through newspapers and television. A thousand people at the rally—mostly black, half of them students— sounded like brownshirts, Nazi sympathizers, in Yorkville, New York, in the 1930s.

One person who was stunned at the machine-gun stereotyping of Jews during that gathering was a Howard University professor named Vera Katz. For the past quarter century she had taught acting and directing in the university's Department of Theater Arts. Among her black students have been Lynn Whitfield (who played in *The Josephine Baker Story*), Charles Brown (from the television sitcom *Here and Now*), choreographer Debbie Allen, and Allen's sister Phylicia Rashad (who, as Clare Huxtable, played opposite Bill Cosby in one of the most popular series in television history).

Vera Katz started teaching at Howard soon after the assassination of Martin Luther King. In a 1990 interview with a reporter for the campus newspaper, the *Hilltop*, Katz recalled, "It was a very angry time. There was a lot of hostility toward me. From some of the black faculty as well as students."

The message she got was that nobody at Howard wanted her there. Tires on her car were regularly deflated. "I was threatened with a knife," she remembered. "And I was spat on one time when I crossed the yard. I used to cry a lot." She also spent a lot of time at the Howard University library learning about black history and black theater.

Vera Katz's mother urged her to quit her teaching post at Howard, but that is not Vera Katz's style. So she stayed. "I learned a lot about myself by being here, and I learned a lot about what it is to be Jewish."

What she learned became vividly evident following the anti-Semitic rally at Howard. "After that night, I came in to work upset and in a rage." To members of the faculty she knew, she said, "Well, here I am, Miss Bloodsucker!" (a reference to Khallid Abdul Muhammad's mention of Jews sucking the blood out of black communities).

Some of Vera Katz's colleagues asked her why she was so upset After all, the law student leading the anti-Semitic fugue was a fanatic, they said.

"It wasn't just him," she answered. "A lot of people were cheering him."

Vera Katz had three classes that day. In each one she taught about stereotypes. "Look at me!" she said to her students at the start of each class. "Look at me! You know me! Am I a bloodsucker?"

She told me, "My students had to look at me. They had to see me *as a human being.* They had to realize they were being taught by a Jewish lady who had been devoted to teaching students at Howard for a quarter of a century."

She told her students how hurt she was that her heritage as a Jew was being maligned and scorned. "I underscored how much they respected their own heritage and their own ancestors. And I told them that having studied their history and culture I also have great reverence for *their* ancestors.

"I also told them I hoped they could see that there are Jews who have fought in the civil rights movement and Jews who teach in inner cities now. I mean Jews who are not just helping but are *interacting with* African Americans."

In response, one of her students said—and he was joined by most of the others—that "it's terrible when you indict a whole group of people. Like how *all* African Americans often get indicted on the news programs for what only some African Americans do. Our whole race is judged by what those people do."

"I know, Professor Katz," a student said, "You can't judge all Jews by what some do. There are many different kinds of Jews."

Sean Wingate, an eighteen-year-old freshman, had told a reporter from the *New York Times* that he was disturbed because some black students, as a test of solidarity, felt they had to agree with—go along with—the anti-Semitism. "They say," Sean Wingate pointed out, "that African-Americans shouldn't think independently because that leads to divisions in the black community."

Wingate shook his head, thinking about this call that all black students should think alike. "But," he said, "how then can we think at all?"

Vera Katz told me that Wingate had said much the same thing in one of her classes. "And he was *heard,*" she emphasized.

There were students in her classes who strongly supported the Nation of Islam. "A very bright young lady in my directing class," Katz said, "spoke of the positive things the Nation of Islam has done. I told her I certainly agree. I recalled that in the late 1960s, when I first came to Howard, I had students who had been into drugs and were straightened out by members of the Nation of Islam. I respected that, I told her, and I said that I wasn't going to indict the entire Nation of Islam because of a particular strain in it."

I asked the professor if she had seen any effects of her teaching about stereotypes after the anti-Semitic rally on campus.

"Some of the students who didn't know me well," she said, "seem to be working harder in class now. They seem to be more open and honest with me. I think that's because I was with them after that rally."

One of her students told a reporter from the *Washington Jewish Week* that Professor Katz "comes from a very honest place. She cares about me as a person, so I am more susceptible to her criticism."

To her students at Howard, therefore, Vera Katz, by honestly relating her reactions to the anti-Semitic rally on campus, was able to cut through the stereotypes of those bigots. And she was able to challenge her students to think for themselves rather than to join, on the basis of solidarity, in the vicious bigotry being spread by some of the other students on campus. Vera Katz used her right to speak to open, rather than to close, minds.

13

SUPREME COURT JUSTICE
ANTHONY KENNEDY

"The Constitution needs renewal and understanding each generation, or else it's not going to last."

In 1878 British Prime Minister William Gladstone called the United States Constitution "the most wonderful work ever struck off at a given time by the brain and purpose of man."

To ensure that this "most wonderful work" would continue to function in ways that would be fair to all Americans, the framers, responding to the demands of the first Americans to be independent of the British Crown, created the First Amendment.

Without freedom of speech and assembly, protests against injustice would be difficult to sustain because established centers of power would suppress them. As Justice Brennan used to say, all our liberties flow from the First Amendment.

Yet this part of the Constitution, as well as many other parts, is largely misunderstood—or not known about at all—by many Americans. As Richard Harwood, the *Washington Post* columnist put it, "Americans, in the mass, believe in 'free speech' and a 'free press' only in theory. In practice they reject them."

I have pointed out throughout this book the difficulties that men and women of conscience—also a First Amendment freedom of belief—have had in maintaining their integrity against the disapproval of the majority. The difficulties have been many and recurring. It is important to note, however, that one of the abiding myths among many liberals in that only those of the political and religious Right are suppressors of free speech and free expression.

The fallacy of that belief struck me with particular force some years ago when I arrived at the small town of Coeur d'Alene in northern Idaho. I was scheduled to speak at a local college on freedom of speech that evening. A civil war was raging in the town over whether a series of reading textbooks, called *Impressions,* were to be used in the public schools. The books included stories and poems that were regarded by some parents and ministers as proselytizing for witchcraft, satanism, and the occult (as later in Grand Saline, Texas).

That afternoon the leader of the opposition, a young bearded lay minister, a carpenter by trade, asked to speak with me. Along with members of his flock, he came to where I was staying.

We talked for some time about the *Impressions* books. Neither of us persuaded the other to reconsider our opinion about even a single paragraph. I told him that when I was a kid, I devoured every book of fairy tales I could find in the public library *because* of the witchcraft and the demons in them. They did me no harm, so far as I could tell.

"But how could you know," he said, "the harm such stories and books do to children more vulnerable than you were?"

Before he left, the minister pointed in the direction of the college where I was going to speak in a few hours and said, "The people who will come to hear you, including the people at this college, think that I—and the people who believe as I do—are kooks, religious nuts. And so they don't think we should have any First Amendment rights. But freedom of speech is for everyone, isn't it?"

In fact, some of the faculty members at the college did indeed believe that the minister and his allies were so consumed by religious zealotry that, in the context of book selection for the public schools, they were demanding that the Constitution be violated. And so the speech of this group, who were in opposition, did not merit attention, if it should have a forum at all.

I told those professors—not all of them wanted to silence the minister—that any attempt to limit the minister's speech would be a violation of the First Amendment. For the rest of my stay in Coeur d'Alene, I became a person under, suspicion by members of both sides of the debate—those who wanted to censor the *Impressions* books and those who wanted to censor the minister.

In 1989 I became even more aware of the disdain for free expression by many liberals, including young people on the Left. Canetta Ivy, a leader of the student government at Stanford and a major in African American studies, declared, "We don't put as many restrictions on freedom of speech as we should."

A few years later, an ecumenical letter appeared in the *Stanford Daily* signed by the Black Law Students Association, the Asian American Law Students Association, and the Jewish Law Students Association. They sternly called for harsh penalties for offensive speech.

Traveling to various campuses, public and private, I heard from students who had censored themselves after asking such questions as the following in class and elsewhere: Is it fair that some of the students benefiting from affirmative action scholarships come from black middle-class homes? After being called racists, those critical students preferred to escape into silence.

The hunters of bad speech, on the faculty and among the students throughout the country, were and are liberals. In my younger days, contempt for the "wrong" kind of speech came from such warriors of the Right as FBI director J. Edgar Hoover. When I finally got to read my FBI files, I found them full of articles I'd written and petitions I'd signed against the Vietnam War. Some of them had been sent directly to the ever vigilant director of the Bureau, with sulfurous notes from FBI field agents.

These days, the political and religious Right make themselves vigorously heard attacking "inappropriate" books in school libraries; inflammatory rap recordings; and perniciously infectious television programs. Some of these watchdogs say they don't intend to censor; however, their aim *is* to censure, and they clearly want to censure their targets out of existence. They don't believe the First Amendment could possibly apply to speech and expression *they* don't like.

Meanwhile, liberal critics of an unfettered First Amendment are growing in number and influence. In a 1997 edition of the *Columbia Journalism Review,* Floyd Abrams, who has often appeared on behalf

196 ★ NAT HENTOFF

of the First Amendment before the Supreme Court, wrote an article titled "Look Who's Trashing the First Amendment."

He cited a declaration by the editors of the *Nation* a proudly liberal publication for many years, that the First Amendment is being used "to thwart progressive reforms such as caps (limits) on campaign spending, public access to the airwaves, and regulation of cigarette advertising." In all these battles, these editors complained, "the wrong side kept winding up with the First Amendment in its corner."

But any corner can use the First Amendment, which doesn't mean that corner will always prevail. If a product is legal, its producers have the right to advertise. (Congress has never made cigarettes illegal as a menace to public health.) Requiring public access to the airwaves puts the government in a position to control part of the content of broadcasting, thereby violating the First Amendment rights of the broadcasters. As for campaign finances, the Supreme Court has declared that contributions to political campaigns can be, with exceptions, a form of free speech.

Yale law professor Owen Fiss is among the non-right-wingers cited by Floyd Abrams who want to constrict free speech. "To serve the ultimate purpose of the First Amendment," Professor Fiss said, "we may sometimes find it necessary to restrict the speech of some elements of our society in order to enhance the relatively [unrepresented] voices of others."

"We must destroy the village," an American army officer said during the Vietnam War, "in order to save it."

Fiss was speaking specifically of restrictions on campaign expenditures. But who will draw these rules of law allowing some people to speak—and not others?

Another believer in using the good-faith offices of government to "enhance" the distribution of free speech through regulation is University of Chicago professor and constitutional law scholar (!) Cass Sunstein.

Wrote Floyd Abrams: "According to Sunstein, the government . . . should be permitted to require the news media to provide a 'right of reply to dissenting views'; and to impose on public universities significant limitations on 'hate speech' on campus."

For government to mandate that the press provide "a right of reply" involves—just as "public access to the airwaves" does—government violation of the First Amendment rights of the press. The idea of a "right of reply" would almost certainly get a large majority vote in a poll of the public. But the First Amendment was not intended to be subject to a vote—or to a revision by a law professor.

Floyd Abrams, aware of the increasing number of "summer soldiers" of the First Amendment, emphasized has point: "It is at the very heart of the First Amendment to deny government the authority to pick and choose among speakers and messages, determining that some may, and others may not, be heard—and how often."

In 1989 Canetta Ivy, insisting that the First Amendment is too generous in its protections of speech, may have been prophetic. Conservatives and liberals, though different in their priorities and strategies, are not averse to uniting against freedom of expression.

It's worth reemphasizing Supreme Court justice Anthony Kennedy's warning: "The Constitution needs renewal and understanding each generation, or else *it's not going to last.*"

At the beginning of this constitutional democracy, one of the framers, Benjamin Franklin, was asked in 1787, "What have you given us?"

"A republic," the eighty-one-year-old Franklin answered. "If you can keep it."

Unless more Americans *know* the Constitution and live the Bill of Rights, the future of the nation as a strongly functioning constitutional democracy will be at risk.

It is also worth recalling a warning that could be a prophecy spoken by Justice William O. Douglas:

> The Constitution and the Bill of Rights were designed to get Government off the backs of the people—all the people. Those great documents . . . guarantee to us all the rights to personal and spiritual self-fulfillment. But that guarantee is not self-executing.
>
> As nightfall does not come all at once, neither does oppression. In both instances, there is a twilight when everything remains seemingly unchanged. And it is in such twilight that we all must be most aware of change in the air—however slight—lest we become unwitting victims of the darkness.

★ THE CONSTITUTION OF THE ★ UNITED STATES OF AMERICA

$\mathcal{W}$e the People of the United States, in Order to form a more perfect Union, establish Justice, insure domestic Tranquility, provide for the common defence, promote the general Welfare, and secure the Blessings of Liberty to ourselves and our Posterity, do ordain and establish this Constitution for the United States of America.

ARTICLE I.

Section 1. All legislative Powers herein granted shall be vested in a Congress of the United States, which shall consist of a Senate and House of Representatives.

Section 2. [1] The House of Representatives shall be composed of Members chosen every second Year by the People of the several States, and the Electors in each State shall have the Qualifications requisite for Electors of the most numerous Branch of the State Legislature.

[2] No Person shall be a Representative who shall not have attained to the Age of twenty-five Years, and been seven Years a Citizen of the United States, and who shall not, when elected, be an Inhabitant of that State in which he shall be chosen.

[Representatives and direct Taxes shall be apportioned among the several States which may be included within this Union, according to their respective Numbers, which shall be determined by adding to the whole Number of free Persons, including those bound to Service for a Term of Years, and excluding Indians not taxed, three fifths of all other Persons.] *(Note: changed by section 2 of the Fourteenth Amendment.)* The actual Enumeration shall be made within three

Years after the first Meeting of the Congress of the United States, and within every subsequent Term of ten Years, in such Manner as they shall by Law direct. The number of Representatives shall not exceed one for every thirty Thousand, but each State shall have at Least one Representative; and until such enumeration shall be made, the State of New Hampshire shall be entitled to chuse three, Massachusetts eight, Rhode-Island and Providence Plantations one, Connecticut five, New-York six, New Jersey four, Pennsylvania eight, Delaware one, Maryland six, Virginia ten, North Carolina five, South Carolina five, and Georgia three.

When vacancies happen in the Representation from any state, the Executive Authority thereof shall issue Writs of Election to fill such Vacancies.

The House of Representatives shall chuse their Speaker and other Officers; and shall have the sole Power of Impeachment.

Section 3. [1] The Senate of the United States shall be composed of two Senators from each State, [chosen by the Legislature thereof,] *(Note: changed by the Seventeenth Amendment)* for six Years; and each Senator shall have one Vote.

[2] Immediately after they shall be assembled in Consequence of the first Election, they shall be divided as equally as may be into three Classes. The Seats of the Senators of the first Class shall be vacated at the Expiration of the second Year, of the second Class at the Expiration of the fourth Year, and of the third Class at the Expiration of the sixth Year, so that one third may be chosen every second Year; [and if Vacancies happen by Resignation, or otherwise, during the Recess of the Legislature of any State, the Executive thereof may make temporary Appointments until the next Meeting of the Legislature, which shall then fill such Vacancies.] *(Note: changed by the Seventeenth Amendment)*

[3] No Person shall be a Senator who shall not have attained to the Age of thirty Years, and been nine Years a Citizen of the United States, and who shall not, when elected, be an Inhabitant of that State for which he shall be chosen.

[4] The Vice President of the United States shall be President of the Senate, but shall have no Vote, unless they be equally divided.

[5] The Senate shall chuse their other Officers, and also a

President pro tempore, in the Absence of the Vice President, or when he shall exercise the Office of President of the United States.

[6] The Senate shall have the sole Power to try all Impeachments. When sitting for that Purpose, they shall be on Oath or Affirmation. When the President of the United States is tried, the Chief Justice shall preside: And no Person shall be convicted without the Concurrence of two thirds of the Members present.

[7] Judgment in Cases of Impeachment shall not extend further than to removal from Office, and disqualification to hold and enjoy any Office of honor, Trust or Profit under the United States: but the Party convicted shall nevertheless be liable and subject to Indictment, Trial, Judgment and Punishment, according to Law.

Section 4. [1] The Times, Places and Manner of holding Elections for Senators and Representatives, shall be prescribed in each State by the Legislature thereof; but the Congress may at any time by Law make or alter such Regulations, except as to the Places of chusing Senators.

The Congress shall assemble at least once in every Year, and such Meeting shall be [on the first Monday in December,] *(Note: changed by section 2 of the Twentieth Amendment)* unless they shall by Law appoint a different Day.

Section 5. Each House shall be the Judge of the Elections, Returns and Qualifications of its own Members, and a Majority of each shall constitute a Quorum to do Business; but a small Number may adjourn from day to day, and may be authorized to compel the Attendance of absent Members, in such Manner, and under such Penalties as each House may provide.

Each House may determine the Rules of its Proceedings, punish its Members for disorderly Behaviour, and, with the Concurrence of two thirds, expel a Member.

Each House shall keep a Journal of its Proceedings, and from time to time publish the same, excepting such Parts as may in their Judgment require Secrecy; and the Yeas and Nays of the Members of either House on any question shall, at the Desire of one fifth of those Present, be entered on the Journal.

Neither House, during the Session of Congress, shall, without the Consent of the other, adjourn for more than three days, nor to any other Place than that in which the two Houses shall be sitting.

Section 6. The Senators and Representatives shall receive a Compensation for their Services, to be ascertained by Law, and paid out of the Treasury of the United States. They shall in all Cases, except Treason, Felony and Breach of the Peace, be privileged from Arrest during their Attendance at the Session of their respective Houses, and in going to and returning from the same; and for any Speech or Debate in either House, they shall not be questioned in any other Place.

No Senator or Representative shall, during the Time for which he was elected, be appointed to any civil Office under the Authority of the United States, which shall have been created, or the Emoluments whereof shall have been encreased during such time; and no Person holding any Office under the United States, shall be a Member of either House during his Continuance in Office.

Section 7. All Bills for raising Revenue shall originate in the House of Representatives; but the Senate may propose or concur with Amendments as on other Bills.

Every Bill which shall have passed the House of Representatives and the Senate, shall, before it becomes a Law, be presented to the President of the United States; If he approve he shall sign it, but if not he shall return it, with his Objections to that House in which it shall have originated, who shall enter the Objections at large on their Journal, and proceed to reconsider it. If after such Reconsideration two thirds of that House shall agree to pass the Bill, it shall be sent, together with the Objections, to the other House, by which it shall likewise be reconsidered, and if approved by two thirds of that House, it shall become a Law. But in all such Cases the Votes of both Houses shall be determined by yeas and Nays, and the Names of the Persons voting for and against the Bill shall be entered on the Journal of each House respectively. If any Bill shall not be returned by the President within ten Days (Sundays excepted) after it shall have been presented to him, the Same shall be a Law, in like Manner as if he had signed it, unless the Congress by their Adjournment prevent its Return, which Case it shall not be a Law.

Every Order, Resolution, or Vote to which the Concurrence of the Senate and House of Representatives may be necessary (except on a question of Adjournment) shall be presented to the President of the United States; and before the Same shall take Effect, shall be approved by him, or being disapproved by him, shall be repassed by two thirds of the Senate and House of Representatives, according to the Rules and Limitation prescribed in the Case of a Bill.

Section 8. The Congress shall have Power To lay and collect Taxes, Duties, Imposts and Excises, to pay the Debts and provide for the common Defence and general Welfare of the United States; but all Duties, Imposts and Excises shall be uniform throughout the United States;

To borrow Money on the credit of the United States;

To regulate Commerce with foreign Nations, and among the several States, and with the Indian Tribes;

To establish a uniform Rule of Naturalization, and uniform Laws on the subject of Bankruptcies througout the United States;

To coin Money, regulate the Value thereof, and of foreign Coin, and fix the Standard of Weights and Measures;

To provide for the Punishment of counterfeiting the Securities and current Coin of the United States;

To establish Post Offices and post Roads;

To promote the Progress of Science and useful Arts, by securing for limited Times to Authors and Inventors the exclusive Right to their respective Writings and Discoveries;

To constitute Tribunals inferior to the supreme Court;

To define and punish Piracies and Felonies committed on the high Seas, and Offenses against the Law of Nations;

To declare War, grant Letters of Marque and Reprisal, and make Rules concerning Captures on Land and Water;

To raise and support Armies, but no Appropriation of Money to that Use shall be for a longer Term than two Years;

To provide and maintain a Navy;

To make Rules for the Government and Regulation of the land and naval Forces;

To provide for calling forth the Militia to execute the Laws of the Union, suppress Insurrections and repel Invasions;

To provide for organizing, arming, and disciplining, the Militia, and for governing such Part of them as may be employed in the Service of the United States, reserving to the States respectively, the Appointment of the Officers, and the Authority of training the Militia according to the discipline prescribed by Congress;

To exercise exclusive Legislation in all Cases whatsoever, over such District (not exceeding ten Miles square) as may, by Cession of particular States, and the Acceptance of Congress, become the Seat of the Government of the United States, and to exercise like Authority over all Places purchased by the Consent of the Legislature of the State in which the Same shall be, for the Erection of Forts, Magazines, Arsenals, dock-Yards and other needful Buildings;—And

To make all Laws which shall be necessary and proper for carrying into Execution the foregoing Powers, and all other Powers vested by this Constitution in the Government of the United States, or in any Department or Officer thereof.

Section 9. The Migration or Importation of such Persons as any of the States now existing shall think proper to admit, shall not be prohibited by the Congress prior to the Year one thousand eight hundred and eight, but a Tax or duty may be imposed on such Importation, not exceeding ten dollars for each Person.

The Privilege of the Writ of Habeas Corpus shall not be suspended, unless when in Cases of Rebellion or Invasion the public Safety may require it.

No Bill of Attainder or ex post facto Law shall be passed.

No Capitation, or other direct, Tax shall be laid, unless in Proportion to the Census or Enumeration herein before directed to be taken. *(Note: see the Sixteenth Amendment.)*

No Tax or Duty shall be laid on Articles exported from any State.

No Preference shall be given by any Regulation of Commerce or Revenue to the Ports of one State over those of another: nor shall Vessels bound to, or from, one State, be obliged to enter, clear, or pay Duties in another.

No Money shall be drawn from the Treasury, but in Consequence of Appropriations made by Law; and a regular Statement and Account of the Receipts and Expenditures of all public Money shall be published from time to time.

No Title of Nobility shall be granted by the United States: And no Person holding any Office of Profit or Trust under them, shall, without the Consent of the Congress, accept of any present, Emolument, Office, or Title, of any kind whatever, from any King, Prince, or foreign State.

Section 10. No State shall enter into any Treaty Alliance, or Confederation; grant Letters of Marque and Reprisal; coin Money; emit Bills of Credit; make any Thing but gold and silver Coin a Tender in Payment of Debts; pass any Bill of Attainder, ex post facto Law, or Law impairing the Obligation of Contracts, or grant any Title of Nobility.

No State shall, without the Consent of the Congress, lay any Imposts or Duties on Imports or Exports, except what may be absolutely necessary for executing it's inspection Laws: and the net Produce of all duties and Imposts, laid by any State on Imports or Exports, shall be for the Use of the Treasury of the United States; and all such Laws shall be subject to the Revision and Controul of the Congress.

No State shall, without the Consent of Congress, lay any Duty of Tonnage, keep Troops, or Ships of War in time of Peace, enter into any Agreement or Compact with another State, or with a foreign Power, or engage in War, unless actually invaded, or in such imminent Danger as will not admit of delay.

ARTICLE II.

Section 1. The executive Power shall be vested in a President of the United States of America. He shall hold his Office during the Term of four Years, and, together with the Vice President, chosen for the same Term, be elected, as follows:

Each State shall appoint, in such Manner as the Legislature thereof may direct, a Number of Electors, equal to the whole Number of Senators and Representatives to which the State may be entitled in the Congress: but no Senator or Representative, or Person holding an Office of Trust or Profit under the United States, shall be appointed an Elector.

[The Electors shall meet in their respective States, and vote by Ballot for two Persons, of whom one at least shall not be an Inhabitant of the same State with themselves. And they shall make a List of all the Persons voted for, and of the Number of Votes for each; which List they shall sign and certify, and transmit sealed to the Seat of the Government of the United States, directed to the President of the

Senate. The President of the Senate shall, in the Presence of the Senate and House of Representatives, open all the Certificates, and the Votes shall then be counted. The Person having the greatest Number of Votes shall be the President, if such Number be a Majority of the whole Number of Electors appointed; and if there be more than one who have such Majority, and have an equal Number of Votes, then the House of Representatives shall immediately chuse by Ballot one of them for President; and if no Person have a Majority, then from the five highest on the List the said House shall in like Manner chuse the President. But in chusing the President, the Votes shall be taken by States, the Representation from each State have one Vote; A quorum for this Purpose shall consist of a Member or Members from two thirds of the States, and a Majority of all the States shall be necessary to a Choice. In every Case, after the Choice of the President, the Person having the greatest Number of Votes of the Electors shall be the Vice President. But if there should remain two or more who have equal Votes, the Senate shall chuse from them by Ballot the Vice President.] *(Note: Changed by the Twelfth Amendment.)*

The Congress may determine the Time of chusing the Electors, and the Day on which they shall give their Votes; which Day shall be the same throughout the United States.

No Person except a natural born Citizen, or a Citizen of the United States, at the time of the Adoption of this Constitution, shall be eligible to the Office of President; neither shall any person be eligible to that Office who shall not have attained to the Age of thirty five Years, and been fourteen Years a Resident within the United States.

[In Case of the Removal of the President from Office, or of his Death, Resignation, or Inability to discharge the Powers and Duties of the said Office, the Same shall devolve on the Vice President, and the Congress may by Law provide for the Case of Removal, Death, Resignation or Inability, both of the President and Vice President, declaring what Officer shall then act as President, and such Officer shall act accordingly, until the Disability be removed, or a President shall be elected.] *(Note: Changed by the Twenty-fifth Amendment.)*

The President shall, at stated Times, receive for his Services, a Compensation, which shall neither be increased nor diminished during the Period for which he shall have been elected, and he shall not receive within that Period any other Emolument from the United States, or any of them.

Before he enters on the Execution of his Office, he shall take the following Oath or Affirmation:—"I do solemnly swear (or affirm) that I will faithfully execute the Office of President of the United States, and will to the best of my Ability, preserve, protect and defend the Constitution of the United States."

Section 2. The President shall be Commander in Chief of the Army and Navy of the United States, and of the Militia of the several States, when called into the actual Service of the United States; he may require the Opinion, in writing, of the principal Officer in each of the executive Departments, upon any Subject relating to the Duties of their respective Offices, and he shall have Power to grant Reprieves and Pardons for Offenses against the United States, except in Cases of Impeachment.

He shall have Power, by and with the Advice and Consent of the Senate, to make Treaties, provided two thirds of the Senators present concur; and he shall nominate, and by and with the Advice and Consent of the Senate, shall appoint Ambassadors, other public Ministers and Consuls, Judges of the supreme Court, and all other Officers of the United States, whose Appointments are not herein otherwise provided for, and which shall be established by Law: but the Congress may by Law vest the Appointment of such inferior Officers, as they think proper, in the President alone, in the Courts of Law, or in the Heads of Departments.

The President shall have Power to fill up all Vacancies that may happen during the Recess of the Senate, by granting Commissions which shall expire at the End of their next Session.

Section 3. He shall from time to time give to the Congress Information of the State of the Union, and recommend to their Consideration such Measures as he shall judge necessary and expedient; he may, on extraordinary Occasions, convene both Houses, or either of them, and in Case of Disagreement between them, with Respect to the Time of Adjournment, he may adjourn them to such Time as he shall think proper; he shall receive Ambassadors and other public Ministers; he shall take Care that the Laws be faithfully executed, and shall Commission all the Officers of the United States.

Section 4. The President, Vice President and all civil Officers of the United States, shall be removed from Office on Impeachment for, and Conviction of, Treason, Bribery, or other high Crimes and Misdemeanors.

ARTICLE III.

Section 1. The judicial Power of the United States, shall be vested in one supreme Court, and in such inferior Courts as the Congress may from time to time ordain and establish. The Judges, both of the supreme and inferior Courts, shall hold their Offices during good Behaviour, and shall, at stated Times, receive for their Services, a Compensation, which shall not be diminished during their Continuance in Office.

Section 2. The judicial Power shall extend to all Cases, in Law and Equity, arising under this Constitution, the Laws of the United States, and Treaties made, or which shall be made, under their Authority;—to all Cases affecting Ambassadors, other public Ministers and Consuls;—to all Cases of admiralty and maritime Jurisdiction;—to Controversies to which the United States shall be a Party;—to Controversies between two or more States;—[between a State and Citizens of another State;—] *(Note: changed by the Eleventh Amendment)* between Citizens of Different States,—between Citizens of the same State claiming Lands under Grants of different States, [and between a State, or the Citizens thereof, and foreign States, Citizens or Subjects.] *(Note: changed by the Eleventh Amendment.)*

In all Cases affecting Ambassadors, other public Ministers and Consuls, and those in which a State shall be Party, the supreme Court shall have original Jurisdiction. In all the other Cases before mentioned, the Supreme Court shall have appellate Jurisdiction, both as to Law and Fact, with such Exceptions, and under such Regulations as the Congress shall make.

The Trial of all Crimes, except in Cases of Impeachment; shall be by Jury; and such Trial shall be held in the State where the said Crimes shall have been committed; but when not committed within any State, the Trial shall be at such Place or Places as the Congress may by Law have directed.

Section 3. Treason against the United States, shall consist only in levying War against them, or in adhering to their Enemies, giving them Aid and Comfort. No Person shall be convicted of Treason unless on the Testimony of two Witnesses to the same overt Act, or on Confession in open Court.

The Congress shall have Power to declare the Punishment of Treason, but no Attainder of Treason shall work Corruption of Blood, or Forfeiture except during the Life of the Person attainted.

ARTICLE IV.

Section 1. Full Faith and Credit shall be given in each State to the public Acts, Records, and judicial Proceedings of every other State; And the Congress may by general Laws prescribe the Manner in which such Acts, Records and Proceedings shall be proved, and the Effect thereof.

Section 2. The Citizens of each State shall be entitled to all Privileges and Immunities of Citizens in the several States.

A Person charged in any State with Treason, Felony, or other Crime, who shall flee from Justice, and be found in another State, shall on Demand of the executive Authority of the State from which he fled, be delivered up, to be removed to the State having Jurisdiction of the Crime.

[No Person held to Service or Labour in one State, under the Laws thereof, escaping into another, shall, in Consequence of any Law or Regulation therein, be discharged from such Service or Labour, but shall be delivered up on Claim of the Party to whom such Service or Labour may be due.] *(Note: changed by the Thirteenth Amendment.)*

Section 3. New States may be admitted by the Congress into this Union; but no new State shall be formed or erected within the Jurisdiction of any other State; nor any State be formed by the Junction of two or more States, or Parts of States, without the Consent of the Legislatures of the States concerned as well as of the Congress. The Congress shall have Power to dispose of and make all needful Rules and Regulations respecting the Territory or other Property belonging to the United States; and nothing in this Constitution shall be so construed as to Prejudice any Claims of the United States, or of any particular State.

Section 4. The United States shall guarantee to every State in this Union a Republican Form of Government, and shall protect each of them against Invasion; and on Application of the Legislature, or of the Executive (when the Legislature cannot be convened) against domestic Violence.

ARTICLE V.

The Congress, whenever two thirds of both Houses shall deem it necessary, shall propose Amendments to this Constitution, or, on the Application of the Legislatures of two thirds of the several States, shall call a Convention for proposing Amendments, which, in either Case, shall be valid to all Intents and Purposes, as Part of this Constitution, when ratified by the Legislatures of three fourths of the several States, or by Conventions in three fourths thereof, as the one or the other Mode of Ratification may be proposed by the Congress; Provided that no Amendment which may be made prior to the Year One thousand eight hundred and eight shall in any Manner affect the first and fourth Clauses in the Ninth Section of the first Article; and that no State, without its Consent, shall be deprived of its equal Suffrage in the Senate.

ARTICLE VI.

All Debts contracted and Engagements entered into, before the Adoption of this Constitution, shall be as valid against the United States under this Constitution, as under the Confederation.

This Constitution, and the Laws of the United States which shall be made in Pursuance thereof; and all Treaties made, or which shall be made, under the Authority of the United States, shall be the supreme Law of the Land; and the Judges in every State shall be bound thereby, any Thing in the Constitution or Laws of any State to the Contrary notwithstanding.

The Senators and Representatives before mentioned, and the Members of the several State Legislatures, and all executive and judicial Officers, both of the United States and of the several States, shall be bound by Oath or Affirmation, to support this Constitution; but no religious Test shall ever be required as a Qualification to any Office or public Trust under the United States.

ARTICLE VII.

The Ratification of the Conventions of nine States, shall be sufficient for the Establishment of this Constitution between the States so ratifying the Same.

Done in Convention by the Unanimous Consent of the States present the Seventeenth Day of September in the Year of our Lord one thousand seven hundred and Eighty seven and of the Independence of the United States of America the Twelfth. In Witness whereof We have hereunto subscribed our Names,

George Washington—President and deputy from Virginia

New Hampshire
  John Langdon
  Nicholas Gilman

Massachusetts
  Nathaniel Gorham
  Rufus King

Connecticut
  Wm. Saml. Johnson
  Roger Sherman

New York
  Alexander Hamilton

New Jersey
  Wil: Livingston
  David Brearley
  Wm. Paterson
  Jona: Dayton

Pennsylvania
  B. Franklin
  Thomas Mifflin

  Robt Morris
  Geo. Clymer
  Thos. FitzSimons
  Jared Ingersoll
  James Wilson
  Gouv Morris

Delaware
  Geo: Read
  Gunning Bedford jun
  John Dickinson
  Richard Basset
  Jaco: Broom

Maryland
  James McHenry
  Dan of St Thos. Jenifer
  Danl Carroll

Virginia
  John Blair—
  James Madison Jr.

North Carolina
   Wm. Blount
   Richd. Dobbs Spaight
   Hu Williamson

South Carolina
   J. Rutledge
   Charles C. Pinckney

Charles Pinckney
Pierce Butler

Georgia
   William Few
   Abr Baldwin

Attest *William Jackson Secretary*

IN CONVENTION
MONDAY, SEPTEMBER 17TH 1787.

Present The States of
New Hampshire, Massachusetts, Connecticut, Mr. Hamilton from New York, New Jersey, Pennsylvania, Delaware, Maryland, Virginia, North Carolina, South Carolina and Georgia.

Resolved,
That the preceeding Constitution be laid before the United States in Congress assembled, and that it is the Opinion of this Convention, that it should afterwards be submitted to a Convention of Delegates, chosen in each State by the People thereof, under the Recommendation of its Legislature, for their Assent and Ratification; and that each Convention assenting to, and ratifying the Same, should give Notice thereof to the United States in Congress assembled. Resolved, That it is the Opinion of this Convention, that as soon as the Conventions of nine States shall have ratified this Constitution, the United States in Congress assembled should fix a Day on which Electors should be appointed by the States which shall have ratified the same, and a Day on which the Electors should assemble to vote for the President, and the Time and Place for commencing Proceedings under this Constitution.
That after such Publication the Electors should be appointed, and the Senators and Representatives elected: That the Electors should

meet on the Day fixed for the Election of the President, and should transmit their Votes certified, signed, sealed and directed, as the Constitution requires, to the Secretary of the United States in Congress assembled, that the Senators and Representatives should convene at the Time and Place assigned; that the Senators should appoint a President of the Senate, for the sole Purpose of receiving, opening and counting the Votes for President; and, that after he shall be chosen, the Congress, together with the President, should, without Delay, proceed to execute this Constitution.

By the unanimous Order of the Convention

George Washington—President
W. Jackson, Secretary

Congress Of The United States
begun and held at the City of New-York, on Wednesday the fourth of March, one thousand seven hundred and eighty nine.

THE Conventions of a number of the States, having at the time of their adopting the Constitution, expressed a desire, in order to prevent misconstruction or abuse of its powers, that further declaratory and restrictive clauses should be added: And as extending the ground of public confidence in the Government, will best ensure the beneficent ends of its institution:

RESOLVED by the Senate and House of Representatives of the United States of America, in Congress assembled, two thirds of both Houses concurring, that the following Articles be proposed to the Legislatures of the several States, as Amendments to the Constitution of the United States, all or any of which Articles, when ratified by three fourths of the said Legislatures, to be valid to all intents and purposes, as part of the said Constitution; viz:

ARTICLES in addition to, and Amendments of the Constitution of the United States of America, proposed by Congress, and ratified by the Legislatures of the several States, pursuant to the fifth Article of the original Constitution. . . .

Frederick Augustus Muhlenberg
    Speaker of the House of Representatives.
John Adams
    Vice-President of the United States,
    and President of the Senate.

ATTEST,
    John Beckley, Clerk of the House of Representatives.
    Sam. A. Otis. Secretary of the Senate.

FURTHER AMENDMENTS TO THE CONSTITUTION OF THE
UNITED STATES

AMENDMENT XI.

The Eleventh Amendment was ratified February 7, 1795.
    The Judicial power of the United States shall not be construed to extend to any suit in law or equity, commenced or prosecuted against one of the United States by Citizens of another State, or by Citizens or Subjects of any Foreign State.

AMENDMENT XII.

The Twelfth Amendment was ratified June 15, 1804.
    The Electors shall meet in their respective states, and vote by ballot for President and Vice President, one of whom, at least, shall not be an inhabitant of the same state with themselves; they shall name in their ballots the person voted for as President, and in distinct ballots the person voted for as Vice-President, and they shall make distinct lists of all persons voted for as President, and of all persons voted for as Vice-President, and of the number of votes for each, which lists they shall sign and certify, and transmit sealed to the seat of the government of the United States, directed to the President of the Senate;—The President of the Senate shall, in the presence of the Senate and House of Representatives, open all the certificates and the votes shall then be counted;—The person having the greatest number of votes for President, shall be the President, if such number be a majority of the

whole number of Electors appointed; and if no person have such majority, then from the persons having the highest numbers not exceeding three on the list of those voted for as President, the House of Representatives shall choose immediately, by ballot, the President. But in choosing the President, the votes shall be taken by states, the representation from each state having one vote; a quorum for this purpose shall consist of a member or members from two-thirds of the states, and a majority of all the states shall be necessary to a choice. [And if the House of Representatives shall not choose a President whenever the right of choice shall devolve upon them, before the fourth day of March next following, then the Vice President shall act as President, as in the case of the death or other constitutional disability of the President—] *(Note: superseded by section 3 of the Twentieth Amendment.)* The person having the greatest number of votes as Vice-President, shall be the Vice-President, if such number be a majority of the whole number of Electors appointed, and if no person have a majority, then from the two highest numbers on the list, the Senate shall choose the Vice-President; a quorum for the purpose shall consist of two-thirds of the whole number of Senators, and a majority of the whole number shall be necessary to a choice. But no person constitutionally ineligible to the office of President shall be eligible to that of Vice-President of the United States.

AMENDMENT XIII.

The Thirteenth Amendment was ratified December 6, 1865.
Section 1. Neither slavery nor involuntary servitude, except as a punishment for crime whereof the party shall have been duly convicted, shall exist within the United States, or any place subject to their jurisdiction.

Section 2. Congress shall have power to enforce this article by appropriate legislation.

AMENDMENT XIV.

The Fourteenth Amendment was ratified July 9, 1868.
Section 1. All persons born or naturalized in the United States and subject to the jurisdiction thereof, are citizens of the United States and

of the State wherein they reside. No State shall make or enforce any law which shall abridge the privileges or immunities of citizens of the United States; nor shall any State deprive any person of life, liberty, or property, without due process of law; nor deny to any person within its jurisdiction the equal protection of the laws.

Section 2. Representatives shall be apportioned among the several States according to their respective numbers, counting the whole number of persons in each State, excluding Indians not taxed. But when the right to vote at any election for the choice of electors for President and Vice President of the United States, Representatives in Congress, the Executive and Judicial officers of a State, or the members of the Legislature thereof, is denied to any of the male inhabitants of such State, being twenty-one years of age, and citizens of the United States, or in any way abridged, except for participation in rebellion, or other crime, the basis of representation therein shall be reduced in the proportion which the number of such male citizens shall bear to the whole number of male citizens twenty-one years of age in such State.

Section 3. No person shall be a Senator or Representative in Congress, or elector of President and Vice President, or hold any office, civil or military, under the United States, or under any State, who, having previously taken an oath, as a member of Congress, or as an officer of the United States, or as a member of any State legislature, or as an executive or judicial officer of any State, to support the Constitution of the United States, shall have engaged in insurrection or rebellion against the same, or given aid or comfort to the enemies thereof. But Congress may by a vote of two-thirds of each House, remove such disability.

Section 4. The validity of the public debt of the United States, authorized by law, including debts incurred for payment of pensions and bounties for services in suppressing insurrection or rebellion, shall not be questioned. But neither the United States nor any State shall assume or pay any debt or obligation incurred in aid of insurrection or rebellion against the United States, or any claim for the loss or emancipation of any slave; but all such debts, obligations and claims shall be held illegal and void.

Section 5. The Congress shall have power to enforce, by appropriate legislation, the provisions of this article.

AMENDMENT XV.

The Fifteenth Amendment was ratified February 3, 1870.
Section 1. The right of citizens of the United States to vote shall not be denied or abridged by the United States or by any State on account of race, color, or previous condition of servitude.
Section 2. The Congress shall have power to enforce this article by appropriate legislation.

AMENDMENT XVI.

The Sixteenth Amendment was ratified February 3, 1913.
The Congress shall have power to lay and collect taxes on incomes, from whatever source derived, without apportionment among the several States, and without regard to any census or enumeration.

AMENDMENT XVII.

The Seventeenth Amendment was ratified April 8, 1913
The Senate of the United States shall be composed of two Senators from each State, elected by the people thereof, for six years; and each Senator shall have one vote. The electors in each State shall have the qualifications requisite for electors of the most numerous branch of the State legislatures.

When vacancies happen in the representation of any State in the Senate, the executive authority of such State shall issue writs of election to fill such vacancies: *Provided,* That the legislature of any State may empower the executive thereof to make temporary appointments until the people fill the vacancies by election as the legislature may direct.

This amendment shall not be so construed as to affect the election or term of any Senator chosen before it becomes valid as part of the Constitution.

AMENDMENT XVIII.

The Eighteenth Amendment was ratified January 16, 1919. It was repealed by the Twenty-first Amendment, December 5, 1933.

[*Section 1.* After one year from the ratification of this article the manufacture, sale, or transportation of intoxicating liquors within, the importation thereof into, or the exportation thereof from the United States and all territory subject to the jurisdiction thereof for beverage purposes is hereby prohibited.

Section 2. The Congress and the several States shall have concurrent power to enforce this article by appropriate legislation.

Section 3. This article shall be inoperative unless it shall have been ratified as an amendment to the Constitution by the legislatures of the several States, as provided in the Constitution, within seven years from the date of the submission hereof to the States by the Congress.]

AMENDMENT XIX.

The Nineteenth Amendment was ratified August 18, 1920.

The right of citizens of the United States to vote shall not be denied or abridged by the United States or by any State on account of sex.

Congress shall have power to enforce this article by appropriate legislation.

AMENDMENT XX.

The Twentieth Amendment was ratified January 23, 1933.

Section 1. The terms of the President and Vice President shall end at noon on the 20th day of January, and the terms of Senators and Representatives at noon on the 3d day of January, of the years in which such terms would have ended if this article had not been ratified; and the terms of their successors shall then begin.

Section 2. The Congress shall assemble at least once in every year, and such meeting shall begin at noon on the 3d day of January, unless they shall by law appoint a different day.

Section 3. If, at the time fixed for the beginning of the term of the President, the President elect shall have died, the Vice President elect shall become President. If a President shall not have been chosen before the time fixed for the beginning of his term, or if the President elect shall have failed to qualify, then the Vice President elect shall act as President until a President shall have qualified; and the Congress may by law provide for the case wherein neither a President elect nor a Vice President elect shall have qualified, declaring who shall then act as President, or the manner in which one who is to act shall be selected, and such person shall act accordingly until a President or Vice President shall have qualified.

Section 4. The Congress may by law provide for the case of the death of any of the persons from whom the House of Representatives may choose a President whenever the right of choice shall have devolved upon them and for the case of the death of any of the persons from whom the Senate may choose a Vice President whenever the right of choice shall have devolved upon them.

Section 5. Sections 1 and 2 shall take effect on the 15th day of October following the ratification of this article.

Section 6. This article shall be inoperative unless it shall have been ratified as an amendment to the Constitution by the legislatures of three-fourths of the several States within seven years from the date of its submission.

AMENDMENT XXI.

The Twenty-first Amendment was ratified December 5, 1933.

Section 1. The eighteenth article of amendment to the Constitution of the United States is hereby repealed.

Section 2. The transportation or importation into any State, Territory, or possession of the United States for delivery or use therein of intoxicating liquors, in violation of the laws thereof, is hereby prohibited.

Section 3. This article shall be inoperative unless it shall have been ratified as an amendment to the Constitution by conventions in the several States, as provided in the Constitution, within seven years from the date of the submission hereof to the States by the Congress.

AMENDMENT XXII

The Twenty-second Amendment was ratified February 27, 1951.

Section 1. No person shall be elected to the office of the President more than twice, and no person who has held the office of President, or acted as President, for more than two years of a term to which some other person was elected President shall be elected to the office of the President more than once. But this Article shall not apply to any person holding the office of President when this Article was proposed by the Congress, and shall not prevent any person who may be holding the office of President, or acting as President, during the term within which this Article becomes operative from holding the office of President or acting as President during the remainder of such term.

Section 2. This article shall be inoperative unless it shall have been ratified as an amendment to the Constitution by the legislatures of three-fourths of the several States within seven years from the date of its submission to the States by the Congress.

AMENDMENT XXIII.

The Twenty-third Amendment was ratified March 29, 1961.

Section 1. The District constituting the seat of Government of the United States shall appoint in such manner as the Congress may direct:

A number of electors of President and Vice President equal to the whole number of Senators and Representatives in Congress to which the District would be entitled if it were a State, but in no event more than the least populous State; they shall be in addition to those appointed by the States, but they shall be considered, for the purposes of the election of President and Vice President, to be electors appointed by a State; and they shall meet in the District and perform such duties as provided by the twelfth article of amendment.

Section 2. The Congress shall have power to enforce this article by appropriate legislation.

AMENDMENT XXIV.

The Twenty-fourth Amendment was ratified January 23, 1964.

Section 1. The right of citizens of the United States to vote in any primary or other election for President or Vice President, for electors for President or Vice President, or for Senator or Representative in Congress, shall not be denied or abridged by the United States or any State by reason of failure to pay any poll tax or other tax.

Section 2. The Congress shall have power to enforce this article by appropriate legislation.

AMENDMENT XXV.

The Twenty-fifth Amendment was ratified February 10, 1967.

Section 1. In case of the removal of the President from office or of his death or resignation, the Vice President shall become President.

Section 2. Whenever there is a vacancy in the office of the Vice President, the President shall nominate a Vice President who shall take office upon confirmation by a majority vote of both Houses of Congress.

Section 3. Whenever the President transmits to the President pro tempore of the Senate and the Speaker of the House of Representatives his written declaration that he is unable to discharge the powers and duties of his office, and until he transmits to them a written declaration to the contrary, such powers and duties shall be discharged by the Vice President as Acting President.

Section 4. Whenever the Vice President and a majority of either the principal officers of the executive departments or of such other body as Congress may by law provide, transmit to the President pro tempore of the Senate and the Speaker of the House of Representatives their written declaration that the President is unable to discharge the powers and duties of his office, the Vice President shall immediately assume the powers and duties of the office as Acting President.

Thereafter, when the President transmits to the President pro tempore of the Senate and the Speaker of the House of Representatives his written declaration that no inability exists, he shall resume the powers and duties of his office unless the Vice President and a majority of either the principal officers of the executive department or of such other body as Congress may by law provide, transmit within four days to the President pro tempore of the Senate and the Speaker of the House of Representatives their written declaration that the President is unable to discharge the powers and duties of his office. Thereupon Congress shall decide the issue, assembling within forty-eight hours for that purpose if not in session. If the Congress, within twenty-one days after receipt of the latter written declaration,

222 ★ The Constitution of the United States of America

or, if Congress is not in session, within twenty-one days after Congress is required to assemble, determines by two-thirds vote of both Houses that the President is unable to discharge the powers and duties of his office, the Vice President shall continue to discharge the same as Acting President; otherwise, the President shall resume the powers and duties of his office.

AMENDMENT XXVI

The Twenty-sixth Amendment was ratified July 1, 1971.

Section 1. The right of citizens of the United States, who are eighteen years of age or older, to vote shall not be denied or abridged by the United States or by any State on account of age.

Section 2. The Congress shall have power to enforce this article by appropriate legislation

AMENDMENT XXVII

The Twenty-seventh Amendment was ratified in 1992.

No Law, varying the compensation for the services of the Senators and Representatives, shall take effect, until an election of Representatives shall have intervened.

★ ACKNOWLEDGMENTS ★

I am grateful to all who are portrayed in this book for their generosity of interview time and their generosity of spirit. I am also indebted to Shirley Sulat not only for her typing skills but also for understanding—and caring about—the nature of individual liberty and what it takes to safeguard it.

In partial form, sections of this book have appeared in the *New Yorker*, the *Washington Post*, and the *Village Voice*.

Through the years, a particular source of information and inspiration has been Don Edwards, a former longtime congressman from California, whose passion to protect the Bill of Rights in the House would have made him a true companion of James Madison and Thomas Jefferson.

★ INDEX ★